THREADS of PEACE

ALSO BY UMA KRISHNASWAMI

The Grand Plan to Fix Everything
The Problem with Being Slightly Heroic

THREADS of PEACE

HOW MOHANDAS GANDHI AND MARTIN LUTHER KING JR. CHANGED THE WORLD

UMA KRISHNASWAMI

A CAITLYN DLOUHY BOOK

ATHENEUM BOOKS FOR YOUNG READERS   New York   London   Toronto   Sydney   New Delhi

A
atheneum

ATHENEUM BOOKS FOR YOUNG READERS
An imprint of Simon & Schuster Children's Publishing Division
1230 Avenue of the Americas, New York, New York 10020
Text © 2021 by Uma Krishnaswami
Front panel illustration © 2021 by David J. Weissberg
Front panel photograph of Mohandas K. Gandhi © Central Press
Front panel photograph of Martin Luther King Jr. © Universal History Archive
Photograph of the March on Washington © Records of the U.S. Information Agency,
1900–2003/National Archive
Illustrations on pp. 5, 35, 43, 47, 48, 98, 134, 150, 152, 159, 167, 204, 242, and 248 by
Irene Metaxatos
Jacket design © 2021 by Simon & Schuster, Inc.
For information about special discounts for bulk purchases, please contact
Simon & Schuster Special Sales at 1-866-506-1949 or business@simonandschuster.com.
The Simon & Schuster Speakers Bureau can bring authors to your live event. For more
information or to book an event, contact the Simon & Schuster Speakers Bureau at
1-866-248-3049 or visit our website at www.simonspeakers.com.
Interior design by Irene Metaxatos
The text for this book was set in Adobe Caslon Pro.
Manufactured in Thailand
0521 SCP
First Edition
10 9 8 7 6 5 4 3 2 1
CIP data for this book is available from the Library of Congress.
ISBN 978-1-4814-1678-8
ISBN 978-1-4814-1680-1 (ebook)

For tomorrow's peacemakers
and in memory of Kedar

Contents

Threads of Peace: The Right to Take a Seat.....01

Mohandas Karamchand Gandhi.....11

1: A Place of Warm Breezes.....13

2: The Ocean of Life.....19

3: Obedience and Disobedience.....28

4: Questions Large and Small.....36

5: A Lawyer Abroad.....46

6: In Search of Truth.....58

7: Marching for Freedom.....72

8: New Cloth, Frayed Fabric.....92

9: "I Must Now Tear Myself Away".....108

Martin Luther King Jr......117

10: The Curtain of Discrimination.....119

11: Message of Truth.....131

12: Don't Ride the Buses.....137

13: AGAINST THE CONSTITUTION.....148

14: ACTIONS LOUDER THAN WORDS.....162

15: IN GANDHI'S FOOTSTEPS.....169

16: AFTER INDIA.....183

17: KNOWING THE ENEMY.....197

18: BOMBINGHAM.....205

19: "FREE AT LAST, FREE AT LAST".....218

20: CHAMPION OF PEACE.....233

21: BLOODY SUNDAY.....239

22: NO COMPROMISE.....250

23: "PRECIOUS LORD, TAKE MY HAND".....259

WHEN THE THREADS BREAK.....275

24: THE ASSASSINS.....277

25: SPINNING NEW THREADS OF PEACE.....290

AUTHOR'S NOTE, ACKNOWLEDGMENTS, TIMELINE, GLOSSARY, BIBLIOGRAPHY, PHOTO CREDITS, SOURCES, INDEX.....301

Threads of Peace

The Right to Take a Seat

"Victory attained by violence is tantamount to a defeat, for it is momentary."

–Mohandas K. Gandhi

"Christ showed us the way and Gandhi in India showed it could work."

–Martin Luther King Jr.

DUBLIN, GEORGIA
April 17, 1944

Light-headed with excitement, fifteen-year-old Martin stepped up to the microphone. His very first public speech! His teacher, Mrs. Sarah Grace Bradley, smiled at him from the audience.

Martin had practiced this speech many times at home. He'd delivered it in school, winning the chance to enter a statewide contest. Now here he was in the First African Baptist Church, nearly 150 miles away, his gaze falling upon the faces of strangers.

Already, Martin's voice was deep and echoing. The subject of his speech was big. Two centuries of slavery in America and the wounds it had left upon Black society—poverty, inequality, sickness, illiteracy, segregation. Slavery ended in 1865, he pointed out, but "Black America still wears chains." Martin talked about the opera singer Marian Anderson. The city of Philadelphia had honored Marian. They had given her a prize for her talent and her generosity in teaching others. Three years had gone by since that award and still, Martin said, Marian was not "served in many of the public restaurants of her home city, even after it has declared her to be its best citizen."

His speech cast a hush over the audience. The words rose and fell. They circled around Martin's big, wide topic, returning again and again to cry out for justice. "So, with their right hand they raise to high places the great who have dark skins, and with their left, they slap us down to keep us in 'our places.'"

Martin demanded equal education and equal rights for Black people. He demanded equality—"fair play" and "free opportunity" for all.

He won the speech competition. But his first real test was yet to come.

At the end of the day, Martin and Mrs. Bradley caught the bus back from Dublin to Atlanta. Like most buses of the time, it was segregated. Black and white people sat in separate rows. If four Black riders sat in a row and a white person wanted a seat there, all four would have to get up. It didn't matter if they were sick or elderly, pregnant or holding babies or toddlers. That is how it was. Segregated buses were just another way to keep Black America slapped down. Martin could see it.

The bus pulled out of Dublin. Soon it stopped to pick up additional passengers. They were white.

The driver looked around. "Get up!" he ordered Martin and Mrs. Bradley.

Mrs. Bradley whispered to Martin that they'd better obey. He hesitated. He longed to stay put. Why did he have to get up for these people? Why did Mrs. Bradley? It was so unfair. It was downright wrong.

"We have to obey the law," Mrs. Bradley said. Martin had no choice.

Still, Martin hesitated. The bus driver began to yell at him. He cursed and threatened. He spewed the coarsest of language. He hurled his words like weapons.

Martin's mind raced. It could be dangerous to disobey. Drivers on these intercity buses sometimes carried guns. The driver's curses slapped down his ideals of justice and equality. Slapped him back down, as if he had no rights at all.

Shaken as much by the turmoil inside him as by the incident itself, he got to his feet. Through the lowering darkness, the full bus rattled toward Atlanta. The entire way, Martin and Mrs. Bradley stood in the aisle. Every lurch over every pothole drummed anger and humiliation into Martin's memory.

Eleven years later, at the age of twenty-six, Dr. Martin Luther King Jr. was the newly appointed pastor of a church in Montgomery, Alabama. He was asked to lead a movement to protest the city's segregated bus system. Black people would refuse to ride the buses. Without the thousands of dimes they plunked into the till, the city would lose money. Surely *then* they would have to allow Blacks to sit where they chose. No more segregated seating. No more having to get up and give your seat to a white passenger.

Dr. King agreed to the boycott, under one condition. All those who took part must do so peacefully.

In meetings and flyers, the boycott organizers told people to stay calm and peaceful. Join

King speaking at Dexter Avenue Baptist Church, Montgomery, Alabama.

the boycott, they urged. Don't ride the segregated buses in Montgomery. Walk. Get a ride. Find some other way to get where you need to go. No fighting. No violence. By your peaceful actions, you will make the city take notice.

How did Dr. Martin Luther King Jr. journey from anger to peaceful protest? Dr. King himself credited a man from faraway India. His name was Mohandas Karamchand Gandhi. Dr. King called him "the guiding light of our technique of nonviolent social change."

PIETERMARITZBURG, SOUTH AFRICA
June 7, 1893

Gandhi began his journey toward peaceful resistance on a train.

The polished wood and brass carriage was empty. In Mohandas Gandhi's pocket was a first-class ticket, compliments of Dada Abdulla, an Indian merchant who lived in South Africa. Abdulla had hired Gandhi to represent him in a legal case against a family member who owed him money. Having left his native India, armed with a newly minted law degree from England, Gandhi had come to South Africa to argue the case.

Gandhi in
South Africa

The train chugged through the green hills of the Natal province. The countryside was dotted with small settlements, clusters of buildings with mud walls and thatched roofs. The train rattled past rocky outcrops and the occasional cascading waterfall. It pulled into the station of Pietermaritzburg, barely a quarter of the way to Gandhi's final destination of Pretoria.

As the wheels creaked to a halt, a railway attendant poked his head around the door. He was ready to fold down the wooden seatback, turning it into a bunk bed. Did Gandhi need a bedding roll, with pillows? Sheets?

"No," said Gandhi. "I have one with me." He was used to train travel in India, where people always carried their own bedding.

Gandhi was settling in for the night when someone else entered—a white passenger. He looked Gandhi up and down. He seemed about to say something, but then he left. When the man returned, he had two railway officials with him. They, too, stared at the Indian as if he were an unexpected pest that had suddenly shown up in their gleaming wooden carriage.

A third man in uniform arrived. "Come along," he commanded Gandhi. "You must go to the van compartment." Coolies—the insulting name for all Indians in South Africa—weren't allowed in first class.

Gandhi objected. He showed them his ticket. If they didn't want him to ride in this carriage, why had the railway issued a first-class ticket in his name? The officials protested. The stationmaster must have made a mistake.

The white passenger fretted and fumed. He wasn't about to spend the night in the same carriage as this impertinent brown-skinned man. The railway officials warned Gandhi they'd throw him out if he didn't leave.

He remained sitting.

Just as the engine hissed, ready to pull out of the station, a police constable pushed his way in. He grabbed Gandhi by the arm. He shoved him out of the train. Gandhi crashed onto the stone slabs of the station platform. His luggage flew out after him. His wooden trunk crashed at his side. His briefcase followed. The train steamed away.

Gandhi was steaming too, from abuse and injury. How long did he lie there? He hardly knew. Slowly, he regained his breath. He picked himself up and went to the waiting room. His trunk was stored away for him, leaving him with only his hand baggage, wondering what he should do next.

Gandhi eventually made it to Pretoria and completed the job he was hired to do, but he could not forget the indignities of that day. He wrote later, "It was winter . . . the cold was extremely bitter. My over-coat was in my luggage, but I did not dare to ask for it lest I should be insulted again, so I sat and shiv-

Pietermaritzburg Station

ered." What should he do? Should he stay in South Africa and fight for his rights? Should he go back to India? His own "hardship was superficial," he wrote. It was "only a symptom of the deep disease." The disease of color prejudice.

Claiming the right to sit anywhere on a bus. Claiming the right to a seat you have purchased on a train. Half a century separated these incidents, yet how unsettlingly similar they are! Martin Luther King Jr. never forgot the driver's contempt and hatred, the feeling of being powerless. Likewise, Gandhi's experience in Pietermaritzburg stayed with him.

The two incidents influenced the actions, the choices, the causes each man made his own. In the end, those actions shaped the history of their native countries.

The two men never met. They were born sixty years apart, in two different centuries, on two different continents. Yet the threads of their lives, as well as their hopes and dreams for the world all people share, weave together in remarkable ways. Their lives and struggles, their beliefs and principles, raise powerful questions that remain valid in our time.

Mohandas Karamchand

GANDHI

1

A Place of Warm Breezes

PORBANDAR, INDIA: 1869

Mohandas Karamchand Gandhi came into the world in a
seaside town called Porbandar in the Kathiawar Peninsula of western
India. It is a place of warm breezes. The land juts out into the Arabian
Sea, its ear turned to the ocean and to the world beyond.

Once a bustling port, Porbandar was now a sleepy town on the
water's edge. Outside its borders, vast tracts of the Indian subcontinent
lay under the rule of the British. Scattered in between were princely
states, large and small, still ruled by Indian kings.

Some were kind rulers, others tyrannical. Some were independent in name. Most quaked at the power of the British Empire on
their doorsteps. In turn, the British kept an eye on the Indian royals,
to make sure that none of them gained any real strength.

The kingdom of Porbandar was too small to pose any threat to
the British. It consisted of a single town, on a coastal strip less than
twenty-five miles wide. Its creamy-white limestone buildings earned
it the name of the "White City."

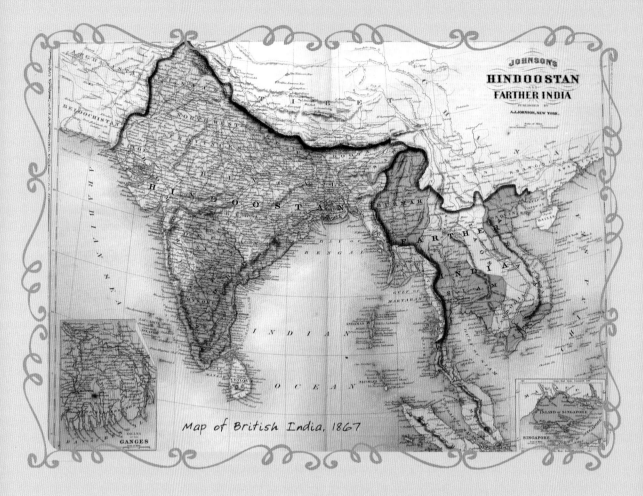

Map of British India, 1867

The British in India

The British came as traders to India—and stayed.

The East India Company had been chartered in 1600 to buy and sell spices. Over the years, the company also traded in tea, indigo, salt, silk, cotton, and other goods—among them, vast quantities of the drug opium, sold to China. Soon the company built permanent offices and took over large areas of land.

By the mid-nineteenth century, the company ran much of the country. It collected taxes. It employed an army. It was the face of the British government in India, and it ruled harshly.

In 1857, twelve years before Gandhi's birth, a rebellion by Indian soldiers in the company army had been brutally crushed by British commanders. The company was dissolved and its powers taken over by the British government. In 1876, Queen Victoria was crowned Empress of India. This was the beginning of the British rule that came to be called "the Raj."

The Gandhi family home, a hundred years old, with twelve rooms and three floors, stood in a narrow lane. Its thick walls kept the interior cool even in the hottest summers. In some rooms, the walls were painted with floral and geometric designs. Evening breezes blew over the rooftop, where the children played.

The women of the household ran the kitchen—chopping vegetables with great curving knife-blades, grinding millet into flour, stirring pots of lentils and rice over crackling wood-fires. They slathered rounds of flat bread with *ghee* made from scalded butter. The fragrance of ground spices, homemade pickles, and chutneys wafted into the central courtyard.

Mohandas lived in this house with his father, Karamchand Gandhi ("Kaba" for short), and his mother, Putliba. Putliba was Kaba Gandhi's fourth wife. The first two had died in childbirth, and the third was childless and ill. Kaba wanted a son, so he had asked and obtained his third wife's permission to marry Putliba. His sick third wife, however, remained living with the family until her death. The white-walled house was also home to two daughters from Kaba's earlier marriages,

Mohandas's mother, Putliba, and Mohandas's father, Kaba Gandhi

Kaba's Wives
Under the law, Kaba Gandhi didn't need his wife's permission to marry again. Hindu men in nineteenth-century India were allowed to have more than one wife at a time.

15

Mohandas's half sisters, and of course to Putliba and Kaba's other children—a daughter, Raliat, and two sons, Laxmidas and Karsandas.

Raliat loved the new baby. She played with Mohandas and carried him everywhere, hardly putting him down for a moment. As he grew to be a toddler, she said her little brother was "restless as mercury," unable to "sit still even for a little while. He must be either playing or roaming about." He was mischievous, too. When they went to the marketplace, he'd chase the neighborhood dogs and tweak their ears.

Kaba Gandhi's father had been the *diwan* to the ruler of Porbandar. Kaba, who held the job of letter writer and clerk, inherited his father's high office upon his death. As a token of the promotion, the ruler presented him with a silver inkstand and inkpot. Kaba could read and write in his native Gujarati language, although, like many Indians of the time, he knew no English.

diwan | (also dewan) *noun* In 19th century India, the chief minister or finance minister of a princely state

Kaba was preoccupied with his work and traveled often. When the fortunes of Porbandar's ruler waned, he began to look for work in other local kingdoms. The new baby saw little of his father.

But the women of the house loved and indulged young Mohandas. Fondly, they called him "Monia." They played with him and teased him. While cooking delicious vegetarian meals for the family, they took care to make special sweets for Mohandas. One of

Mohandas at age seven

the household servants in particular, Rambha, doted on him. She became his loving nurse.

Mohandas adored his mother. She was gentle yet strong. Once, a poisonous scorpion got into the house and ran over her bare feet. Everyone panicked. Mohandas cowered. But his mother simply scooped the insect up and threw it out the window.

Scorpions were not the only things Mohandas feared. Even in the embrace of a loving family, he was timid and struck by frequent terrors. He was afraid of the dark and of ghosts, evil spirits, and demons. He was sure they waited for him around every dark corner or lurked in twilight shadows. His nurse, Rambha, tried her best to bolster his courage. She told him to repeat the name of Rama, the god-prince of Hindu mythology, so good and noble that chanting his name was said to drive away all evil.

"Rama, Rama!" The boy intoned the holy name over and over. It did no good. Come nightfall, he could not shake his fear.

Yet the same excitable imagination that stoked anxiety also drew him to the faith of his mother. Most Hindu families mainly worshipped one—or at most a few—of the many gods in the Hindu tradition. Putliba worshipped them all! She took her son to numerous temples in the area. She even took him to one where the walls were inscribed with writings from both Hindu scriptures and the Muslim holy book, the Quran. A shy boy paying attention to his mother's words and actions, Mohandas likely absorbed some of her open-minded religious views.

“ The outstanding impression my mother has left on my memory is that of saintliness. She was deeply religious. She would not think of taking her meals without her daily prayers. Going to the temple was one of her daily duties. It was a Vaishnava Hindu temple, dedicated to the god Vishnu, filled with carved images, the sounds of bells, and the murmurs of ancient chants. She took vows to fast for religious holidays, and kept them meticulously. Illness was no excuse for relaxing them. . . . To keep two or three consecutive fasts was nothing to her. ”

—M. K. Gandhi

2

The Ocean of Life

RAJKOT, INDIA: 1876

When Mohandas was seven, his father took a new job in the court of the city kingdom of Rajkot. He moved the family there. Rajkot was about a hundred miles inland from Porbandar. Kaba built a spacious new house in which the family settled down.

Before the move, Mohandas had attended an informal private school off and on—a *dhool shala,* or "school in the dust," where he learned to write Gujarati letters on the ground with a stick, but not much more. Now he was enrolled in a local primary school with other boys—in that place and time, schools for girls did not exist.

Over the next few years, Mohandas attended two different schools, sometimes willingly and sometimes less so. Once, a bout of fever kept him home. At other times, he was absent for no good reason. In third grade, he was near the bottom of his class. Despite his spotty attendance, he got through, but of his early education, Gandhi later wrote, "My intellect must have been sluggish and my memory raw."

As he grew older, Mohandas studied arithmetic, history, and the Gujarati language. He began to work harder. He memorized poetry. He learned to spell and to spot the rivers and towns of western India on a map. He did a little better with each passing year. But he was very shy and did not make friends easily. At the end of the school day, he would run home as fast as he could, before anyone tried to talk to him.

In 1880, Mohandas took the entrance test to nearby Kattywar High School, which admitted pupils at eleven years of age and graduated them after they had completed seven grades. In addition to other subjects, the school taught boys to read, speak, and write English, because the British Raj needed educated Indians to fill office jobs in its vast bureaucracy.

Somehow, Mohandas not only passed the test but did quite well. He was not sure what to expect in this new school. What he found surprised him. Kattywar High School expanded his world.

Of the many castes into which Hindu society is divided, the Gandhi family belonged to a community called Banias. They were part of the middle Vaisya or merchant caste in Hindu society.

The Hindu Caste System

Caste divisions have existed in India perhaps as far back as 1500 BCE. The word "caste" comes from the Portuguese *casta*, meaning "race" or "lineage." Caste divisions may have been based on skin color or birth status or both.

Caste groups may have begun as occupations:
- Brahmins: priests, scholars, teachers
- Kshatriyas: kings, warriors
- Vaisyas: traders, merchants, moneylenders
- Sudras: laborers, farmers, artisans

Beyond these four castes, and seen as inferior to all others, are the untouchables (now known as Dalits), scavengers doing dirty work that no one else will do.

Castes exist even today. People of various castes speak different dialects of the same language, eat different foods, and worship differently. Traditionally, people did not marry outside their caste. Today, that is changing.

It is now illegal to discriminate against people of lower castes that have been identified by the government as needing legal protection. But social inequality related to caste still exists in India.

In his new school, for the first time, Mohandas met boys who were not of his caste or even his religion. A Muslim boy, Sheikh Mehtab, became his closest friend. Mehtab was in fact a friend of Mohandas's brother Karsandas. The pair of them had failed their exams and been held back a grade. It wasn't the first time this had happened, but they were now in Mohandas's class.

During their years at Kattywar High School, Mohandas and Mehtab spent many hours together. One day, Mehtab suggested to Mohandas that he ought to try eating meat—surely he knew that he was weak and short because he didn't! Didn't the Gujarati poet Narmad say so? Mehtab recited a popular satirical verse to prove his point:

Mohandas Gandhi and Sheikh Mehtab

> *"Behold the mighty Englishman,*
> *He rules the Indian small,*
> *Because being a meat-eater,*
> *He is five cubits tall."*

It was true that Indians chafed under British rule. Mohandas himself had seen the agonies his father faced in dealing with local British officials for his royal employer. Once, the British agent in Rajkot made Kaba put on English clothes—breeches and stockings and tight, torturous boots—in honor of a high-ranking visitor. Another time, an Englishman had made a rude remark about Kaba's employer, the king of Rajkot. Kaba objected. The Englishman demanded an apology. When Kaba refused, he was tied to a tree and kept there for hours before being released. Could eating meat help to right these wrongs?

Mehtab said he had convinced Mohandas's brother Karsandas to eat meat. Mohandas thought about that for a while. He himself was skinny. His older brother was starting to grow strong and muscled. Had eating meat done that? Mohandas wondered if Mehtab was strong on account of the meat *he* ate. Mehtab boasted he could hold live serpents in his hands. He wasn't afraid of thieves or ghosts.

Mohandas thought about all the fears that danced in his own mind. He'd been raised strictly vegetarian, but maybe he ought to give meat a try. Maybe if everyone in India ate meat, they could chase the British away!

The two boys hid in a place far from the Gandhi house, and Mehtab cooked up some goat meat for his friend. The alien food turned Mohandas's stomach, and the experience made him feel guilty and even more ill. That night, he had a nightmare that live goats were bleating in his stomach. He woke up with a start, feeling dizzy and nauseous. He calmed down only by telling himself that meat-eating was practically a duty, so he could defeat the British and free India.

Mehtab cooked Mohandas several meals after this. Though Mohandas got over his early revulsion, the experiment led to other problems. His mother wanted to know why he wasn't hungry and wouldn't eat the meals she'd cooked. He had to pretend he was sick, and he hated himself for lying. Finally, he confessed to Mehtab that he couldn't go on eating meat on the sly. He'd have to find some other way to get the British out of India.

Mohandas and Karsandas also broke another strict parental rule—no smoking! They picked up cigarette butts thrown away by an uncle, lit them, and choked with delicious pleasure on the smoke. They stole money to buy *bidis*, hand-rolled Indian cigarettes. Terrified of getting caught, they smoked them behind the house.

One day, Mohandas and his brother started talking about their own lack of freedom. Life, they agreed, was unfair. Grown-ups made all the rules. They decided they had to do something. But what? They settled on a grand, tragic act. They would kill themselves! The enormity of suicide made it feel like a heroic deed.

Years later, Gandhi described the event: "But how were we to do it? From where were we to get the poison? We had heard that Dhatura seeds were an effective poison."

Hearts pounding, the boys walked to the city's edge. It was quite a distance. They hunted among the scrubby trees and dangling vines. At last, they spotted what they were looking for: the jimsonweed plant,

Dhatura flowers

called *dhatura* in India, with its white trumpet flowers. And there it was! They handled its prickly brown dried seedpod carefully and managed to crack it open. Despite some scratches, they harvested a few seeds.

That evening, with precious, deadly seeds in hand, they cut across the lane behind the house, taking shortcuts to bypass the main road. In ten minutes, they arrived, breathless, at the temple to the Hindu god Shiva. They added an offering of ghee to the holy lamps and bowed before the stone image of the fierce and powerful god. Considering themselves blessed, they walked to a lonely corner and swallowed a couple of seeds apiece.

Nothing happened. What now? What if they ate the lot and didn't die at once? Would it be painful? More painful than living with the rules of the adults? They agreed it was better to stay alive.

Mohandas was now tortured by guilt for the things he'd done— smoking, stealing money, trying to kill himself! He longed to confess to his father but couldn't imagine how he would even broach the topic. In the end, he wrote a note.

Kaba Gandhi was ill at the time. He was lying in his bedroom, on a plank of wood that served as a bed. Mohandas took the note to his father. He handed it to him. He waited for anger, for punishment, for *some* consequences for his actions.

Instead, his father sat up. Slowly, he read the note. As he did so, tears rolled down his cheeks. He closed his eyes for a moment, then opened them. He tore up the note and lay down again in silence.

His father's tears were "pearl-drops of love." They convinced Mohandas that he was forgiven, but he also knew his actions had hurt his father deeply. He couldn't undo his misdeeds, but he vowed not to repeat them. He quit smoking.

Occupied as he was with schooling and teenage pranks, Mohandas was drawn as well to traditional stories from Hindu mythology. He read a book of his father's about a boy whose parents were poor, aging, and blind. They asked their son to take them on a pilgrimage to forty holy places, to purify their souls before they died. Unable to afford a horse carriage, the boy made a sling out of twin baskets tied to opposite ends of a bamboo pole. He carried them on his shoulders, making the journey slowly and painfully, and yet with joy. The boy's tragic death during the pilgrimage, and the parents' terrible grief upon hearing it, reduced Mohandas to tears.

Another such story presented by a traveling theater group was of a noble king who gives away his kingdom, his wife, and his child, and ends up enslaved. He loses everything in order to be truthful and keep a promise he has made. After watching the play, Mohandas was so struck by the noble character of the king that he dreamed of him. In his waking hours, he replayed the scenes in his mind and struggled to understand what they meant.

Something else in his life was distracting Mohandas from his studies. At not quite thirteen, his marriage was arranged. It was common for parents in India at that time to arrange marriages between their children—sometimes when the children were still infants! Mohandas had been betrothed to two other girls before this one, but both had died. That, too, was not uncommon. In some parts of India in the nineteenth century, half of all children died before the age of five. Countless others never made it to adulthood.

At the time of his wedding, Mohandas was thirteen years old. His new bride, Kastur, was a few months older than him. Her family, from the same caste as his, also came from Porbandar, where the wedding was celebrated. Simultaneous ceremonies for Mohandas;

Indian wedding procession, from a children's book published in England, 1873

his brother Karsandas, sixteen; and a cousin, Motilal, seventeen, saved on the rental for the space.

While the brides waited in the wedding hall, their grooms, garlanded with flowers and mounted on richly decorated mares, rode in a slow, winding procession through the streets of Porbandar. The mares stepped carefully, each led by a minder, since none of the young grooms really knew how to ride. Drummers brought up the rear, pounding the beat as pipers played sweetly yearning wedding music. Crowds joined in until the streets were overrun with revelers.

Upon his arrival, Mohandas was sprinkled with rose water and greeted with lighted oil lamps and platters of flowers by the women of his child bride's family. His forehead was anointed with *kumkum*, the sacred red paste, and he was led to the wedding canopy.

Meanwhile, Mohandas's father, held up at his employer's royal court, was late to the triple wedding. The exact time of the ceremony had been carefully planned in consultation with astrologers. Postponement was out of the question.

Just as panic was setting in, Kaba appeared—limping and covered with bandages! Guests shrieked in alarm. Kaba explained. The royal horse-drawn coach that hurried him to the wedding had rolled over during its three-day journey. Yes, yes, he was injured, but he was here, wasn't he? The weddings could proceed.

Mohandas had never before seen the girl he was about to marry. Now, at the start of the ceremony, he caught only a brief glimpse of Kastur through her veil. They exchanged garlands. The priests chanted marriage vows in the ancient Sanskrit language. The bride's father placed her hand in the groom's. The pair took seven steps around the sacred fire—their first steps taken together as husband and wife. They placed portions of sweetened wheat *halwa* into each other's mouths. And just like that, they were married.

Mohandas and Kastur would live together for sixty-two years. Later, Gandhi would write that they were "two innocent children all unwittingly hurled into the ocean of life."

3

Obedience and Disobedience

Now Kastur Kapadia was part of the big Gandhi household in Rajkot, trying to be a good daughter-in-law. At thirteen, she had a title added to her name in honor of her status as a married woman. To everyone around her, she was now Kasturbai.

Until the wedding, the young bride had lived in her parents' home in Porbandar. She had never been to school.

In nineteenth-century India, literacy was considered unnecessary for girls and women. Only a few royal families educated their daughters, sending them abroad to study. Like other women in her own family and her husband's, Kasturbai could neither read nor write. To Mohandas, her illiteracy created a great gap between them.

Never mind that he himself hadn't been the most eager of students. He wanted to "*make* my wife an ideal wife." To his mind, that meant teaching her how to read and write.

To his dismay, Kasturbai did her best to duck his "lessons." They usually took place at the end of a long day, which he spent in school and she in the kitchen with her mother-in-law and sister-in-law. Was Kasturbai worried that the Gandhi women might disapprove of this instruction with slate and chalk, alphabets and words? Might Putliba and Raliat think she was trying to be better than they were? Or was she just tired? Whatever the reason, she pushed slate and chalk and lessons aside.

Other conflicts arose in Mohandas's yearning heart. Arranged marriages were social alliances between families and not necessarily romantic relationships. But Mohandas now fell utterly in love with his young wife. This turned him, at the age of fourteen, into a petty, jealous tyrant. One day, he announced to Kasturbai that she could not go anywhere without asking his permission. She had to tell him where she went and when, with whom, and why.

Kasturbai was outraged. Why was he making such demands? Mohandas explained that it was all about being faithful to each other. He pledged he would never look at another woman, so it was his duty to make sure that Kasturbai, in turn, remained true to him. Therefore, he had to keep track of her every movement.

Traditional Women's Names in Gujarat
In the region of India that is now the state of Gujarat, girls were known by their given names, sometimes with the added suffix of ben, or "sister." When they married, the suffix changed to bai, or "wife." When they had children, that changed to ba, which means "mother." So Kastur became first Kasturbai and then Kasturba. Women today do not add the titles of wife and mother to their names as they once did, but it is still common in Gujarat to follow a woman's name with the title of ben. Today, bai in Gujarat and neighboring states just means "lady."

She couldn't believe her ears. What did loyalty and fidelity have to do with her freedom to go where she pleased? She protested that she'd always be faithful. But she didn't promise to obey him.

The next day, not bothering to ask Mohandas for permission, Kasturbai went to the temple with her mother-in-law. She went again the following day, and the day after that. Then she visited friends, together with her sister-in-law and other women in Mohandas's family. Her actions made it clear that she did not appreciate the restrictions her new husband was trying to place on her.

Mohandas was incensed. Kasturbai pointed out that his mother had invited her to visit the temple and she had accepted. How could he possibly object? "Are you suggesting that I should obey you and not your mother?" she asked.

What could he say in reply? Finally, he had to admit that his attempts to be an authoritative Indian husband had failed. Mohandas realized something about his quiet new wife. She had a mind of her own. Unless he could convince her that his requests were reasonable, she would quietly ignore them. He canceled his "orders." Life resumed more normally. It is possible that this small domestic rebellion on Kasturbai's part was Gandhi's very first lesson in the ways of civil disobedience.

Meanwhile, Mohandas was doing well in school. That year, he skipped a grade level, then found himself "completely at sea" in the new class. Mathematics, in particular, defied him. He even considered going back a grade. But he didn't want to disappoint the teacher who had recommended him for this "leap promotion," so he persevered.

The work paid off. Algebra was difficult, but geometry, he found, was "pure and simple use of one's reasoning powers." At the age of sixteen, to everyone's surprise including his own, he did very well on his examinations. He ranked third in his class on one exam, sixth in the next. He scored high in mathematics and Sanskrit. English grammar and composition stumped him, but he did well enough to win a cash award from two princes of Kathiawar.

His life at home was calmer too. His young wife was expecting their first baby. Mohandas and Kasturbai were both sixteen years old.

Later that year, Mohandas's father fell ill. His children took turns staying at his bedside in the family home. They massaged his arms and legs, trying to keep him comfortable. But when it was Mohandas's turn, he could think only of his wife, who he now loved passionately. He longed to be with her. When an uncle offered to give him a break, Mohandas left eagerly. Only a few minutes later, a servant knocked on

High School attended by Mohandas Gandhi

the door of their bedroom to inform the young couple that the patriarch of the household, Kaba Gandhi, had died.

Years later, Gandhi remained guilty and ashamed that he had not stayed with his father until the moment of his death. Weeks after Kaba Gandhi's death, Kasturbai lost her baby in a miscarriage. She grieved in silence. But in Mohandas's mind, the two tragedies connected inexplicably. Ever after, he felt somehow responsible for both of these deaths.

The loss of his father jolted young Mohandas into adulthood. His older brothers worked to support the family, but neither made much money, so it was up to Mohandas. The family agreed that his schooling was the key to a good future job.

This was his final year in school. He had to sit for an important examination, the ticket to the rest of his life: the matriculation examination of Bombay University.

In 1887, at the age of eighteen, Mohandas caught a train to the city of Ahmedabad and made his way to the exam center. He was shown to his seat. He had to write forty lines in English "on the advantage of a cheerful disposition," define words like "pleonasm" and "metaphor," and solve difficult math equations. Chemical formulae, maps, British history—this was the hardest test he'd ever taken!

pleonasm | *noun* the use of more words than necessary to convey meaning (e.g. see with one's eyes), for style or emphasis

metaphor | *noun* describing an object or action by naming another that is not directly related (e.g. a heart of gold)

Part of the test required Mohandas to translate a passage from English to his native Gujarati. As he read the passage, he found himself quite interested. Instead of erecting statues to Queen Victoria, the passage suggested, the Golden Jubilee of her reign should be celebrated by raising a fund "enabling India to take her place in the new industrial world." What a good idea! His nervousness deserting him, Mohandas plunged into translation.

Passing the exam, Mohandas enrolled the following year in Samaldas College, the first college to grant degrees in Kathiawar. It was over 150 miles away from his home in Rajkot. He traveled there by camel cart and train and stayed in a rented room.

At Samaldas College, Mohandas attended five hours of lectures a day, in English, mathematics, physics, logic, and history. He was homesick and performed badly, appearing for only four exams out of seven, barely scraping by in English. As in high school, algebra defied him. He wondered what this education was worth. Where could it lead him?

In addition to schoolwork, Mohandas was reading Gujarati writers, among them the poet Narmad—the very same one whose verse had influenced him to try eating meat! Narmad saw British rule as a challenge to Indians. He urged Indians to discard their outmoded traditions and move into the modern era.

Mohandas read books by Narsing Mehta, a fifteenth-century poet whose work was now in print for the first time. One of these poems would become a beloved song, bringing peace to Gandhi's mind in times of struggle. In it, the poet suggests that true followers of God are those who feel the suffering of others, help people who are in pain, and never let pride into their hearts. Between school and home, these voices and ideas, chiming and clashing with each other, gave Mohandas plenty to think about.

That year, 1888, Mohandas's wife gave birth to their first son, Harilal. At eighteen, Mohandas was a father. It wasn't until he came home for the summer holidays that he saw his three-month-old son for the first time. His life was changing so fast, it made his head spin.

More change was on the horizon. A family friend, Mavji Dave, came to visit. He suggested to Putliba that Mohandas should leave Samaldas College and go farther for an education—much farther. He should go to London, England. A degree from London would assure him a high-ranking job.

London! The family exploded with questions and objections. It was too far—there was an ocean in between! London was filled with temptations for a Hindu boy who knew nothing of the world. And what would he study?

Mohandas himself suggested medicine. It was not a serious interest; rather, he was guessing wildly, trying to find something that would be better than the slog at Samaldas.

Dave recommended another path. Hadn't Mohandas's late father reached the high post of diwan at the court of Porbandar? A comparable job at that very court would be a worthy goal for young Mohandas. "[T]he medical degree will not make a Diwan of you, and I want you to be Diwan, or if possible something better." He should study law.

In London, Dave said, he could get a law degree in half the time it would take to gain a bachelor of arts at Samaldas College. Mohandas was excited by the thought of studying abroad. "I . . . was a coward. But that moment my cowardice vanished before the desire to go to England, which completely possessed me."

The Gandhis' Bania caste group buzzed with the news. Their strict religion forbade travel abroad. Crossing the ocean, the so-called "black water"—the only way to travel to London at the time—was thought to pollute the traveler. Relatives and acquaintances did their best to threaten, coax, and dissuade Mohandas. They pronounced him an outcast. This only made him determined to sail as soon as he could.

Putliba made her son swear that he would not drink wine or eat meat, that he would stay faithful to his wife. Only then did she give her consent. With his mother's blessing, Mohandas got ready for a life-changing journey to the land of the people who ruled India. Saying good-bye to his sobbing wife and new baby, fighting back his own tears, he set off for Bombay, where ships set sail across the ocean to European ports.

He was not quite nineteen years old, and he was ready to see the world.

4

Questions Large and Small

The shipboard world of the SS *Clyde* gave Mohandas a chance to prepare for life in a strange new country. He made a few friends. He gained the courage to speak in English. It wasn't easy. "[E]ven when I understood I could not reply. I had to frame every sentence in my mind before I could bring it out."

At first, he hardly dared to leave his cabin. But after a few days, Mohandas grew fidgety. When he did venture out, he found himself fascinated by the world of the ship. The sailors on deck worked constantly. How skilled they were, looping and knotting great lengths of rope, checking the rigging. It was all very mysterious to him. He enjoyed the fresh air on deck. On the passenger deck, he watched European travelers playing chess, cards, and draughts (the British form of checkers). He worked up the courage to plink the keys of the shipboard piano, an instrument he had never seen in his life.

Gandhi marveled as the ship entered the mouth of the Suez

Canal. Snaking through the desert, a feat of engineering connecting Asia to Europe, the Red Sea to the Mediterranean, the waterway had been completed the very year he'd been born.

When the SS *Clyde* anchored in the city of Aden (in the present-day country of Yemen) and Gandhi went ashore for a quick tour, he found that "the currency was English. Indian money is quite useless here." He had indeed left his homeland.

Brindisi, on the heel of Italy's boot; Malta, in the Mediterranean Sea; and Gibraltar, on Spain's southern coast. Finally, the SS *Clyde* sailed into the chilly fog of the south of England. And here was London, at last, the imperial capital itself! It had factories that made furniture and leather, rubber goods, cork, and paper. Printshops churned out newspapers and books. Tailors and drapers and milliners crafted clothes and linens and hats for the wealthy. It was a city of six million people, its streets crammed with horse carriages and milling crowds, its air smoky from the soot of chimneys.

Gandhi and two shipmates took a train from the port to a hotel they had heard about on board ship. They were dazzled by the Victoria Hotel's massive stone façade and its electric lights.

The hotel manager ushered his guests through a set of doors. Gandhi wrote later, "The doors were opened and I thought that was a room in which we were to sit for some time." To his astonishment, with some creaking and grinding, the "room" began to move, and "to my great surprise we were brought to the second floor." He had just ridden in an elevator, which the English called a "lift."

London was a living textbook for young Gandhi. He learned lessons in English manners from an Indian friend: "[N]ever address people [as] 'sir' whilst speaking to them as we do in India; only servants and subordinates address their masters that way." He read English newspapers from cover to cover and was surprised to find a whole range of opinions in them, for and against the government. His English improved.

Many of the people he met, both English and Indian, tried to talk him into eating meat and drinking wine. It was the only way to survive in such a cold place, they told him. At first, he felt embarrassed at the attention, but he argued back and kept his promises to his mother—no meat, no alcohol. The porridge and boiled vegetables tasted unbearably bland, and he missed the rich flavors of his homeland.

As much as the city and its people were teaching him, there was more important learning to be done. He was here to study the law. Gandhi registered at the Inner Temple, a professional organization for lawyers in training. The place was awe-inspiring, and it tested his newfound confidence. He walked in hushed silence through its great inner courtyard. Parts of these august buildings were forbidden to him, a lowly student. But for a young man fresh from India, the courtyard offered a refuge from the bustle and dirt of the city, and the larger-than-life statues of knights in armor were stories in stone from England's past.

As in India, England's colleges and professions were filled with men. Women were not eligible to become lawyers, so the Inner Temple had no female members.

The Inner Temple had strict rules. To be admitted to the legal profession, to "the Bar," Gandhi was required to do more than study. He had to "keep terms." This meant attending six out of twenty-four

Inner Temple

dinners each year in the great dining hall—as Gandhi put it, "eating one's terms." At meals, he had to mingle with other young lawyers in training and with senior members.

A porter announced each formal meal by blowing a horn. Members and students, dressed in their legal gowns, filed into the dining hall. Everyone stood in silence until the highest-ranking lawyers took their seats at the high table. Members sat in assigned seats

Admission book, Inner Temple. Gandhi started writing on the wrong line and had to strike out his first attempt. His signature is second from the bottom, with the false start above it.

on lower benches. Students sat down to eat in the lowest seats of all.

When the food arrived, most of it was meat. Gandhi ate only boiled potatoes, cabbage, and bread. He noticed platters of fresh produce being served to those sitting at the upper tables. After a while, he and a fellow vegetarian plucked up the nerve to ask for some of the grander fare. Speaking up worked. "[W]e began to get fruits and . . . vegetables." Since Mohandas did not want his wine, his table companions got to drink it for him, which kept everyone happy.

Gandhi did find a vegetarian restaurant in London, and he found himself welcomed by the Vegetarian Society of London. The English people he'd known so far had been authority figures, both in India and in the legal training grounds of London. Here, at last, he made English friends. Vegetarianism became the first of many causes that came to matter to him.

His new friends held firm values. Live simply, they told him. Don't spend on luxuries. These values echoed those of home—other than the women's jewelry, mostly now pawned to finance Mohandas's education, the Gandhi family owned few expensive possessions. When he first arrived in England, Gandhi had taken care to dress well, in order to fit in and make a good impression. He brushed and ironed his coat. He made sure his shirt collars were starched and his shoes polished. He even begged his brother to send him a gold watch chain for his pocket watch.

Now, sorry for his own careless extravagance, he cut corners. He gave up starching his laundry. He shaved himself instead of going to

Gandhi as a law student in London

a barber. He stopped buying newspapers and instead began reading them at the public library.

His new friends wanted to talk about religion. They begged him to explain the Bhagavad Gita, a sacred text of his own Hindu faith. Surprised at their interest—the English people he'd met in India generally thought little of Indian religions—Gandhi was also ashamed to admit that he had never read it. He decided to make up for that at once. He began to read an English translation, keeping up, chapter by chapter, with his friends as they met to discuss the text.

With members of the Vegetarian Society in London, 1890

The Bhagavad Gita impressed Gandhi deeply. Many of its verses rang true to him. "Let right deeds be thy motive," he read. Seek "the truth of truths" and "live in action," with "noble purpose." Later in his life, Gandhi would read the Gita every day, seeking in it answers to questions large and small.

He also determined to read the Christian Bible. The Old Testament was tough going. Some chapters put him to sleep. He plodded through them anyway. But the New Testament thrilled him, "especially the Sermon on the Mount which went straight to my heart." The message of Jesus Christ moved him to tears. He began to think about what it meant to turn the other cheek, to face greed with generosity and evil with love. He began to think that love, perhaps, had the power to transform the world.

When he was not reading or meeting new people, Gandhi took long walks through the city. Once, he calculated that he walked an average of eight miles a day.

He was also studying for the bar examinations.

The exams were said to be easy, but Gandhi ended up making them difficult for himself. He read every single recommended text. He also decided to study Roman law in the Latin language! He had picked up a smattering of it while studying for the Bombay matriculation exam. As a boy, he had not cared for school lessons. Now he set to work eagerly, trying to find the "noble purpose" of his life.

BAR EXAMINATION A BAR EXAMINATION IS A TEST TO DETERMINE IF A PERSON IS QUALIFIED TO PRACTICE LAW. GANDHI HAD TO TAKE TWO OF THEM, ONE IN ROMAN LAW AND ONE IN BRITISH COMMON LAW.

The studying paid off. He sat for the exams and passed both, standing 6th out of 46 in the first and 34th out of 109 in the second.

His confidence was increasing, yet Gandhi remained shy. He hated speaking in public. But he discovered another way to employ words: in writing. The editor of the Vegetarian Society's newsletter asked Gandhi to write an article for the publication.

Gandhi wrote not one article, but six. He pondered over the task, choosing his words with care. How could he best inform an English audience about India's customs and people? He dipped his nib pen in ink and wrote. Many people in England believed "all Indians are born vegetarians." On the contrary, Gandhi wrote, "some are so voluntarily and others compulsorily . . . there are thousands who live on bread and salt, a heavily taxed article." How, he asked, could they afford meat even if they wanted it? He circled around to the idea that meat was a food obtained violently, by the killing of an animal. He argued that one could grow strong on a vegetarian diet.

From philosophy, Gandhi slipped into the kitchen. One of his articles described how to make the *roti*, or flatbread, common across much of India. Divide the dough, he wrote, "into small equal parts, each as big as a tangerine. These are rolled into thin circular pieces about six inches in diameter with a wooden stick made specially for the purpose. Each piece is separately and thoroughly baked in a flat dish. It takes from five to seven minutes to bake one cake."

The articles made him something of a celebrity in the growing community of vegetarians in England. Not bad for someone who had never heard English spoken in his home, didn't start learning the language until he was eleven, and had been deemed weak in English composition and grammar.

Until that time, Gandhi's schooling had required him to memorize facts and reproduce them. Now writing these articles drove him to reflect upon his own ideas and to make connections between them. Most of all, writing made Gandhi want to speak the truth as he saw it and to communicate with others about things that mattered to him. He began to realize something else. Here in England, in contrast to the arrogant East India Company officials at home, some white people treated Gandhi as if he was their equal and their friend.

Gandhi finished his studies and attended his dinners. By June 10, 1891, he was a qualified lawyer. The next day, he enrolled at the High Court. He gave a farewell restaurant dinner to his fellow vegetarians, at which he made a speech. The next morning, triumphant at his success, he left for home.

Three and a half weeks after its departure from London, Gandhi's ship reached the port of Bombay in the middle of a monsoon rainstorm. The turmoil within him was every bit as stormy as the weather. He was about to see his wife again, and his son, Harilal, who was now two years old. Would he even recognize his father? Gandhi felt an aching need to see Putliba, his sweet mother, to tell her that he had kept his promises.

He needed to get a job. His legal training had prepared him—for what? To be an English gentleman? He worried that he'd learned a lot of lofty ideals and nothing practical at all. Nothing about the law in India. The future suddenly felt as unstable as the ship's deck slanting beneath his feet.

The ship docked in a downpour. There among the crowds of people, Gandhi spotted the face of his brother Laxmidas. He could see at once that something was wrong.

Laxmidas brought news. The family could have sent Mohandas a letter or a telegram, but they hadn't wanted to disrupt his studies. Now he had to face a terrible loss. While Mohandas had been in England, his mother had become seriously ill and had passed away.

5

A Lawyer Abroad

Back at home, mourning his beloved mother, Mohandas Gandhi could not find work. He took on legal jobs for the prince of Porbandar. In the process, he had to deal with English officials. In England, he had made friends with so many white people, but the English in India lost no time reminding him who was in charge.

He felt like a failure. He took it out on his wife, arguing with her about trivial things. As a mother, Kastur had a new status now and even a new name. She was no longer "bai," but "Kasturba." She had missed him terribly when they were apart, yet living with him now was hardly easy. She bore his bouts of temper with patience.

On the advice of friends, Gandhi sought work at the High Court in Bombay, over five hundred miles away. There, he made friends with other lawyers, but found no clients. When he was finally hired to argue a case in court, he became so tongue-tied that he could not even speak coherently.

After six frustrating months in Bombay, he returned to Rajkot. In England, Gandhi had thrown himself into the hundreds of tasks required to make him a lawyer. Now he faced rejection in his chosen profession. So he tried setting up a business that could put his writing skills to work. A few clients came to him, then a few more. He wrote petitions, mostly about land disputes, and earned around three hundred rupees a month. He needed this to support his growing family—the couple's second son, Manilal, was born in 1892. At least now Gandhi did not have to depend on loans from his brothers, who in turn were managing to support themselves.

One day, the mail brought a letter all the way from South Africa. It was from an Indian businessman, Dada Abdulla. He needed a lawyer fluent in both English and Gujarati. He offered round-trip ship's fare, room and board, and a fee in British currency of £105.

Gandhi was only just reconnecting with his wife and family. He was sorry to leave, but he felt he had no choice. In truth, it was also a "tempting opportunity of seeing a new country, and of having a new experience." He accepted the offer, sailing once again from Bombay, arriving a month later in the port of Durban.

Within a week, he found himself thrown off the train to Pretoria.

Dumped off the train, Gandhi collected himself. From the station, he sent two telegrams. One was a complaint to the railway authorities. The other was to Dada Abdulla, his employer. Abdulla in turn

HOW MUCH MONEY IS THAT? IF YOU HAD 300 RUPEES IN THE 1890S IN INDIA, YOU COULD BUY AS MUCH AS YOU CAN BUY IN THE U.S. TODAY WITH ABOUT $4,000. IN 1890S BRITAIN, £105 HAD THE SAME SPENDING POWER AS $10,000 TODAY.

contacted Indian merchants in Pietermaritzburg. They came to the station to sympathize with Gandhi. Indians, they told him, were often treated badly in South Africa.

That evening, Gandhi resumed his journey to Pretoria with an uneventful train ride to Charlestown. There, he tried to board a stage-coach to Johannesburg. At first, the man in charge of the coach gave him his own seat, next to the driver, while he himself sat inside with the white passengers. Gandhi was furious but held his tongue. Then, at

Sea routes taken by Gandhi to South Africa and England. (The city of Bombay is now called Mumbai.)

THE BRITISH IN SOUTH AFRICA THERE WERE FOUR BRITISH COLONIES IN SOUTH AFRICA: CAPE COLONY, NATAL COLONY, TRANSVAAL COLONY, AND ORANGE RIVER COLONY. THE BRITISH ESTABLISHED A SOUTH AFRICA COMPANY, LIKE THE EAST INDIA COMPANY AND THE VIRGINIA COMPANY, TO EXPLORE AND TRADE ON THE CONTINENT.

a midpoint stop, the coachman changed his mind. Maybe he wanted to get a smoke or fresh air. Whatever the reason, he put a dirty cloth on the footboard of the coach. "You sit on this," he said to Gandhi. "I want to sit near the driver." Gandhi protested. At this, the coachman leaped on him, hit him in the head, and tried to push him off the stagecoach.

The coach began to move. Gandhi hung on to the brass rails for dear life all the way to the next stop. There, he got off, shaking with anger. Once again, local Indian merchants comforted him, but the ordeal was not over. In Johannesburg, he was denied a hotel room. On the train from Johannesburg to Pretoria, he was asked to move to third class. He refused. A white passenger said he was willing to share the compartment with him. At last, Gandhi completed his journey.

The lawyer with whom Gandhi was supposed to work on Dada Abdulla's case was a white man, Albert Baker. In addition to his law practice, he was also a Christian preacher. He introduced Gandhi to other Christians. Gandhi found them friendly but was soon dismayed when they tried to convert him.

Gandhi wore a necklace of wooden beads that had been given to him by his mother. Baker's friends tried to convince him that the talisman was a sign of superstition. They told him to break the necklace and throw it away. Politely, Gandhi refused. Baker and his friends were good people. Their opinions came from deeply held beliefs. He could understand how they felt. He just didn't have to agree with them.

While he made new friends, Gandhi threw himself into his work. Dada Abdulla was suing his cousin, Khan Mohammad Tayob, claiming Tayob owed him £40,000. Gandhi wrote briefs for Baker and others to argue the case in court. He translated piles of Gujarati letters and documents into English. And he realized something. Even if Abdulla won, the case could drag on for months. Everyone would lose. Only the lawyers would profit.

After mulling it over, Gandhi suggested an alternative. Why not work on settling the case out of court? There was a process for that. It was called "arbitration." "I strained every nerve to bring about a compromise." At last, the cousins agreed. An arbitrator was appointed. The case was argued before him—and Dada Abdulla won.

This did not satisfy Gandhi. If his client pressed his cousin for the money, it would ruin Tayob. The Muslims of that area were a proud people. They considered bankruptcy to be an unbearable disgrace. Death was thought to be better than such ruin. What if Tayob were to kill himself? Gandhi persuaded Abdulla to let his cousin pay him on an installment plan. Everyone was happy, no one more than Gandhi. He felt he had truly understood the law and worked within it to help everyone concerned. "I realized that the true function of a lawyer was to unite parties riven asunder."

Once he had helped to settle Dada Abdulla's case, Gandhi planned to go back home to India. Dada Abdulla held a farewell dinner for him. But at that dinner, the talk turned to a bill being considered by lawmakers in the South African province of Natal. The bill would strip Indians living there of the right to vote. The merchants offered to pay Gandhi to stay on in Durban and help them fight the bill.

To Gandhi, racial prejudice in South Africa was as jolting as being thrown off a train. In India, the British ruled, but they were outnumbered. In London, the very seat of the empire, Gandhi could meet and eat and talk with Englishmen. Exotic and strange as he was to them, the liberal English he met treated him as their equal.

Some South African provinces were ruled by the British, others by the Boers—descendants of Dutch settlers who spoke the Afrikaans language. But here, there was no question of equality between the races. Most white South Africans believed that native black-skinned people were only fit to be servants.

Indians had been brought to South Africa to work on the sugar plantations as indentured laborers since the 1860s. Other so-called "passenger Indians," mostly Gujarati like Gandhi, came as traders. Indian businesses were now growing in number.

In the late nineteenth century, Indians began to register to vote. Having colonized the land and completely subjugated local Black people, white South Africans were taken by surprise at the very idea that dark-skinned people might want to be treated as equals. The white minority promptly

Indentured Labor

Laborers brought to South Africa from India were bound to their employers by contract. A worker was obliged to work for his employer until he had paid off the cost of his passage from his home country. That could take years, sometimes a lifetime. The children of a laborer could "inherit" his indenture. Then they had to continue working for the same master.

It wasn't slavery, but it came close. The work was backbreaking. Employers were often brutal. If an escaped laborer was caught, he was tried in criminal court and sent to jail.

enacted laws to curb the freedom of the new arrivals. In some places, Indians could not be on the streets after nine o'clock unless they carried passes. They were pushed off sidewalks, kicked and beaten, forced to live in slums.

So, when the merchants at Abdulla's gathering begged Gandhi to stay and oppose the new law, he accepted.

Gandhi drafted a petition to the Natal Assembly questioning the new bill. Hundreds of copies were written out by hand. Over eight thousand Indians signed it. The local newspaper published it. It was not a fiery piece. Gandhi wrote that Indians were not "propagandists of agitation" but "British subjects, who have come from India and settled in the Colony." He was trying to be reasonable, appealing to the goodwill of the government.

The petition was ignored. The bill became law, stripping Indians of the right to vote. But by now, Indians in South Africa saw twenty-five-year-old Gandhi as a leader.

He founded a political party, the Natal Indian Congress, named after the Indian National Congress. An important part of its business, in Gandhi's words, "was propaganda. This consisted in acquainting the English in South Africa and England and people in India with the real state of things in Natal." Words had the power to persuade, he knew. He would use them to make people understand one another.

THE INDIAN NATIONAL CONGRESS THE INDIAN NATIONAL CONGRESS WAS FOUNDED IN INDIA IN 1885. IT WAS MEANT TO GIVE INDIANS A LEGAL WAY TO CONVEY THEIR GRIEVANCES TO THE BRITISH RULERS.

At the same time, Gandhi applied to the Natal Bar Association to try to practice law. The association tried to stop him on grounds of race, but the Supreme Court granted his license. As a lawyer trained in London, he was one of a kind—the only Indian in all of South Africa who could speak across racial boundaries.

Gandhi with members of the Natal Indian Congress, 1895

One day, a man came to see Gandhi. He was an indentured laborer: "[A] Tamil man in tattered clothes, head-gear in hand, two front teeth broken and his mouth bleeding, stood before me trembling and weeping." He had been beaten by his employer. Gandhi got medical help, then got in touch with the employer. Instead of filing a lawsuit, he arranged a new job for the worker. He interviewed the new employer to make sure there would be no more abuse. The laborer, his client, was deeply grateful.

Word got around. Indian laborers began to flock to Gandhi for help, "and I came to be regarded as their friend." Some, who had managed to complete their indenture terms and were trying to go into business, were forced into closure by the government's punishing tax. The Natal Indian Congress fought the tax and got it reduced.

All along, Gandhi read books on religion and philosophy— nearly a hundred in a year. He discovered the great Russian writer Leo Tolstoy, who wrote that following one's conscience is better than obeying the rules of churches or the laws of kings and generals. He wrote about Christ's Sermon on the Mount—a call to the meek, the pure at heart, the peacemakers. With his conscience as guide, Gandhi grew convinced that he didn't have to follow anyone else's spiritual path. He could find his own. More importantly, he began to think of peacemaking as a strength rather than a weakness.

In 1896, having decided to stay in South Africa, Gandhi traveled to India so he could bring Kasturba and the children back with him. During the trip, he spoke to eager audiences about the plight of Indians in South Africa. Once, the crowd was so large that his voice failed to reach the back of the room. Others had to read his written speech.

" The only means of deliverance from violence lies in not taking part in it. " — Leo Tolstoy

He met important people from both Hindu and Muslim communities, leaders of India's newly formed political parties. Everyone praised his work in South Africa.

He published a flyer about the struggles of Indians in South Africa. It became known as "The Green Pamphlet" for the color of its cover. To save money, he got his children to fold hundreds of copies and stick on the stamps. He mailed the pamphlet to major newspapers in India and to all the political parties. It was quoted in the Indian papers and then in England. News of Gandhi's pamphlet made its way overseas, all the way back to far-off Natal.

While Gandhi was in India, plague, carried by infected rat fleas, broke out in the western provinces. To contain the disease, Gandhi helped the sanitation department inspect people's homes and improve drains and bathrooms. His sister Raliat's husband was stricken. Gandhi nursed him personally, but could not save him.

Despite this tragic event, Gandhi and his family—his wife and

A 1922 commemorative edition of Gandhi's Green Pamphlet

sons, along with Gokuldas, his sister's son—had to get ready for their trip to South Africa. He taught the boys to sing the British national anthem, "God Save the Queen." Kasturba and the boys were used to eating with their fingers. Now Gandhi made them eat with knives and forks and wear a blend of Indian and European-style clothes, including stockings and shoes. The boys found the shoes torturous. Kasturba said of her aching feet, "What a heavy price one has to pay to be regarded as civilized." But Gandhi still believed in the British Empire. He questioned its unfair laws, yet felt he and his family should be loyal subjects.

When the Gandhi family arrived in Durban, their ship, coming from a port afflicted by plague, was placed in quarantine. Groups of white protesters crowded on the shore, infuriated by the publication of "The Green Pamphlet." Mobs gathered, five thousand strong. They shouted, "Send the Indians back!" They yelled for Gandhi, intending to beat him up. The attorney general of Natal spoke to the crowd. He assured them Natal would remain a white colony, no matter what the Indians wanted.

After twenty-three days on board, the passengers were finally allowed to disembark. Because Gandhi was warned he might be the target of angry white people, he sent Kasturba and the children ahead, directing them to take a carriage to the house of an Indian businessman who would give them shelter. Off the ship at last, he was pushed and jostled by a gang of white boys. Crowds pelted him with stones, bricks, and eggs. They beat and kicked him. Someone lashed at him with a whip.

When Gandhi tried to escape, the mob threw mud and stale fish at him. He nearly passed out. Finally, a white woman, Jane Alexander, wife of the Durban police superintendent, got between him and his attackers. She protected Gandhi with her parasol as he was escorted to the police station. The superintendent diverted the crowd, which by then was singing, "We'll hang old Gandhi on the sour apple tree."

From the police station, dressed up in a government worker's uniform, his face blackened and covered by a scarf, Gandhi was spirited to the safety of his friend's house.

6

In Search of Truth

Traumatic as their arrival in South Africa had been, the Gandhi family finally entered their new home—Beach Grove Villa, a rented five-bedroom house overlooking the bay, in a fashionable, mostly European section of Durban. The two-story house with shuttered windows had no familiar courtyard, no flat rooftop. Gandhi showed the boys the swings and parallel bars they could play on in the backyard.

Gandhi began work, walking daily to his office, writing letters for professional Indians—a typist, a doctor—seeking government jobs. An Indian merchant had been beaten by white attackers. Gandhi obtained compensation for him.

As his practice grew, Gandhi worried about his sons' and nephew's education. The best schools were for whites only. Missionary schools would accept the boys, but the teachers might try to convert them to Christianity. He decided to school them at home. He hired an English

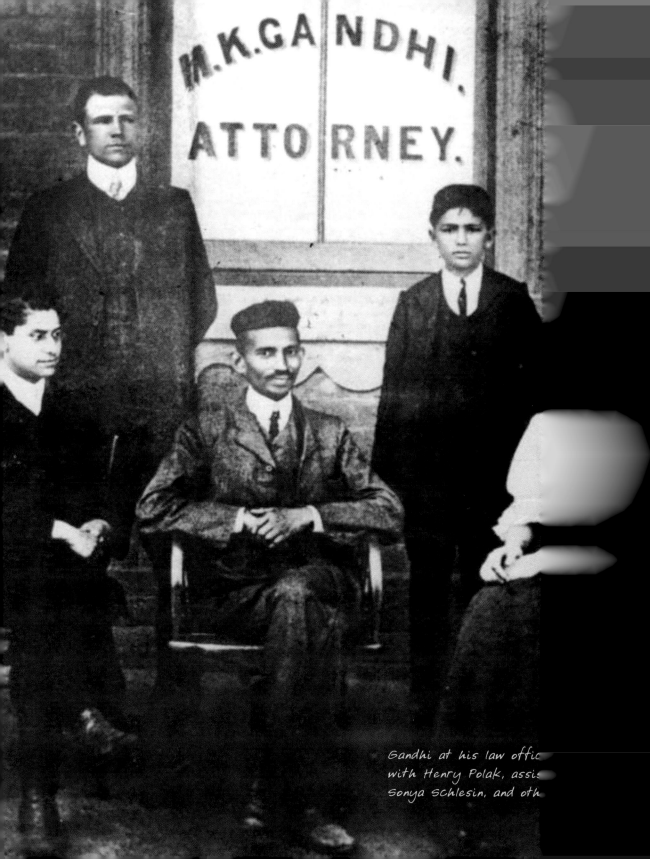

M.K.GANDHI.
ATTORNEY.

Gandhi at his law offic
with Henry Polak, assis
Sonya Schlesin, and oth

governess. He himself would teach the boys their Gujarati language.

That was the plan. In practice, Gandhi was too busy with legal work and social causes; the children often got overlooked. Meanwhile, the family grew. A new baby, Ramdas, was born in 1897, and three years later came the Gandhis' last child, Devadas.

When Kasturba was expecting Devadas, Gandhi decided to "have the best medical aid at the time of her delivery." He convinced Kasturba to allow a strange male doctor in the birthing room. Just in case, he studied the passages on childbirth in a medical book written in Gujarati. As it turned out, Kasturba went into labor early; the doctor was not available, "and some time was lost in fetching the midwife." With a calm akin to his own mother's handling of scorpions, Gandhi delivered the baby himself.

He began to do his own chores rather than hiring servants as others did—he washed his own clothes, starched his shirts. When visitors arrived, often for long stays, they, too, were expected to work alongside the family.

In those days, there was no indoor plumbing. In India, people who cleaned toilets were despised, considered so impure, they

Durban around
1885

were called "untouchables." In South Africa, bedrooms had chamber pots that needed to be emptied. Instead of hiring help for the job, Gandhi insisted everyone should take their own chamber pots outside, empty the smelly contents, wash the pots, and return them to their places.

Once, a new visitor arrived. He either did not know or did not follow the house rule. Gandhi decided that he himself, with Kasturba's help, would empty the guest's used chamber pot. Kasturba refused. Gandhi was enraged. He nearly pushed his wife out the door. Weeping, she protested. Did he know what he was doing? Had he no shame? Just in time, he pulled himself together. Later, he felt sorry for having shown so much anger. He cringed at the way he had shouted at her.

Kasturba with the children and her husband's nephew, around 1899, before the birth of Devadas

Outside home and work, Gandhi volunteered in a local physician's clinic. When a man stricken with leprosy, a dreaded disease, came to his door, Gandhi took him in and dressed his wounds. He sent him to the hospital only when it became clear that he could not keep him at home forever.

While Gandhi worked with the Natal Indian Congress, the Anglo-Boer War broke out. On one side were Afrikaans-speaking Boers, demanding independence from Britain; on the other, the British, determined to squash the rebellion. Although Gandhi secretly sympathized with the Boer cause, he decided to remain loyal to the

British Empire. He raised an ambulance corps of 1,100 Indians to support British forces. The corps served for six weeks, rescuing wounded soldiers from behind the firing line. Sometimes they had to march for twenty-five miles, carrying the wounded on stretchers to the nearest clinic. The experience opened Gandhi's eyes to the brutality of war. Yet British soldiers he had met on the battlefield had been kind to him and grateful for his help. Why were they not as kind in peacetime?

With troop reinforcements from England assuring British victory, the ambulance corps was no longer needed. Gandhi decided to return to India. His merchant friends showered him with gifts—gold watches and gold and diamond jewelry, including a necklace for Kasturba. Gandhi felt he couldn't possibly accept such expensive presents. But what about his wife? Would she agree? He doubted it.

Gandhi approached this dilemma like a general planning a campaign. First, he involved his sons: Harilal, eleven, and Manilal, seven. He persuaded them to take his side.

As he had suspected, Kasturba was indignant. "What about my daughters-in-law?" she demanded, pointing to her baffled boys. "They will be sure to need them. . . . And who knows what will happen tomorrow?"

In the end, he won. "I am definitely of the opinion that a public worker should accept no costly gifts." In fact, he was not a public worker. He had been hired by the merchants and was paid by his clients. But that is how he saw himself.

In October 1901, the family sailed for Bombay. They stopped in the Indian Ocean island of Mauritius, also a British colony where Indians had been brought to work on the sugar plantations. Gandhi

urged them to take part in local elections, to strive for "a place in the sun under the pavilion of liberty." He believed liberty could be won at the ballot box and in the courtroom. Diplomacy and compromise were tools he knew how to use.

Back in India, Gandhi attended a session of the Indian National Congress in the city of Calcutta (now Kolkata). One of its leaders, Gopal Krishna Gokhale, encouraged Gandhi to speak about his work in South Africa. He did, urging the party to pass a resolution, addressed to the British government in India and in England, in support of their fellow Indians in South Africa. To his surprise, the resolution passed. It affirmed Gandhi's growing belief that peaceable demands gained strength from numbers.

A health crisis marred the family's homecoming. Gandhi's second son, Manilal, fell ill with typhoid. Gandhi and Kasturba gave the boy hot baths and watched over him constantly. Gandhi prayed, murmuring the name of the god Rama as his nurse, Rambha, had taught him long ago. Finally, the fever broke. "I had no fear now." His faith in God grew strong—a personal, loving God, not Hindu nor Muslim nor Christian, but above all these.

Once Manilal was well, Gandhi looked for work. But employers in his native Gujarat were unimpressed by his experiences overseas, and no one wanted to hire him. It was almost a relief to receive a letter from the Natal Indian Congress. Now that South Africa was under British control, the government postponed the question of franchise for native Blacks and altogether ignored the matter of votes for Indians. Gandhi was needed. Would he please return? He accepted. Kasturba and the boys could stay on in Bombay until he got himself situated.

Arriving once more in South Africa, Gandhi set up a law practice in Johannesburg and began writing petitions on behalf of Indians complaining of discrimination. He hired clerks and a secretary. He rode a bicycle to court and to meet clients. In his spare time, he started a journal named *Indian Opinion*.

Soon Kasturba and three of the boys arrived from India, along with a couple of Gandhi nephews. Ramdas had broken his arm on the ship. Gandhi set it himself, caring for him until the arm healed. His oldest son, Harilal, now a teenager, remained in school in Bombay. At this point, he was closer to his uncles than to his own father, whom he hardly knew.

In 1904, pneumonic plague broke out in Brickfields, an Indian settlement, home to some of Gandhi's clients. At once, he rode out on his bicycle to join a relief team at a makeshift hospital. Many people were saved, but twenty-one died. "It was a terrible night—that night of vigil and nursing," Gandhi wrote.

While Gandhi helped the sick, he tried to educate people in Brickfields. Keeping their surroundings clean could help prevent disease. Overcoming her shyness, Kasturba visited women in the settlement and convinced them to help clean the temporary hospital.

Gandhi wrote to the press, criticizing the municipality for neglecting Brickfields and causing the outbreak. One day, when he was dining in a vegetarian restaurant in Johannesburg, a young man introduced himself. His name was Henry Polak. He had read Gandhi's letter.

Printing Press founded by Gandhi in South Africa, now a historic site

Polak loaned Gandhi a book, *Unto This Last*, by English writer John Ruskin. The book blamed capitalist societies for the terrible conditions in which poor people lived. Ruskin believed that people should be generous and cooperate with one another. Gandhi was as moved by Ruskin as he had been by Tolstoy. He began to think of the two of them as his teachers. He decided to live by Ruskin's teachings. He moved his newspaper, *Indian Opinion*, to a farm outside the city. He called it the Phoenix Settlement.

Gandhi invited others to join him there. Everyone would work on the farm and the paper. People of all races and nationalities would be treated as equals. Henry Polak joined him. So did two of Gandhi's nephews and other relatives from India. Soon the community bustled with market gardens, a dairy, and of course the newspaper. Everyone was paid a wage of £3 a month.

All the while, Gandhi continued his law practice, shuttling between city and farm. He rented a larger house. Henry Polak and his wife, Millie, moved in. Kasturba was ill at ease sharing her home with Europeans, especially with her husband gone so much. But it also opened her eyes to the world. Millie Polak believed passionately in women's rights. She and Kasturba had long conversations. They sometimes disagreed but became friends.

In 1906, a new law in the Transvaal province of South Africa called Gandhi to action once again. The Asiatic Registration Act required Indians and other Asians to register their fingerprints and carry registration certificates or face deportation. Those affected were outraged.

At a mass meeting at the Empire Theatre in Johannesburg, Gandhi laid out a new approach to resistance. He called upon Indians to defy

The Zulu Rebellion

In 1906, a leader named Bambatha led his Zulu people in a rebellion against a new poll tax. The government sent troops to subdue them. Instead of siding with the Black African rebels, Gandhi organized Indians to carry stretchers and help wounded soldiers in the battlefield. At the time, he still believed that "the British Empire existed for the welfare of the world."

That loyalty began to erode as Gandhi was sickened by the violence in the battlefield. He heard "rifles exploding like crackers in innocent hamlets." The simple villages of the Zulu people reminded him of villages in India. As a stretcher-bearer, sometimes marching forty miles a day, he was overcome with guilt at being on the side of the oppressors in this struggle. He decided to help all the wounded—Zulu, Indian, and white.

He was doubly disheartened when the Zulu rebellion was brutally crushed and the leader, Bambatha, executed.

the law in an entirely new way: No one should take up arms. Rather, they should simply disobey the unfair law. If they were arrested, they should go cheerfully to jail.

It was a serious thing to ask, and he knew it. He was asking them to disobey the authorities, much as young Kastur had disobeyed him years ago when he had been unfair. Only this enemy had far greater power than a foolish young husband. In this new movement, Gandhi was asking for heroes.

He called his passive resistance strategy *satyagraha,* or "holding fast to truth." Truth in Gandhi's mind equaled justice, and every waking minute, justice was what he sought. He even traveled to London, hoping to persuade the British to reject the unfair law. He met with a high-ranking official named Winston Churchill but returned to Johannesburg disappointed. Instead of giving up, however, Gandhi launched the promised protests.

SATYAGRAHA A POLICY OF PEACEFUL POLITICAL RESISTANCE, ESPECIALLY THAT ADVOCATED BY MAHATMA GANDHI, AGAINST BRITISH RULE IN INDIA.

Thousands of Indians went on strike. They refused to register with the authorities. Many were arrested. The jails filled rapidly. Gandhi received his own sentence in a courtroom where he had once argued a case as a lawyer.

To negotiate, the government sent a senior minister named Jan Christiaan Smuts. If Indians registered voluntarily, Smuts said, the law would be repealed. Some registered. Many did not. The law remained in force, as did an annual tax of £3 first levied on Indians in 1895.

In return, Gandhi called on Indians to burn their government registration cards. Thousands turned the cards in. Others brought them to a meeting at a Muslim place of worship, the Hamidia Mosque in Johannesburg. People tossed the cards into a cauldron. Someone poured paraffin on the pile, struck a match, and threw it in. Flames crackled. The *Daily Mail* of London reported that it was something like the Boston Tea Party, when Americans had protested unfair taxes by throwing English tea into the harbor.

As Indians—Gandhi among them—tried to travel without their cards, they found themselves in jail. Some were flogged. A few were shot. Gandhi himself was arrested, released, and then rearrested. In prison, he broke stones for roadwork, dug holes for planting trees, and sewed caps for prison uniforms on a sewing machine. He also read an essay titled "Civil Disobedience" by an American writer named Henry David Thoreau, who had died before Gandhi was born, yet seemed to have walked the same road as him. Thoreau had even read Gandhi's beloved Bhagavad Gita!

Once released from prison, Gandhi found philosophy of little use. The South African government was refusing to budge on the new Transvaal law. How could Gandhi argue cases in court when he was opposing the government on moral grounds? He decided to give up his law practice and turn to the pursuit of truth—satyagraha. An architect friend, Hermann Kallenbach, donated a tract of farmland near Johannesburg to the movement and called it Tolstoy Farm, in honor of the writer and philosopher whose work Gandhi so admired.

To Gandhi, Tolstoy Farm, with its many fruit trees, its wells and sparkling spring, was an "experiment with truth." He invited peaceful resisters and their families to join this new community. He shuttled

Violence in England

On July 1, 1909, an Indian student named Madanlal Dhingra shot and killed a British army officer and former government official. At his trial, Dhingra asked to be sentenced to death, "for in that case the vengeance of my countrymen will be all the more keen." He was found guilty and executed by hanging.

Gandhi condemned both deaths—the murder and the execution—but on a trip to London, he met Indians who praised Dhingra. Among them was Vinayak Damodar Savarkar, who said India should gain freedom by any means, including violence.

between the farm and the city, while Kasturba and the boys remained in Natal, in the Phoenix Settlement. For three years, eighty people or more lived on the farm. They belonged to many faiths and spoke many languages. They pledged to work hard, live simply, and resist injustice.

Injustice kept demanding Gandhi's attention. In 1913, he organized a "Great March" from Newcastle in northern Natal, in support of Indian coal miners protesting the annual tax on Indians. The authorities had cut off light and water from the houses of the striking miners, who had called on Gandhi to help.

Until then, satyagraha had been carried on mainly by men. Now Gandhi invited women to join. Kasturba did, along with fifteen-year-old Ramdas and three other women from the Phoenix Settlement.

Gandhi planned to lead a group of marchers across the Natal-Transvaal border to Tolstoy Farm. But at the border, special trains waited to send them back to Natal. Gandhi, Kallenbach, and Polak were arrested. Gandhi was charged with conspiring to smuggle indentured laborers out of the province.

In jail, he served time with murderers and thieves. Given a sentence of "hard labor," he dug a stony field until his hands were blistered. He

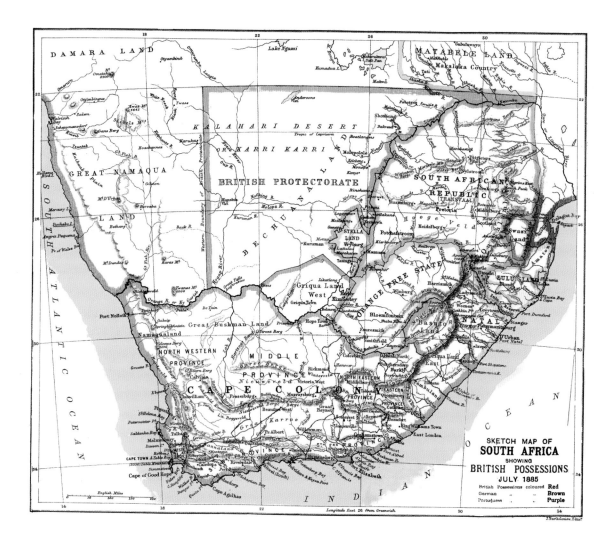

Map of South
Africa showing
British territory
and the Natal-
Transvaal border,
1885

worried about his fellow resisters—among them an eleven-year-old boy with a fourteen-day sentence and a seventy-five-year-old man. How could he sleep when the heroes he'd summoned were hurting on his account?

In response to Gandhi's arrest, Indian-owned stores closed. Prisons overflowed with protesters. Newspapers in South Africa and overseas published reports of the arrests. Indian leaders sent encouraging letters, as did Black South Africans. "Our sympathies go out to our oppressed fellow subjects," said an article in the Black-run *Basutoland Star*.

The British government urged the colonial rulers to settle with the strikers. Gandhi was released from jail to negotiate with none other than Jan Smuts. The £3 tax was scrapped. Immigration laws were relaxed. Resisters were pardoned.

Freed at last, Gandhi suspended the South African satyagraha movement. He was exhausted by the nearly decade-long struggle. He was forty-five years old. The Gandhis had four sons, and Kasturba was tired of raising them so far from extended family.

It was time for Gandhi to go home, and home, without a doubt, was India. As for Jan Christiaan Smuts, now General Smuts, he wrote to a colleague, "[T]he saint has left our shores—I sincerely hope for ever."

Protesters marching in Transvaal

On march through Volksrust.

7

Marching for Freedom

Gandhi's ship pulled into the dock at Bombay, India, to the welcoming cheers of thousands. Admirers presented him with garlands of flowers. To them, he was a hero. He had stood up to the British who ruled South Africa. He cared about the rights of Indians abroad. Now he had come home.

Local businessmen threw parties in his honor. Instead of his usual suit, he came dressed in a seamless Indian *dhoti* and a plain shirt, with a turban on his head. When his hosts honored him with speeches in English, Gandhi replied in his native Gujarati. He hoped his deliberate choices of dress and language would convey his growing belief that Indians could not gain pride and dignity by imitating the British.

If the British rulers of India noticed such subtle hints, they ignored them and joined in welcoming Gandhi home. They awarded him the Kaiser-i-Hind, or "Emperor of India," gold medal for his work with the Indian Ambulance Corps in South Africa.

Gandhi was ready to continue in India the work of building community while pursuing truth and justice. Someone he hoped would help was Gopal Krishna Gokhale, a member of the party seeking greater power for Indians in India: the Indian National Congress.

Gokhale, a teacher, social reformer, and well-known politician, believed Indians should work with the British to achieve their goal of independence. Gandhi had been corresponding with him since their first meeting in 1896. He hoped Gokhale would help him raise money to establish a retreat like the Phoenix and Tolstoy sites in South Africa. Gokhale pledged his support, but he had questions. Was Gandhi sure about his plans? He had been away from India for so long; did he truly know what Indians wanted and needed? Gokhale suggested that Gandhi should spend some time traveling around all of India. The land and her people would be a living lesson for him.

Gandhi took the advice to heart. He crisscrossed India, traveling mostly by train, in third-class cars where he could meet ordinary people. The trains were dirty, the food inedible, the passengers packed so tightly that it was impossible to sleep.

DHOTI: A RECTANGULAR LENGTH (10–15 FT.) OF UNSTITCHED CLOTH, WORN BY MEN IN A VARIETY OF REGIONAL STYLES, WRAPPED AROUND THE WAIST AND SOMETIMES THE LEGS, PLEATED, KNOTTED IN THE FRONT OR BACK

Once, he bought a ticket but found no room on the train. A porter shoved him in through a window. Passengers helped him to his feet. There were no empty seats, so he stood for hours, holding on to a chain. Third-class travel in India was a far cry from the South African first-class carriage where he had once tried to sit.

Third-class travel was more than Gokhale had advised—just as studying Roman law in Latin had been more than any law professors in London required. But Gandhi never did anything halfway.

A few weeks into 1915, Gandhi received sad news: Gokhale had passed away. Gandhi had hoped to learn more from this generous, liberal man. Now he felt alone on an uncharted road, so train travel became an antidote.

On these travels, Gandhi met peasants and landlords, students and teachers. At a train station, he met a young man named Jawaharlal Nehru, who would go on to become India's first prime minister. Sometimes one of Gandhi's sons joined him, as did Kasturba. Their oldest son, Harilal, and Gandhi did not always get along. Harilal was drinking, telling lies—behaviors that Gandhi found despicable. Kasturba was happy when Harilal accompanied them. The train trips connected Gandhi and Harilal, if only briefly.

Gandhi began to listen for stories of poverty and injustice. He followed those stories. They led him to Champaran, a district in the northern province of Bihar. There, rich landlords owned the land and poor tenant farmers worked it. The landlords forced the farmers to plant *indigo*, an expensive cloth dye, instead of food crops. The farmers could not afford to pay the taxes they owed. Without food crops, they could not afford to eat.

Gandhi in peasants' clothes

Gandhi and
Kasturba, 1915

The peasants welcomed Gandhi. A group of lawyers from the region offered to join him in speaking to the government on the peasants' behalf. Gandhi told the lawyers they should charge no fees. They agreed. Soon Gandhi was busy talking to everyone concerned—the peasants, the planters, the British officials. At the same time, he began to work with the farmers to clean their surroundings, to build schools and hospitals. Kasturba joined him.

While the peasants were grateful to Gandhi, the police began to follow him. When he complained, he was served with an order to leave. He refused, insisting he did not mean to make trouble. He was promptly arrested for causing unrest and released with a trial date.

A FUTURE PRESIDENT ONE OF THE LAWYERS WHO WORKED WITH GANDHI IN CHAMPARAN WAS RAJENDRA PRASAD, WHO WOULD LATER BECOME THE FIRST PRESIDENT OF FREE INDIA.

At the trial, Gandhi said he was following "the higher law of our being—the voice of conscience." Outside the court, crowds demanded his release. Gandhi wrote, "[T]he people had for the moment lost all fear of punishment and yielded obedience to the power of love."

Perhaps the authorities sensed the change. The case was dropped. The government allowed Gandhi to complete his inquiry into the problems of the indigo farmers. They also included him on an official panel of inquiry. On the panel's recommendation, the government abolished the forced planting of indigo and cash crops.

Next, Gandhi joined with Congress leader Vallabhbhai Patel to help peasants in Gujarat take similar action against repressive taxes. World War I was raging in Europe, Africa, and parts of China. The British Empire's resources were stretched, so Gandhi took care to keep all protests limited and local. Although the Congress Party had begun to talk about *swaraj*, or independence, Gandhi was not yet ready to make such demands.

Instead, he turned to his dream of an *ashram*, a service community like Phoenix and Tolstoy Farm where Hindus of all castes, and people from all other religions as well, could live and work together. His dream was realized with the help of a generous donation from a lawyer friend. Among those who joined Gandhi at this time was Mahadev Desai, a lawyer and scholar who became his personal secretary.

Soon after the ashram opened in the city of Ahmedabad in Gujarat, an untouchable couple joined the community. Some members protested. Others left rather than live with people who were seen as unclean. Even Kasturba objected. In South Africa, she had accepted all kinds of people into her home, but here in India, she balked at breaking ancient traditions. Sternly, Gandhi told her that if she could not accept these changes, she could leave him "and we should part good friends." She stayed.

An outbreak of plague followed, and Gandhi decided to look for a different site. With over twenty members willing to join, and yet another generous donor offering to pitch in, Gandhi found a site atop cliffs overlooking the Sabarmati River. A British prison stood nearby.

On the day Gandhi visited the site, thunderclouds loomed. Lightning flashed. The rain pelted down. Greeted by the stormy weather, Gandhi determined that here, in sight of a symbol of foreign oppression, was the spot to plant a seed of defiant hope.

It was 1919. World War I had ended, but the passage of a new law was about to shake India. It was called the Rowlatt Act, and it gave the British government in India sweeping powers. It clamped down on the freedoms of Indian people.

Gandhi called for a public strike to protest the act. When strikers began to riot, however, he called the protest off. He wanted discipline, restraint—no violence. Indians, he concluded, were not yet ready for peaceful resistance.

Violence led to still more violence. In the northern Punjab province, an anti-government protest spun out of control. In the city of Amritsar, mobs killed five Europeans and attacked an Englishwoman. Local authorities appealed to the British Raj for help. The army was called in, under General Reginald Dyer. He imposed a curfew. Gatherings of more than four people were forbidden.

Inspired by the ideals of satyagraha now spreading across India, the people of Amritsar planned a massive gathering. As the city got ready for Baisakhi, a holiday for people of the Hindu and Sikh religions, the celebration gained a

The Rowlatt Act

Gandhi dubbed the Rowlatt Act the "Black Act," a term that had also been used, back in 1906, to describe the Asiatic Registration Act in Transvaal, South Africa. The Rowlatt Act:

- Extended the use of wartime "emergency measures," including those related to public gatherings
- Gave the government tight control of the press
- Allowed the police to make arrests without warrants and hold those arrested indefinitely without trial
- Allowed juryless trials for "political acts" (no one would know what happened at those trials)

new purpose. In Jallianwala Bagh, a walled garden, a crowd of around twenty thousand people—among them women and children—gathered peacefully to protest the Rowlatt Act.

Hurrying to the site of the illegal gathering, General Dyer blocked off the garden's sole entrance, which stood between two pillars. Then he did the unthinkable. He ordered his men to fire. They hesitated. He shouted at them. Shots rang out. Panicked people trampled one another, trying in vain to escape. Some jumped, screaming, into a well to avoid the shower of bullets. They drowned.

Dyer's men shot 1,650 rounds of ammunition into the unarmed crowd. Even by a low government estimate, they killed 379 people and wounded 1,137. Other estimates ranged as high as 1,500 dead.

The Jallianwala Bagh massacre sent a bitter message to Indians. The British Raj could no longer pretend to be benevolent. Over in England, some saw Dyer as a savior of British rule in India. A London newspaper launched a fund to collect money for his legal expenses—famous English writer Rudyard Kipling donated £10. But others were horrified. Even Winston Churchill, the British official who had disappointed Gandhi in London, called the Jallianwala Bagh massacre "an extraordinary event, a monstrous event." General Dyer was demoted to a lower rank and forced to retire.

Throughout World War I, Gandhi had supported the British, taking care to limit civil disobedience until the end of hostilities. Dyer's massacre of innocent people caused a quake inside him. Greater freedom under British rule was no longer enough. India deserved complete independence.

The British government tried to make amends. It proposed elected councils to govern British-ruled Indian provinces. But Gandhi had made up his mind.

In 1920, Gandhi launched what he called the Non-cooperation Movement. He used a word that would find its way into dictionaries of the English language: "nonviolence." It was the best way he could express an ancient word, *ahimsa*. In the Sanskrit language, *himsa* means "injury" or "harm," so *ahimsa* means the opposite—doing no harm, causing no injury.

Gandhi's movement was driven by a single action: boycott. He called on all Indians to refuse British products and avoid British institutions. And Indians responded. By the thousands, they boycotted British schools, jobs, courts, and councils. They burned clothes made in England. They refused to pay taxes. Gandhi himself returned the

Kaiser-i-Hind medal like the one returned by Gandhi

80

Kaiser-i-Hind medal he had received for his service during the Boer War in South Africa.

A year passed, then two. Protests continued. Ten thousand Indians went to jail. But some lost sight of Gandhi's guiding principles—doing no harm, causing no injury. In 1922, in a northern town called Chauri Chaura, marchers found themselves facing the police. They shouted slogans. The police fired into the air. The crowd retaliated by throwing stones. The police fired into the mass of people, killing three men. The mob exploded, burning down a police station and killing twenty-two policemen.

Grief-stricken, Gandhi halted the movement. Still, he was promptly arrested. In court, he freely admitted to rallying people against the government and asked for "the severest penalty." The judge sentenced him to six years in Yerwada Central Prison, near his late friend Gokhale's hometown of Poona. Gandhi served less than two years. Hospitalized for appendicitis, he was released on account of his poor health.

Meanwhile, Muslims and Hindus, instead of uniting to free India, grew further apart. Hindus complained that Gandhi had deserted his own faith, challenging age-old traditions of caste. Old resentments erupted anew, reaching back centuries to a time before the coming of the British, when Muslim kings had ruled India. Muslims in turn distrusted and feared the Hindu majority, of whom Gandhi was one. Riots flared between the religious groups.

Kasturba and son Ramdas, 1920. While Gandhi was busy, Kasturba, aided by their son Ramdas, handled many daily chores at Sabarmati ashram. She took special care of the young women and children who came there.

In response, Gandhi fasted. He stayed at the house of a Muslim friend, eating nothing, drinking only water. Newspapers ran the story. Crowds rallied in the streets, anxious for updates on his health. Only at the end of twenty-one days, when Hindu and Muslim leaders pledged friendship and unity once more, did Gandhi finally begin to eat.

FASTING MEANS DELIBERATELY REFUSING TO EAT. GANDHI USED FASTS AS A WEAPON OF PEACEFUL PROTEST. HE FASTED TO PROTEST UNFAIR LAWS, TO SEEK BETTER CONDITIONS IN PRISON, TO URGE HINDUS AND MUSLIMS TO WORK TOGETHER, AND TO OBJECT TO HIS OWN FOLLOWERS' BEHAVIOR WHEN THEY LAPSED INTO VIOLENCE. HE FASTED A TOTAL OF SEVENTEEN TIMES BETWEEN 1913 AND 1948. HIS FASTS LASTED FROM ONE TO TWENTY-ONE DAYS.

Restless, Gandhi traveled across India again, on foot, by train, and in bullock-carts, with a new message. Since returning to India, he had become more and more intrigued by a humble folk tradition he encountered in many places: spinning. He himself had learned to spin. His idea was simple. Why should Indians feed the English economy by buying foreign-made clothes? If instead they spun thread, wove cloth, and made their own clothes, they would not

The Yerwada Charkha, Gandhi's suitcase model, 2015

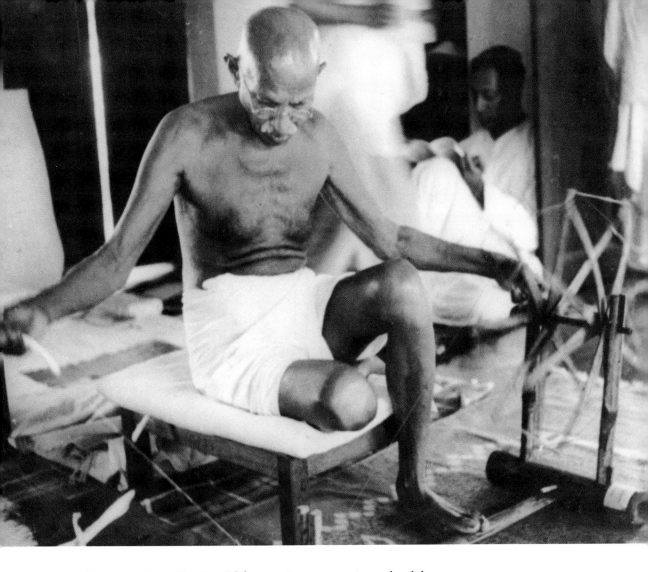

need imports from England. The *charka*, or spinning wheel, became a symbol of unity and freedom.

Gandhi and Kasturba spun for hours on end. While in prison, Gandhi even designed a portable spinning wheel that packed into its own case.

Wherever Gandhi went, he collected money for the movement. He sold his autograph to children, persuaded women to donate their gold jewelry. He used the money to buy spinning wheels. He set up centers to teach spinning.

But some questioned his principles. His old antagonist Vinayak Damodar Savarkar was back in India after serving time in a prison colony for the murder of a British officer. Savarkar argued that true patriots were those who saw India as both a homeland and a holy land. That ruled out Christians and Muslims. Savarkar and his followers refused to make pledges of friendship with Muslims. Instead, they called on Hindus to take up arms and defend themselves—against the British, but also against Muslims.

Similarly, Muslims armed themselves. In 1923 alone, there were eleven major Hindu-Muslim riots. Many other Muslims who did not advocate violence still joined the Muslim League, whose members believed they were best off representing themselves.

The untouchables had their own leader—Dr. Bhimrao Ramji Ambedkar, a brilliant lawyer. He disagreed with Gandhi on many grounds, including the name by which Gandhi had begun to call untouchables: Harijan, meaning "child of God."

HARIJAN ONCE GANDHI HAD MET AN UNTOUCHABLE PEASANT WHO BEGGED HIM TO CALL HIM ANYTHING BUT A "COOLIE." THE MAN SUGGESTED THE POETIC TERM HARIJAN. GANDHI USED IT AFTER THAT. IN INDIA TODAY, DR. AMBEDKAR'S SUGGESTED NAME OF DALIT IS PREFERRED, YET PEOPLE IN DALIT COMMUNITIES STILL EXPERIENCE VIOLENCE AND DISCRIMINATION.

Ambedkar saw the term as patronizing. He urged the use of a different name: Dalit, or "the oppressed." By choosing this name, Ambedkar boldly proclaimed his people's right to speak for themselves rather than be defined by upper-caste Indians like Gandhi.

With each new conflict that threatened to rip the fragile fabric of Indian resistance to British rule, Gandhi's heart sank. How was it possible to coax the deeply divided people of India to speak out with one voice against a powerful empire? For Gandhi, the answer lay in something so common, so necessary to everyday food, that everyone needed it. Salt.

In British India, salt was taxed. No one was allowed to use salt that had not been processed, taxed, and sold by the government. The tax

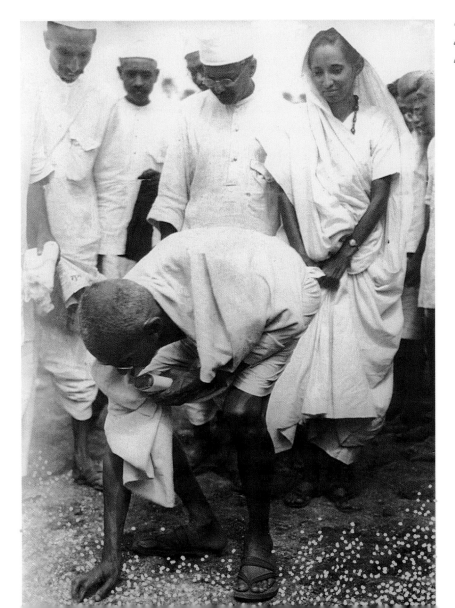

On the seashore at Dandi, picking up salt

had been protested before, to no effect. Gandhi determined that this time would be different.

He planned a protest march, from Sabarmati to the salt flats of Dandi on the Gujarat coast, over two hundred miles away. Pamphlets and newsletters spread the word. From all over Gujarat and neighboring provinces, people began traveling to Sabarmati to join the march. On March 12, 1930, seventy-eight people fell in line behind Gandhi. "You must be prepared to die," he warned them. Reporters and photographers stood at the gate, ready to go along. Kasturba shivered in the morning sunshine. Brass platter in hand, she walked to the head of the line. She anointed her husband's forehead with red kumkum paste for luck and for a safe return, then moved down the line, touching her finger to each marcher's forehead, placing on it the sacred Hindu mark. Then the march began.

At each village where the group stopped, more and more people joined, until the line of marchers was twelve thousand strong, walking twelve miles a day in blistering sun to reach the shore. At dawn on April 6, 1930, Gandhi and his followers waded into the sea. To the hiss of photographers' flashbulbs, Gandhi bent and picked up a fistful of coarse grayish-white crystals. He said, "With this salt I am shaking the foundations of the Empire."

Up and down three thousand miles of coastline, millions of people began making their own salt. Women, who rarely took part in politics, swarmed to the seashore along with the men. The government arrested the salt-marchers.

When one group of marchers tried to occupy the grounds of a salt-processing plant in Gujarat, police beat them back with batons.

As each row fell, the next moved up. Bloodied and bruised, yet calm and unresisting, two hundred protesters were dragged to jail in a single day. Within a month, sixty thousand had been arrested, including Gandhi himself.

The Raj could not afford to arrest this many people. Police stations, courts, and jails were overwhelmed.

In a panic, the British government negotiated with Gandhi and the Indian National Congress. Gandhi signed a deal with the viceroy, Lord Irwin, agreeing to stop protesting. Restrictions on public gatherings were lifted. Gandhi would join a group of Indian leaders at one of the Round Table Conferences in England that would engage Indians in governing their country. The tax on salt remained.

THE VICEROY IN 1857, WHEN THE BRITISH EMPIRE TOOK OVER THE DIRECT RULE OF INDIA FROM THE EAST INDIA COMPANY, AN ENGLISH OFFICIAL BY THE TITLE OF "VICEROY" WAS PLACED IN CHARGE OF GOVERNING INDIA. HE REPRESENTED THE BRITISH CROWN AND ANSWERED TO THE ENGLISH PARLIAMENT.

In 1931, for the fourth time in his life, Gandhi sailed to England. On board the ship, he dressed in his customary loincloth and shawl. He had begun remaining silent on Mondays, not speaking at all, for any reason. He said silence concentrated his mind: "[T]he vow of silence helps in the search for truth." He also spent many hours turning out lengths of cotton thread on his wooden spinning wheel.

In England, Gandhi found sympathizers. Mill workers turned out to greet and cheer him. They knew he was on the side of working people. Children from a community center gave him birthday presents—"a woolly lamb, a little doll's cradle and some other things."

Gandhi with textile mill
workers in Darwen,
Lancashire, England

Not everyone was as welcoming. Winston Churchill, the British official whom Gandhi had met twenty-four years earlier, was now an outspoken politician who believed that the British Empire was good not only for Britain, but for the world. Churchill despised Gandhi for opposing British rule in India. He found it "alarming and nau-

seating" to see this little man "striding half-naked up the steps of the vice-regal palace . . . to parley on equal terms with the representative of the king-emperor." And now here Gandhi was in London.

Asked about his dress, he is said to have quipped that the King had on enough for both of them.

Speaking to students at Eton, a famous English school, he said, "It can be no pride to you that your nation is ruling over ours. No one chained a slave

Imagined version of Gandhi's meeting with King George V, print (artist unknown)

without chaining himself." He said that if the Round Table Conference failed, civil disobedience would start again.

The conference stood little chance of succeeding. Representatives of every princely state in the region, every religious group, and every political party attended. Ambedkar demanded separate elections for Dalit people. Muhammad Ali Jinnah wanted special safeguards for the rights of Muslims. Landlords, industries, labor, even women had their own delegation. There were just too many negotiators. The conference failed.

While Gandhi was returning home by ship, Congress leaders Jawaharlal Nehru and Khan Abdul Ghaffar Khan, both Gandhi's friends and allies, were among those arrested in India for urging tenant farmers to refuse to pay punitive rents until the government stepped in to help them. Massive protests resumed. The jails filled up once more.

Gandhi was jailed too, his arrest warrant citing merely "good and sufficient reasons." In jail, he prayed, walked when he could—and spun. Family concerns also haunted him. His son Devadas, also jailed in another part of the country for civil disobedience, contracted the infectious disease typhoid. Letters Gandhi wrote to him were held up for weeks by jail censors who could not read Gujarati. In South Africa, Manilal, too, was ill with an unspecified sickness, and the oldest Gandhi son, Harilal, was quarreling with relatives.

On the national front, Gandhi felt equally helpless. He wanted Hindus to unite. He believed that Ambedkar's demand, separate elections for Dalits, would only divide them further. He longed to wipe untouchability out from within the Hindu fold, yet Ambedkar, disillusioned and distrusting caste itself, declared his desire to leave that fold altogether. In September 1932, Gandhi began a new fast, one meant to "sting the Hindu conscience." If Hindus kept discriminating against untouchables, they should let Gandhi die.

Years ago, in South Africa, he had asked others to step up and be heroes. Now more than ever, as his wife led women's protests and was herself arrested and rearrested, Gandhi was ready to put his own life on the line.

8
New Cloth, Frayed Fabric

Released from jail and hosted at a friend's house, Gandhi kept on fasting. As news of the fast spread, Hindu temples across the country began to open their doors to Dalits, who had for centuries been denied this equal access. Under pressure from Gandhi's followers, Ambedkar gave up his demand for a separate electorate. Instead, seats would be reserved for untouchables in a general election in which everyone could vote. As Congress leaders, including Gandhi's friend Jawaharlal Nehru, made anti-government speeches and went in and out of jail, Gandhi ended his fast. Were Hindus in India ready to move beyond the evils of caste segregation?

Through all his jail terms and fasts, Gandhi replied to a deluge of mail from all over the world. In between, he wrote to family members. He advised Manilal, in South Africa, not to become bitter over a disagreement with a friend. In letters to several people, he mentioned with some pride that Devadas had a job with a newspaper in

Delhi, the *Hindustan Times*, at a monthly salary of 250 rupees.

Then, in the summer of 1934, this routine was shattered by unexpected violence. Gandhi was in the western city of Poona to receive an award from the city council. People crammed into the municipal hall to hear him. A car pulled up. Thinking Gandhi was in it, a Boy Scouts' band played a welcome. Suddenly, a grenade thudded onto the hood of the car, bounced off into the street, and exploded. In the chaos, no one could tell who had thrown it. Ten people were injured, but Gandhi, arriving a few minutes later in another vehicle, escaped. He called the failed attack an "insane act," but said he had "deep pity" for the unknown thrower of the bomb.

While the botched assassination attempt fueled temporary headlines, a young Black minister, Howard Thurman, prepared to travel to India at the invitation of a Christian student group. Thurman's hosts hoped to learn how Black people, adopting the religion of their oppressors, had made it authentically theirs. Thurman's itinerary was packed. Still, he knew of Gandhi's work to free India from British rule, and he was eager to meet Gandhi.

Thurman and his wife, Sue Bailey Thurman, along with a friend, met Gandhi in Bardoli, a small town near Bombay where the Congress Party had set up temporary offices. As their car pulled up, Gandhi himself came out to greet them.

He invited them into his tent, which was furnished only with a mattress, a lap-desk, and a spinning wheel. The visitors sat on the floor with Gandhi. He pulled an old watch out from under his shawl, saying to his guests, "[W]e have much to talk about and you have only three hours before you have to leave to take your train back to Bombay."

He peppered them with questions. How had Black people in America survived the horrors of slavery? Would they ever get voting rights? Was it true that people of different races were not allowed to marry? Was education unequal for Black and white people? The churches, the laws—he knew so much and wanted to know even more.

Thurman told Gandhi about Booker T. Washington, who had founded a college and advised presidents, and about W. E. B. Du Bois, scholar and writer, who believed Black people around the world should unite. About Benjamin Mays, dean at Howard University in Washington, DC, who had long admired Gandhi.

Gandhi referred to a passage from the Bible about the greatest of all forces, love. He talked about nonviolence and civil disobedience—ahimsa and satyagraha. To him, nonviolence was an active force, "more positive than electricity," accessible to all who strive to live by it. He held his guests spellbound.

Finally, three hours were up. Sue Bailey Thurman said to Gandhi, "We want you to come to America . . . we have many a problem that cries for solution and we need you badly."

"How I wish I could," he replied, saying that his work in India was still unfinished. He gave Sue a basket of tropical fruit.

Howard Thurman was intrigued by Gandhi's spinning wheel. He knew that Gandhi spun cotton thread daily. It was like a meditation. He

Gandhi's Watch

During his lifetime, Gandhi owned two watches, one of them the so-called "dollar watch" made by the American company Ingersoll. This was the watch for which, during his law student days in London, he begged a gold watch chain from his brother Laxmidas. By the time Thurman met Gandhi, that chain was long gone. It had been donated to the cause of satyagraha along with most of Gandhi's personal possessions. The watch hung on a string, attached to his clothes with an outsize safety pin.

Gandhi was always punctual. As he put it, "You may not waste a grain of rice or a scrap of paper, and similarly a minute of your time. It is not ours. It belongs to the nation and we are trustees for the use of it."

was deeply moved by Gandhi's belief that nonviolent protest included changing one's own life, making that life "a living sermon." The wheel was a symbol of that effort. Thurman said, "I would like a piece of cloth woven out of material that you yourself have spun from the flax." Gandhi smiled as his secretary, Mahadev Desai, took notes.

Before leaving, Thurman and his group sang two hymns, "Were You There When They Crucified My Lord?" and "We Are Climbing Jacob's Ladder." Their voices filled the canvas tent as Gandhi listened with bowed head and closed eyes. They ended with prayers.

Gandhi's final words were a blessing or a prophecy or both. It would be through Black people, he is reported to have said, "that the unadulterated message of nonviolence will be delivered" to the world. The Thurmans' meeting opened doors to many other African Americans who visited India over the next decade, seeking to learn from Gandhi.

Several months after returning home, Thurman received a parcel from Mahadev Desai. It contained a length of cloth from Gandhi's own loom. The cloth became one of Thurman's most treasured possessions.

There was something wonderfully symbolic in the gift. Thurman and his group carried back across the oceans a feeling in their hearts that they had encountered someone extraordinary, with an extraordinary message for the world. They went eager to learn. They left inspired. Thurman became a greatly respected preacher, writer, and teacher. The words exchanged by Gandhi and Thurman did not stop when their conversation ended. Those words still had a long way to travel.

Soon after the Thurmans' visit, Gandhi decided to withdraw from politics. He had been in and out of jail a dozen times, starting with his early arrests in South Africa. Often Kasturba had joined him. Going to jail was a critical part of the satyagraha movement, but all the time in prison had weakened both of them. Gandhi was tired. It was all he could do to reply to the hundreds of letters that arrived for him daily. Some days, he wrote with his left hand when the right one got tired.

He moved to a small village called Segaon near the town of Wardha in central India, longing for peace and solitude. But he could not long remain inactive. Once he settled into a new, bare hut, he began what he called his Constructive Program. Gandhi and Kasturba urged the peasants of Segaon to educate their children and clean their streets and yards. Gandhi renamed the village Sevagram, "village of service."

Gandhi told the peasants to work with the local village councils, traditionally run by upper-caste Hindus. At the same time, he talked to council members, urging them to include people of all castes—even untouchables. Change, he insisted, grows from small actions.

While Gandhi worked locally to bring people together, Hindus and Muslims all over India grew further apart. Leaders like Savarkar attacked Gandhi for not being Hindu enough. Muhammad Ali Jinnah and the Muslim League saw the Congress Party, and Gandhi, as being too Hindu. The rhetoric of politicians fueled the clash of mobs in the streets.

Outside India, Europe and Asia had been on the brink of war for several years. The war front grew when, in 1936, Italy invaded Ethiopia and formed a partnership with Germany and Japan that came to be called the Axis. World War I was supposed to have been the war to end all wars, but now the world braced again for conflict.

In 1939, Germany invaded Poland. In retaliation, Britain declared war against Germany.

Because India was part of the British Empire, that meant India was at war too. In the past, Gandhi had supported the South African government in wartime. He had curtailed the civil disobedience movement during World War I. What should he, and India, do now, in the face of the horrific menace of Nazi Germany?

In the early years of World War II, Gandhi maintained, "I do not believe in any war." He even suggested that European Jews should practice satyagraha in the face of the Nazi atrocities. Then rumors began to spread of gas ovens, of hundreds—even thousands—going into concentration camps and never emerging alive. Hearing this news, Gandhi grew more sympathetic toward England's position in the war, although, like others across the world at that time, he may not have fully understood Hitler and the German Third Reich. Communications were far less advanced than they are today, and the true numbers—millions!—of Jews and other minorities exterminated were not widely known until years later. Gandhi wanted to believe that everyone had good in them, even people who committed evil deeds. He had no idea just how far Hitler would go in destroying everyone who stood in the way of his desire to dominate the world.

After some vacillation, Gandhi proposed unconditional nonviolent support for the British in the war, much like the ambulance corps of the Boer War days. But the Congress Party had shifted direction, and his proposal was defeated. Instead, Indians favored conditional support—after the war, they wanted Britain to give India complete independence.

The Indian Army
in World War II

During World War II, two million Indians fought with the Allies in Europe, North Africa, and on the Pacific front.

Many volunteered for the money. The war had brought about food shortages in India, and the army provided soldiers with salaries so they could support their families. To those with professional qualifications, it offered military careers that had until then been open only to white officers. Some joined despite personal doubts. More than 87,000 died.

Even though the Indian independence movement was a thorn in the side of the British, they had to pay attention. Gandhi's old adversary Winston Churchill was now the British prime minister. In the spring of 1942, Churchill sent a special representative, Sir Stafford Cripps, to India. Unlike many others in the British government, Sir Stafford knew several Congress leaders and was sympathetic to the Indian cause. Britain, he said, was willing to give Indians immediate representation. At the war's end, India would become a British dominion, independent but with the king of England as its head of state.

But the Cripps proposal also stated that Indian provinces, princely states, and religious minorities could negotiate separately with the British: Each province and princely state, each minority group, could choose not to join the new country. How could this possibly work? Gandhi wondered, aghast. The map of India would be full of holes, a ragged quilt containing within its borders a patchwork of states that had chosen not to join. He turned down the proposal, calling it a "perpetual vivisection of India."

Disappointed, betrayed by a British government he had once trusted, Gandhi began a new campaign: the Quit India Movement. The Congress Party demanded that the British withdraw from India at once. The new viceroy, Lord Linlithgow, promptly arrested Gandhi, Nehru, and the entire Congress Working Committee.

Protests broke out. Some turned violent. Mobs stormed government buildings and police stations, looted them, set them on fire. They cut rail tracks and telegraph lines. They attacked, wounded, and even killed British officials.

Gandhi was under house arrest in the palace of the Aga Khan, the wealthy hereditary leader of a Muslim sect with Persian origins. The British had taken his palace over for wartime use. It was outside the city of Poona, not far from Yerwada Prison, where Gandhi had previously been held. Others held along with Gandhi were his wife, Kasturba, whom everyone now called "Ba," or "mother," his secretary Mahadev Desai, and a young Englishwoman who had joined the Indian independence movement. Gandhi called her "Mirabehn." Mirabehn taught Kasturba how to play *carom*, a board game. They sang and prayed together.

Gandhi was allowed to walk the palace grounds. He received visitors and wrote many letters to the viceroy. As India erupted into flames, Gandhi condemned the spreading violence. He denied that he had stoked it. Instead, he insisted it was the viceroy's response to the Quit India campaign that was responsible for the fury of the mobs.

A personal loss crushed Gandhi as well. His beloved secretary, Mahadev Desai, was at work as usual one day when he suddenly collapsed. Gandhi rushed to his side, took Desai's head in his lap, called his name. But he was dead. Gandhi was grief-stricken. Desai had been the most careful and caring of assistants. They had worked together for twenty-five years. How would Gandhi manage now, without Mahadev's perfect penmanship, his attention to detail, his common-sense advice?

Kasturba cried. Her husband had lost "his left hand and his right hand." Desai was cremated within the palace grounds.

Outside the grounds, the country remained in ferment. The Congress Party was banned. The government censored newspapers and radio broadcasts and forbade public meetings.

In February 1943, at the age of seventy-three, Gandhi announced that he would fast for twenty-one days. He said he wished to invite God to settle his "misunderstanding" with the viceroy. Linlithgow was infuriated. So was Winston Churchill. He told the viceroy that if Gandhi insisted on fasting, he should let him starve to death. It is said that

the government even made secret arrangements for his funeral.

Gandhi survived. In October 1943, he spent his second birthday in a row under house arrest. His fellow detainees decided to celebrate. They decorated the dining room. Kasturba wished she could wear her one special *sari,* the customary female garment in India. It had a red border and was woven out of thread spun by Gandhi. At first, no one could find it, but then Manu, Gandhi's teenaged grandniece, remembered where it had been left at the ashram in Sevagram. The sari was found, and Ba wore it for the seventy-fourth birthday party of her husband, a man whom people around the nation were beginning to call Bapu—"father."

But Kasturba herself had been weakened by repeated jail terms. In January 1944, she suffered two heart attacks. Sure her end was near, she wanted to see her children before she died. Devadas came from Delhi and Ramdas from his home in Nagpur, in central India. Manilal, still in South Africa, could not make the journey in time to see his mother.

As for Gandhi's troubled and troubling oldest son, Harilal, upon hearing his mother was ill, he came one day to the palace prison gates. He had been drinking. His speech was slurred and he could not walk straight. The guards turned him away. But Kasturba longed to see Harilal, so the police hunted him down and brought him to the palace. He looked pale and ill. Kasturba hugged her firstborn son. On a second visit, he was so shaky that she cried in despair.

Kasturba coughed constantly. In addition to her heart condition, she had contracted bronchitis. Devadas managed to obtain a shipment of *penicillin,* a new medicine that was said to work miracles in treating bacterial infections. Devadas pleaded that Ba should be given this life-saving medicine. The drug would have to be administered every four to six hours by injection. Gandhi hesitated. The injections would be painful. He did not want to cause more pain. If Devadas insisted, he said, he would not refuse. But Devadas backed off. On February 22, 1944, Kasturba died in Gandhi's arms.

Might the new miracle drug have saved Kasturba's life? The doctors had said she was beyond help. She, too, was cremated on the palace grounds. From then on, Gandhi referred to the place as "sacred."

For over half a century, Kasturba had worked and suffered at her husband's side. She had put up with his eccentric, unpredictable ways. She had spoken the truth to him when others hesitated. Together, from the time in Porbandar when the young Kastur had refused to let her bossy young husband dictate where she could go and with whom, they had traveled a long, hard road. In reply to a letter of sympathy, he wrote: "[S]he became truly my *better* half . . . my teacher in the art and practice of non-violent non-cooperation."

In May 1944, after Gandhi contracted malaria, the British released their most famous prisoner on grounds of ill health. For the last time, he walked out of his house arrest at a prison that he complained was far too luxurious for his taste. In all, he had spent almost six and a half years in prison—2,089 days in India, 249 in South Africa. He joked that the prisons were "His Majesty's hotels."

The years between 1944 and 1947 saw many changes. World War II ended. The Allies defeated Nazi Germany and the other Axis powers, Japan and Italy. But years of war had left Britain impoverished. The empire was simply too expensive to maintain. The British were ready to transfer power into Indian hands, and Gandhi was hopeful once more.

Those hopes were dashed when the Muslim League—the party now led by that other lawyer from Gujarat, Muhammad Ali Jinnah—refused to cooperate. The league demanded a separate homeland for Muslims: an independent country carved out of Muslim-majority areas of India. They had a name for this newly proposed country:

Mahatma Gandhi pays homage to Kasturba Gandhi at Aga Khan Palace, 1945.

Pakistan, which meant "land of the pure." The announcement sparked riots. Mobs of Muslims, Sikhs, and Hindus clashed in many cities. More than five thousand people were killed.

For two centuries, the British Raj had divided the people of India along lines of religion, language, and culture. They had pitted Hindus against Muslims, native ruler against native ruler. Now, after decades of boasting that India was the jewel of their imperial Crown, the British were suddenly in a great hurry to leave. In March 1947, a new representative arrived from England—the last viceroy of India, Lord Mountbatten. He had instructions to set up a commission headed by a lawyer, Sir Cyril Radcliffe, with the purpose of dividing India into two countries: a Hindu-majority India and a Muslim-majority Pakistan. Sir Cyril would draw the boundaries of the two new countries.

Radcliffe had never been to India before. He had six weeks to redraw the region's maps. On the west, the border would cut through the province of Punjab; in the east, it would divide the province of Bengal. Between West Punjab and East Bengal would lie the rest of India. It was a gargantuan task. Existing maps were mostly out of date. Worst of all, millions of people would be affected by the strokes of Radcliffe's pen.

The borders he drew split villages, towns, neighborhoods, families. No matter how he drew them, many Muslims remained in Hindu-majority India. Many Hindus found themselves in Muslim-majority Pakistan. Guards had to protect Sir Cyril's house from possible assassins, so incensed were people in all of the affected areas. The map was finished and submitted less than a week before the announced independence dates of both countries. Before he left India, Radcliffe burned his notes.

On August 15, 1947, the Parliament of the United Kingdom passed the Indian Independence Act, creating a newly independent India. A day earlier, a parallel law had created the new country of Pakistan. The fabric of a united India, for which Gandhi had worked all his life, was now in tatters, ripped apart by violence and bitter religious rivalries. Only after independence was the infamous salt tax repealed.

Sir Cyril Radcliffe

Gandhi with Lord Louis Mountbatten and Lady Edwina Mountbatten

9

"I Must Now Tear Myself Away"

India's partition left chaos in its wake. Suddenly, Hindus in Pakistan and Muslims in India felt unsafe in places where their families had lived for generations. The redrawn borders threw people into panic. Over fourteen million fled their towns and villages to cross those newly drawn lines, Hindus racing to India and Muslims to Pakistan. Rumors flew. *Protect your children! If you don't leave at once, you'll be robbed or killed. If you're Hindu, you can't trust a Muslim. If you're Muslim, all Hindus are now your enemy.*

Gandhi tried to appeal for good sense and calm. No one was listening. In the wake of the rumors, Hindus and Muslims turned once more upon each other. Neighbor attacked neighbor. This time, over half a million people died. Another million were left homeless. Gandhi said, "I feel as if I was thrown into a fire pit and my heart is burning." But the deed was done, the maps were drawn, and despite all of Gandhi's pleas, the violence appeared unending.

Refugees from West Punjab in Delhi, 1947

The native rulers who ruled India's princely states at the time of partition, some Hindu and others Muslim, were also in turmoil. Most had already signed treaties with the British government, promising to cooperate with them. Now they were told they must join one of the two newly formed countries, India or Pakistan.

The kingdom of Kashmir, bordering both India and Pakistan, had a Hindu king, Maharaja Hari Singh. He could not make up his mind. Should he join India? He did not trust the Congress leaders, even though most of them were Hindu like himself. He couldn't join

Pakistan, surely, since that would put his family and his Hindu subjects at risk. Yet most of his subjects were Muslims! What if they rose up against him?

When the Maharaja jailed the Muslim leader of a local political party, Gandhi suggested that the "people of Kashmir should be asked whether they want to join Pakistan or India. Let them do as they want." The ruler should hold a public vote. The people should vote to join Pakistan or India. "The ruler is nothing. The people are everything."

In October 1947, two months after partition, Maharaja Hari Singh was still fretting when armed tribesmen from across the Pakistan border invaded Kashmir. The border would become heavily fortified in years to come, but at the time, there were no fences, no markers, no signs. In desperation, Hari Singh asked the government of India for help. In return, he agreed to join India. By December, Indian army units had killed 320 "raiders" who had crossed the border into the newest Indian state.

The conflict over Kashmir distressed Gandhi deeply. He felt that "the two dominions should come together with God as witness and

Kashmir, Then and Now

For more than a year after independence, India and Pakistan fought over Kashmir. The war ended when the United Nations intervened.

This was the first of many wars between the two countries over Kashmir. The United Nations called for a public vote as Gandhi had done. It has never been held.

Today, large parts of the state remain disputed territory. Both countries claim them. The southern half of Kashmir is under Indian rule; the northwest is administered by Pakistan. An icy northern sliver has been annexed by China.

find a settlement." No one on either side, however, was ready to do that.

While Jawaharlal Nehru, Vallabhbhai Patel, and others were forming a working Indian government in Delhi, Gandhi went to the eastern city of Calcutta, where Hindus and Muslims had clashed. Gandhi fasted and prayed. He made it a point to stay at the home of a Muslim League leader, Huseyn Shaheed Suhrawardy.

People who learned that Gandhi was in the city held their peace, at least for a while. But by the end of the month, mob frenzy erupted again. Suhrawardy's house was attacked, its windows broken, bricks thrown at its doors.

Gandhi decided to fast again. At the age of seventy-eight, he was frail and tired. If he continued this fast, he could die. Within three days, politicians of all parties crowded into his room, promising to stop the fighting, promising that it would not start again. In other parts of India, Muslims and Hindus threw rocks at each other, burned each other's houses. But Calcutta remained calm.

Gandhi left for Delhi. He wanted to stay with untouchables there, in their slums. The Congress leaders would not allow it. He would be an easy target for those who hated him enough to want him dead. They persuaded him to stay in the home of a well-known businessman, G. D. Birla. At Birla House, Gandhi held daily prayer meetings. He read from the texts of many religions, including the Hindu Bhagavad Gita, the Christian Bible, and the Muslim Quran. He longed for people of all of India's faiths to pray and work together.

To Gandhi, the raging war in Kashmir was a symptom of the new nation's ills. He urged politicians on both sides to try to settle disputes

peacefully as only satyagrahis, followers of satyagraha, knew how to do. "Today the poison around us is only increasing. Kashmir has added more poison." No one listened. In January, he began yet another fast. If he could not stop the poison from spreading, he would willingly die. "I yearn for heart friendship between Hindus, Sikhs, and Muslims," he said. He planned to end the fast "when and if I am satisfied that there is a reunion of hearts of all communities."

Gandhi lost several pounds. News of his fast spread through the city. Doctors warned him that his kidneys were failing. He insisted he could not eat again until his vision was made real, until friendship grew between religious groups.

"Gandhi is dying," people whispered to one another. Gradually, crowds began to gather outside the walls of Birla House. Crowds of Hindus, Sikhs, and Muslims. They stood in vigil. Some wept. They promised to trust and love one another as they trusted and loved Gandhi. They begged him to eat once more. He demanded a guarantee in writing.

On January 18, 1948, five days after Gandhi had begun his fast, one hundred Indian leaders signed a declaration of peace and friendship between people of all faiths. Their pledge convinced Gandhi. He began to eat again.

Two Languages, One Promise
The declaration was written in two languages, Hindi and Urdu. They shared a grammar and many basic words. Hindi is spoken by Hindus and contains many loanwords from the ancient language of Sanskrit, whose script it uses. Urdu has loanwords from Persian and Arabic and uses a script related to Persian. Hindus and Muslims joined to write this statement. That made it doubly meaningful.

Two days later, Gandhi resumed his prayer meetings on the lawn of Birla House. That morning, an explosion rocked the garden, not seventy-five feet from where he sat. The crowd panicked, but Gandhi calmed them. In the melee, six men managed to slip away from the garden.

A few people spotted three of them as they rushed out of the gate and jumped into a waiting taxi. Witnesses later said they were young and well-dressed.

A small boy was sure that he remembered the cab's license plate number. When he gave it to the police, however, it proved to be incorrect. The police could not trace the vehicle. Later, it turned out that a young man named Madan Lal Pahwa had planted the bomb. He was a Hindu refugee from Pakistan who belonged to Savarkar's radical group.

Ten days after the explosion, on the morning of January 30, Gandhi was up as usual by 3:30 a.m. He sipped some lemon water and honey. He led early-morning prayers. He read and wrote a little.

He took a bath. He ate a spare meal—goat's milk, boiled vegetables, tomato, radish, and orange juice. As the time for the daily prayer meeting approached, he was deep in talks with a special visitor. Vallabhbhai Patel was the home minister of independent India. He was clashing with the prime minister, Jawaharlal Nehru. Both had been Congress leaders for years, but they disagreed in many ways. Patel did not always agree with Gandhi, either, but he respected him greatly. On this day, he had come to Gandhi for advice.

As the men talked, Gandhi's grandniece, Abha, fidgeted. It was time to wrap up the conversation. Five minutes passed, and the two men continued talking. Abha held up her great-uncle's watch so he could see that it was time for the morning prayer meeting.

At last Gandhi paid attention. "I must now tear myself away," he said to Patel.

Abha and Gandhi's other grandniece, Manu, led him out of the house. He walked slowly, leaning on them as he went. Abha joked, "Bapu, your watch must be feeling very neglected. You would not look at it."

"Why should I," he replied, "since you are my time-keepers?"

Entering the garden, they joked and laughed. It was a day like any other. It had its challenges. It followed a set routine.

That routine was about to be brutally disrupted.

That same morning, one of the six men who had hurried away on the day of the bomb returned to the garden of Birla House. His name was Nathuram Vinayak Godse. Young and well-built, dressed in khaki, he pushed his way to the front of the crowd and folded his hands in the Hindu greeting: *Namaste.* But he did not speak to Gandhi, as visitors so often did, seeking advice or blessings. Nor did he bend down to touch Gandhi's feet, another common and respectful greeting.

Instead, Nathuram Godse opened his folded hands to reveal a pistol in his grip. He aimed squarely at Mahatma Gandhi's bare chest and fired three bullets. Gunsmoke curled through the air. Gandhi's foot hit the ground mid-stride. He staggered and crumpled, blood pouring from his wounds.

Panic erupted. Several people in the crowd grabbed Godse and pushed him toward the police.

Aroused from their shock, those nearest Gandhi supported his sagging frame. By the time they hurried him into the house, he was dead.

Gandhi's funeral procession, the open bier bedecked with flowers. Millions turned out to mourn his passing.

Martin Luther

KING JR.

10

The Curtain
of Discrimination

Just as Gandhi lived and chafed under foreign rule in India, young Martin Luther King Jr. grew up enduring the everyday insults of racial discrimination in the United States. When King was born in 1929, slavery had been abolished for sixty-four years, but its effects persisted, a blight still infecting America. Laws discriminating against Black people remained on the books. Dubbed "Jim Crow laws," they enforced strict racial segregation, especially in the South. Although Black and white people lived in the same cities, they inhabited different—and unequal—worlds. Black people could not eat at the same restaurants, drink from the same drinking fountains, or use the same swimming pools as whites. Neighborhoods were segregated. Black children attended segregated schools that were often ill-equipped and poorly staffed.

In many states, Black people were prevented from voting. They were charged poll taxes they could not afford to pay. So-called literacy

Outside County
Courthouse,
Halifax, NC, 1938

tests were forced on them. These "tests" were random and unpredict-able. They sometimes asked for information that was difficult, even impossible, for anyone to know offhand, like the names of all the judges in a district or the number of bubbles in a bar of soap. Some-times they were administered in a group. If one person got an incor-rect answer, the entire group was turned away.

In this America, a country whose laws were cruelly unfair to

its largest minority, in an Atlanta, Georgia, neighborhood named Sweet Auburn, the child who grew up to be Dr. Martin Luther King Jr. was raised with loving care. He hadn't yet acquired his famous name.

Ebenezer Baptist Church, 2016

He was born Michael King. Everyone called him "Little Mike." His father and his maternal grandfather, Adam Daniel Williams, prayed that this new baby would, like them, someday become a preacher.

Martin Luther King Jr. wrote, "The community in which I was born was quite ordinary in terms of social status. No one in our community has attained any great wealth." But no one was desperately poor, either. Within Atlanta's segregated society were neighborhoods of middle-class Black people. They were ministers and teachers and own-

The house in Atlanta, Georgia, where Martin Luther King Jr. was born

ers of businesses lining the streets— an insurance company, newspapers, churches, and nightclubs. At the intersection of Auburn and Jackson Streets stood Ebenezer Baptist Church, where King Sr. preached.

The church was a second home to Little Mike, with its gracious redbrick walls and its interior bursting with sound—the peals of the organ and the powerful rising notes of the choir. The rafters just about

trembled to the stirring sermons of Little Mike's father, known to all as "Daddy King."

As well as being a rousing preacher, Daddy King cared about civil rights. He headed up the Atlanta chapter of the National Association for the Advancement of Colored People (NAACP), organized voter registration drives, and supported the demands of Black teachers for the same salaries as their white colleagues. He often defied Jim Crow laws, using city hall elevators marked whites only and refusing to ride the segregated buses. The son of sharecroppers (tenant farmers who paid their rent with a portion of each harvest), he'd lived a hard life. He'd seen the landowner cheat and bully his father. He'd seen his father drink and fly into a rage. He'd seen his mother cower in fear.

Daddy King had sworn to give his own children a better life. In return, he expected good behavior, even if that required a belting now and then.

While Daddy King alternately inspired and intimidated his son, Little Mike's mother, Alberta King, instilled in her children a sense of self-respect. She was the only daughter of A. D. Williams, who had founded Ebenezer and was then its pastor. Not only did

NAACP
The National Association for the Advancement of Colored People was founded at the turn of the twentieth century to fight in the courts for equality for Black people. Today, NAACP attorneys continue to challenge racial discrimination against minorities.

he look after his congregation, but he was also a respected member of the Black community. Alberta was a teacher, and she taught her son to read before he even entered school. "You are as good as anyone," she told him. He took her words seriously.

The year that Little Mike turned five, the church rewarded his father's work with a summer tour of Europe and the Holy Land. The trip included a ministers' conference in Germany. There, Daddy King was struck by the teachings and legacy of the great sixteenth-century European monk and scholar Martin Luther. Upon his return, he renamed himself "Martin Luther King." He also renamed his young son. No official change was registered, but young Mike became Martin. Martin Luther King Jr. he remained, for the rest of his life.

Martin Luther King Sr. and Alberta Williams King celebrating their twenty-fifth wedding anniversary in 1951

MARTIN LUTHER (1483-1546) FELT THAT THE MEDIEVAL CATHOLIC CHURCH WAS UNTRUE TO THE BIBLE. HE WROTE THAT TO BE FREED FROM SIN, PEOPLE SHOULD BELIEVE IN JESUS CHRIST WITHOUT HAVING TO PAY THE CHURCH. HIS WRITINGS HELPED USHER IN NEW BRANCHES OF CHRISTIANITY AND THE ESTABLISHMENT OF NEW CHURCHES.

A plump child with a round face and eyes that family friends described as "watchful" and "glistening," Martin loved home cooking—greens and grits and fried chicken. He played the piano and was quite taken with opera. He liked wrestling. His mind was forever roaming and inquisitive. He was careless in his spelling and grammar. And books—how he loved books! His father said he liked to have them around him even before he had learned to read.

When he began to read, stories sent his imagination flying beyond the here and now. As an adult, he would recall how books had given him windows into the rest of the world. India in particular held a magical allure. "Even as a child, the entire Orient held a strange fascination for me—the elephants, the tigers, the temples, the snake charmers and all the other storybook characters."

Martin as a child with his sister, Christine

The richness of spoken language also captivated him. One Sunday, a visiting preacher came to the church. His sermon was dramatic and splendid, overflowing with many fancy words. Martin listened, took it all in. Later that day, he announced to his mother, "Someday I'm going to have me some big words like that."

He did indeed cultivate his vocabulary. He could stump anyone with his ten-dollar words. Martin even learned to talk himself out of fights. He was growing into a self-assured boy, finding his own way to relate to the world.

But the world beyond the security of family and home was a harsh one. Segregation intruded early upon young Martin's life. Martin had a white friend, a boy he'd played with since they were both toddlers. The boy's father owned a store across the street from the King home. At six, both boys entered first grade—in separate schools, of course. One day, Martin's friend told him they could no longer play together: His father wouldn't allow it.

Martin was shocked. They were best friends! Why would his friend's father want to break up their friendship? At the dinner table, he asked his parents. Over supper, his parents talked to him about race. About how white people didn't want their children to play with those who were Black. About insults they themselves had to endure on account of their race. "Here for the first time I was made aware of the existence of a race problem. I had never been conscious of it before."

Hearing his parents talk, Martin felt his anger flare. He decided that from that moment on, he would hate every single white person. He said so.

His parents would have none of it. Hatred was wrong, they told him. It was his Christian duty to love all people. That made no sense at all to young Martin. How could he love a race of people who hated him purely for the color of his skin? Hated him enough to force him apart from his childhood friend? The question would burn for years in his mind.

When he was about eight years old, Martin's mother took him to a downtown store. She shopped. He dawdled, distracted by his surroundings, daydreaming. Suddenly, a hand struck his face! He jumped. The slap stung. It was from a white woman. She flung a racist slur at him, a word that white people used when they meant to wound and demean Blacks. She insisted he'd stepped on her foot.

Young Martin was startled. He hadn't stepped on her foot! Had he gotten in her way without realizing it? What had he done that was so wrong? He froze. "I wouldn't dare retaliate when a white person was involved." But it bothered him, so he told his mother about it. Alberta King was upset, but by the time she had comforted Martin, the woman who had slapped him had left. His mother whisked Martin out of the store. It was a hard lesson for an eight-year-old—that no matter how unfair it might be, if you were Black, you were best off getting out of the way of an angry white person.

As Martin grew older, his mother told him about the nation's history of slavery and how it had ended with the Civil War and Emancipation. She explained that they had to put up with the system of separate facilities and spaces for Black and white people, but that did not mean it was right. It was a burdensome system created by people—it wasn't how God meant the world to be. At the same time, Martin also saw the adults in his life refusing to take racial slurs and affronts from white people. Once, a traffic policeman stopped Martin's father when he was driving and addressed him as "boy." Daddy King retorted, "If you persist in referring to me as boy, I will be forced to act as if I don't hear a word you are saying."

Another time, Daddy King and Martin went to buy shoes. They were sitting down when a clerk ordered them to move to the back of the store. Martin's father snapped, "We'll either buy shoes sitting here or won't buy any shoes at all." As they walked away, his father muttered, "I don't care how long I have to live with this system, I will never accept it."

Dignity. Self-respect. Resistance to injustice. These were important values in Martin's life. They helped to shape him into the boy who traveled to Dublin, Georgia, with his teacher in 1944. The boy who made a winning speech, his strong young voice filled with certainty: "We cannot have an enlightened democracy with one great group living in ignorance. We cannot have a healthy nation with one-tenth of the people ill-nourished, sick, harboring germs of disease which recognize no color lines—obey no Jim Crow laws."

In making that speech, Martin, at fifteen years old, was expressing ideas instilled in him since childhood. In his own voice, he was trying out the sounds of resistance.

He quoted the teachings of Jesus. He insisted that it was impossible for people to be truly Christian unless they loved their brothers. He argued that if Black people were given the vote, "they will be vigilant and defend, even with their arms, the ark of federal liberty from treason and destruction by her enemies."

The ark of federal liberty. He was comparing the ideal of liberty to the biblical ark that lifted Noah to safety above the flood. In affirming that Black people would defend liberty with "arms" or weapons, was he as yet unready to embrace nonviolent resistance? Or was this a reference to the military service of Black citizens, even when they were treated as unequal to their white counterparts?

He ended the speech by looking forward to the day when "I with my brother of blackest hue possessing at last my rightful heritage and holding my head erect, may stand beside the Saxon—a Negro—and yet a man!"

But then of course, on the bus ride back to Atlanta, he had to stand the whole way, having had to give up his seat to a white passenger.

At Booker T. Washington High School, across town from familiar Auburn Avenue, Martin was doing so well he'd skipped his first year. But to get to school, he had to take the bus over to the West Side, and he had to sit in the back: "I would end up having to go to the back of the bus with my body, but every time I got on that bus I left my mind up on the front seat." As a Black boy growing up in America in the 1940s, Martin kept falling into the chasm that yawned between his ideals of liberty and the reality of life. He said to himself, "One of these days, I'm going to put my body up there where my mind is."

He became increasingly sensitive to the injustice all around him.

" I would end up having to go to the back of the bus with my body, but every time I got on that bus I left my mind up on the front seat. "

—Martin Luther King Jr.

When he took a summer job at a mattress company, he was saddened and frustrated to see how badly the Black employees were treated. He quit another job at the Railway Express because a superintendent kept calling him by a racist name. Like Black people all over America, Martin was the target of racial baiting and insults.

Despite the obstacles that racism placed in the way, Daddy King believed that education would give his son the tools to succeed in life. During his junior year in high school, Martin applied to Morehouse College, an institution with a fine history of educating young Black men. He was granted early admission, so he skipped his last year of high school and got ready for college.

The summer before entering Morehouse, Martin went to Simsbury, Connecticut, to earn a little money by working on a tobacco farm. He wrote to his father about the northbound trip: "After we passed Washington there was no discrimination at all the [sic] white people here are very nice. We go to any place we want to and sit any where we want to."

Booker T. Washington High School, Atlanta, Georgia, 2019

One Sunday, in Simsbury, he went to church. He noticed that he and other boys working on the farm were the only Blacks there. Not about to let that stop him, he joined the choir and began to take a leading role. He even performed once on the radio.

Yet, despite the absence of enforced segregation, Martin found racism in the North to be alive and well, even if it was more masked than in his native Georgia. Here, too, there were people who believed in white supremacy, who were convinced that Black people were inferior to whites, that this was natural and acceptable. Once, the owner of a diner in New Jersey refused to serve Martin and his friends. The man made them leave—at gunpoint!

The train journey home at the end of that summer cast a pall of despair over fifteen-year-old Martin. From Connecticut to Washington, he could sit anywhere he liked. But once he was south of the nation's capital, Martin had to switch to a Jim Crow car. In the dining car, he was made to sit behind a curtain, out of sight of the white passengers. In years to come, Martin wrote, "I felt as if the curtain had been dropped on my selfhood."

Back in 1897, W. E. B. Du Bois had written about feeling similarly excluded, shut out by a kind of veil from the dazzling opportunities in the world of white people.

The truth was that separate would always be unequal.

11
Message of Truth

The year was 1944. World War II was raging. The papers were full of it—American soldiers were invading France, liberating it from Nazi German occupation. The U.S. Navy was capturing strategic islands in the Pacific, putting the Japanese capital, Tokyo, within range of American bombers. Thousands of men, including many young Black men, were away at war. But for Martin, college held hope and excitement. It was a world away from the drama and tragedy in the news. It offered new horizons for a boy fresh out of high school and younger than his classmates.

When Martin first arrived at Morehouse College at the precocious age of fifteen, he did not study very hard. He was too busy having a good time. He took care to dress well. He liked to throw big words around and impress young women with his fancy vocabulary. He often wore broad-brimmed hats, snazzy two-toned shoes, and sports jackets. He was known for his stylishly tailored suits, which earned him the nickname of "Tweed."

His professors found him promising, but not outstanding. One weekly event he attended was a chapel service at which Benjamin Mays, the president of Morehouse College, spoke about the struggle for equal rights. Mays told students, "I wouldn't go to a segregated theater to see Jesus Christ himself."

It was Mays who first introduced Martin to the work of Henry David Thoreau. Thirty years earlier, in prison in South Africa, Gandhi had been moved by Thoreau's ideas. Now Martin was drawn to them. Thoreau wanted the U.S. government of his time to abolish slavery and stop waging war. He protested by refusing to pay taxes. Reading his words, Martin was convinced that people of conscience should resist an evil system.

While big social questions filled his mind, Martin had life decisions to make. He needed to decide on a college major, but he couldn't make up his mind. He considered medicine, then decided on pre-law

Martin Luther King Jr. with parents, brother A. D. King, sister Christine, and uncle Joel King, on Morehouse Campus, 1948

sociology. The study of society—its history, structure, functions, and problems—was a big field. Could he perhaps follow the path of Thurgood Marshall? Marshall was a lawyer who represented the NAACP. If Martin became a lawyer, he could argue cases for Black rights in the courtroom.

In his senior year, at eighteen years of age, Martin changed his mind. Instead of law, he decided to enter the ministry. The decision was "not a miraculous or supernatural something." Rather, he began to feel an "inner urge calling me to serve humanity." The church would allow him to bring messages of racial and social protest to a wide audience.

He was also striving to grow himself, to become different from his father. He didn't want to preach like Daddy King, delivering fire-and-brimstone sermons, threats from the pulpit about sin and punishment. He would be more thoughtful, more restrained. He would preach a gospel of freedom and equality.

Despite their different approaches to religion, Daddy King was delighted at his son's decision. He promptly arranged for Martin to be ordained as a minister at Ebenezer Baptist Church. At the young age of nineteen, while he was still a student, Martin began preaching in his father's church.

" I was well aware of the typical white stereotype of the Negro, that he is always late, that he's loud and always laughing, that he's dirty and messy, and for a while I was terribly conscious of trying to avoid identification with it. If I were a minute late to class, I was . . . conscious of it. . . . Rather than be thought of as always laughing, I . . . was grimly serious. "

—Martin Luther King Jr.

After he graduated from Morehouse, Martin applied to Crozer Theological Seminary in Chester, Pennsylvania, moving there to begin his studies in 1948. Crozer was a small, integrated school, with fewer than one hundred students and less than a quarter of them Black. Arriving as a new Black student in a mostly white school, Martin was keen to make a good impression. He took care to keep his room spotless, his shoes perfectly shined, his clothes immaculately pressed.

He wrote in a letter to his mother: "You stated that my letters aren't newsy enough. Well, I don't have much news. I never go anywhere much but in these books. Some times [sic] the professor comes in class and tells us to read our assignments in Hebrew, and that is really hard."

He studied much harder than he'd done at Morehouse. He read the works of major European philosophers: the ancient Greeks Plato and Aristotle; French thinker Jean-Jacques Rousseau; English philosophers Thomas Hobbes, John Locke, and Jeremy Bentham; and John Stuart Mill, an early champion of individual freedom, women's rights, and the abolition of slavery. Martin questioned each of their writings, but he also found much to admire. For the first time in his life, he began "a serious intellectual quest for a method to eliminate social evil."

He studied the writings of Karl Marx and of Vladimir Lenin. Marx raised important questions for him about "the gulf between superfluous wealth and abject poverty." That gap disturbed Martin. He thought that *capitalism*, the market system of the American economy, placed business profit over the welfare of people. It felt unfair. He thought there must be a better way. But Marx rejected religion, and Martin could not accept that. The church was too important in his life. He questioned his father's way of preaching, but he believed deeply in the existence of God.

Martin began to read and question, to explore new ideas. He found himself engrossed by the writings of a Christian pastor and theologian, Walter Rauschenbusch. Rauschenbusch wrote that religion should be concerned not only with people's souls, but with their bodies as well. If families were strangled by economic hardship, then religion must care about that. Martin wrote, "Therefore, I must be concerned about unemployment, slums, and economic insecurity."

In addition to his classes, Martin attended lectures by guest speakers. He was especially moved by a speech given by former clergyman and social activist A. J. Muste. Muste had once led a strike of thirty thousand textile workers in Massachusetts. Police pulled him from the picket line. They questioned and clubbed him. They arrested him. Even so, he advised striking workers to smile while passing the machine guns and the police. Now Muste spoke about pacifism, shunning war, and resisting injustice peacefully.

Martin was intrigued by Muste's words, but he was also full of doubts. Could nonviolent resistance ever be practical?

"During this period I had almost despaired of the power of love in solving social problems. The 'turn the other cheek' philosophy and the 'love your enemies' philosophy are only valid, I felt, when individuals are in conflict with other individuals; when racial groups and nations are in conflict a more realistic approach is necessary."

Martin spent a long time thinking about life and its meaning, and what he could do in the world to make a difference. The campus at Crozer was a peaceful place. Martin often strolled through the grounds, walking past the buildings to the woods and fields beyond so he could "commune with nature."

> " Sometimes I go out at night and look up at the stars as they bedeck the heavens like shining silver pins sticking in a magnificent blue pin cushion. There is God. Sometimes I watch the sun as it gets up in the morning and paints its technicolor across the eastern horizon. There is God. Sometimes I watch the moon as it walks across the sky as a queen walks across her masterly mansion. There is God. "
>
> —Martin Luther King Jr.

Not for another two years did nonviolence become central to Martin's thinking. In 1950, he would attend a sermon by Dr. Mordecai Johnson, the first Black president of Howard University, a leading Black college in Washington, DC. Dr. Johnson, just returned from a trip to India, would speak about the life and work of a man unknown to many in his audience: Mohandas K. Gandhi.

Martin had heard of Gandhi from his father's friend Howard Thurman, who had first told him about the engaging old man he'd met in 1935 in India, a man who had spun cotton and spoken about peace. Benjamin Mays, now president of Morehouse College, had likewise met Gandhi in 1936 and mentioned him often during his weekly chapel talks. Martin had even written an essay on Gandhi but had not yet studied his writings in any depth.

Dr. Johnson's lecture would leave Martin electrified. Johnson would tell of how Gandhi had transformed India and galvanized its people into a massive wave of opinion, demanding and getting freedom from the yoke of imperial British rule—and of Gandhi himself falling to an assassin's bullet.

Johnson's words would not fully resolve Martin's doubts, but they would promise truth and love. They would give Martin hope.

12

Don't Ride
the Buses

read the *New York Times* headline. For a second, the article stated, the crowd remained stunned. A young man from the American embassy, Tom Reiner, was reportedly among those who pushed the assassin toward a group of police guards. Confusion ensued, but the shooter was finally arrested. Most American papers ran the story. Morehouse College buzzed with the news. In years to come, King would refer again and again to the assassination of his hero, Gandhi.

In 1948, the year of Gandhi's death, Martin Luther King Jr., at nineteen, with a BA degree in sociology, entered Crozer Theological Seminary. By May 1951, he earned his degree in divinity—with flying colors. He graduated with the highest grade point average in his class. Delighted, his father presented him with a shiny new car: a green Chevrolet equipped with "powerglide."

In his fancy car, Martin went north to enroll in the doctoral program at Boston University. The school was known for advocating peace, peacemakers, and social justice. Martin came to campus eager to learn from the famous religious scholars who taught there.

But when he tried to find a place to live, to his surprise, Martin ran headlong into racial bias. He trudged down the streets, noting the phone numbers on the signs—ROOMS FOR RENT—posted on apartment buildings. He'd call and get an appointment. When he showed up, landlords would tell him—apparently upon seeing the color of his skin—that the rooms were already rented out. He finally found an apartment on Massachusetts Avenue, across from the Savoy Ballroom. The dance hall often stayed open all night, and its stomping music filtered into Martin's apartment, even through closed windows.

Martin soon settled into classes and a schedule. But he was also looking for something else in his life: romantic love. He met quite a few girls in Boston, but none of them took his fancy. He asked a friend from Atlanta, Mary Powell, if she knew any "nice, attractive young ladies." Mary was a student at the New England Conservatory of Music. She gave Martin the phone number of a friend of hers. The young woman's name was Coretta Scott. She was from Marion, Alabama, and had gone to college in Ohio before getting a scholarship to study music in Boston.

Martin called Coretta on the telephone and introduced himself. He told her their mutual friend Mary had said wonderful things about her. "I'd like very much to meet you and talk to you," he said. They talked for a while. Then Martin startled Coretta by declaring, "You know every Napoleon has his Waterloo. I'm like Napoleon. I'm at my

Waterloo, and I'm on my knees. I'd like to meet you and talk some more." He suggested lunch.

Perhaps Coretta was amused at this grand, dramatic speech. At any rate, she agreed. He went to pick her up in his new green Chevy.

At lunch, they talked about many things. Coretta was swayed by Martin's eloquence. He certainly had a way with words. His sweeping sentences built vivid images and stories. He wasn't very tall, but his words lifted him, made him larger than life.

As for Martin, he fell completely and instantaneously in love. Coretta had character, intelligence, personality, and beauty. After only an hour, he proclaimed, "You have everything I ever wanted in a woman. We ought to get married someday."

Young Coretta Scott, 1948

The two young people spent hours together. They went to concerts and plays. They found that they shared a yearning for a larger cause. They had heartfelt discussions about racial and economic injustice and about peace—how it was lacking, how much it was needed, and whether it could ever be achieved.

Martin told his mother, "Coretta is going to be my wife."

Martin's father was not immediately pleased. He had hoped his son would marry a girl from Georgia, from a family the Kings already knew. It took some time to bring him around. When Martin brought Coretta home to meet his parents, his father promptly informed Coretta that his son had dated many girls from right there in his home state. Why, he'd even proposed to a few of them! Coretta was a bit taken aback, but she smiled and carried on the conversation.

Martin's parents met with Coretta once more before giving their blessings. Finally, on June 18, 1953, before his final year of study, the couple were married on the lawn of Coretta's family home in Marion, Alabama. Martin's father was the officiating minister.

In Marion at the time, there were no hotels with bridal suites that would accept a Black newlywed couple. They spent their wedding night in the guest bedroom of friends who owned a funeral parlor. For years, Martin would joke, "Do you know, we spent our honeymoon at a funeral parlor."

Returning to Boston to begin their life together, both Martin and Coretta had goals to meet. Martin had to complete his coursework. Coretta had to finish her degree in voice and piano from the New England Conservatory of Music.

During that year, Martin looked for employment. He wanted to be a pastor in a church. He found an opening at the Dexter Avenue Baptist Church in Montgomery, Alabama. He applied and was invited to visit and deliver a sermon.

In the old church, with its gleaming woodwork and tall windows, he preached about what a complete life meant. Life, he said, is a great triangle. At one corner stands the individual. At the second corner are all other people. At the third is God. He urged the congregation to look inward for their own welfare, outward for the welfare of others, and upward, reaching for God.

The congregation and the pulpit committee were impressed by Martin's sermon. They offered him the job.

Though Martin Luther King still had to finish his doctoral dis-

Martin and Coretta on their wedding day

sertation, Coretta had just earned her degree, so the couple decided to move to Montgomery. He could write his dissertation there and travel back to Boston when necessary. It took him nine more months of writing and rewriting, then appearing before a committee to defend his work, but he earned that degree. He was now Dr. Martin Luther King Jr.

Moreover, at the age of twenty-five, after being in school for nineteen years without a break, he now had his own church—he was

WEDDING VOWS IN A REQUEST THAT WAS MOST UNUSUAL FOR THAT TIME, CORETTA ASKED THAT THE PROMISE TO "OBEY" HER HUSBAND BE REMOVED FROM THE WEDDING VOWS. SHE HAD HER WAY.

Reverend King. The solid-brick building of Dexter Avenue Church filled regularly with worshippers. Ironically, it stood at an angle across the square from the elegant dome of the state capitol—the very building where generations of Alabama legislators had once defended the rights of white people to own slaves.

Reverend King had a busy schedule. An early riser, as Gandhi had been, he woke before six each morning, preparing his sermons, memorizing them, then rehearsing them in a full-length mirror. But while Gandhi had been a timid speaker, more comfortable with pen and ink than the podium, King could be a thunderous and rousing orator. His words from the pulpit moved those who listened.

A year of working, settling in, building community, ended on a note of personal joy. In November 1955, Coretta gave birth to their first child, a girl. They named her Yolanda. King called her "Yoki." He said she was a "big little girl. She kept her father quite busy walking the floor."

Brown v. Board of Education

In 1954, the U.S. Supreme Court ruled unanimously that racial segregation in public schools was unconstitutional. Almost immediately, Southern white political leaders condemned the decision and vowed they would not obey it. Some Virginia schools shut down rather than let Black children in. For years, Southern schools resisted integration. The governor of Arkansas called in the state's National Guard to block the entry of nine Black students into Central High School in Little Rock.

Meanwhile, King remained haunted by the desperate condition of Black people. A fourteen-year-old boy, Emmett Till, was brutally murdered in Mississippi, for supposedly flirting with a white woman. His murderers, who boasted about their terrible deed, were found innocent by an all-white jury.

National laws were starting to mandate integration, yet schools and communities remained stubbornly segregated. That included the buses. In Montgomery, by law, the first four rows of bus seats were reserved for white people. If you were Black, it didn't matter how tired you were, or if you were ill or elderly or had a disability. If you were Black, you could not sit in those seats.

In December, a woman named Rosa Parks was arrested for refusing to give up her bus seat to a white passenger. Mrs. Parks was an activist and a member of the National Association for the Advancement of Colored People. The driver of the bus, James Blake, had ordered Rosa

Parks off his bus before in order to accommodate white riders.

On this night, the bus filled up, Black people in the back and white in the front. Blake ordered four Black passengers to give up their seats so that a lone white man left standing could sit down without having to share his row with people of color.

Three of the Black passengers obeyed the driver's command. Rosa Parks did not, even though she knew that drivers in Montgomery, Alabama, carried guns. She was promptly arrested.

Rosa Parks's arrest set off a ripple of indignation in the Black community. The Women's Political Council, an organization of Black women working to reform racist local policies, drafted a letter in support of Mrs. Parks. Activist Edgar D. Nixon phoned King, inviting him to join a movement to boycott the bus system. King was reluctant, saying he would need to think about it for a while. Nixon called Ralph Abernathy, a close friend of King's and pastor of Montgomery's oldest Black Baptist church. Abernathy called King to tell him he must get involved.

Rev. King hesitated, because he hadn't made up his mind about the method of the boycott. Was it a Christian thing to shut the buses down, thereby depriving other riders of a necessary service? Would

A Seat on a Bus

Rosa Parks was not the first Black person to be arrested for refusing to yield a seat to a white rider. In March 1955, a fifteen-year-old girl named Claudette Colvin had been arrested for the same reason. Today, Claudette, in her eighties, says many people worked and sacrificed to integrate Southern buses: "Young people think Rosa Parks just sat down on a bus and ended segregation, but that wasn't the case at all."

Girl, 15, Guilty In Bus Seat Case

the drivers get paid if they didn't have work? In the past, White Citizens' Councils across the South had threatened to boycott schools and public facilities because they wanted to *keep* them segregated. Having been used to perpetuate a cruelly divided society, was the method itself corrupt? Still, he said he would help if he could be of some service.

The teachings of Jesus Christ filled King's mind. He thought as well of Thoreau's essay "Civil Disobedience." He gave in, offering his church for the initial meeting.

Still unsure—had he done the right thing?—he hurried home to his wife and baby. He told Coretta of the day's events. She assured him that she would support him in whatever he did.

Later that day, animated voices filled a crowded meeting room at Dexter Avenue Church. All those who attended agreed to spread the word about the boycott. Sensitive to the mood of the group, King was sure that something important and unusual was about to happen.

A mimeograph machine ran for hours, churning out leaflets, seven thousand of them, containing much of the letter written earlier by the Women's Political Counsel. The leaflet urged readers: "Don't ride the buses to work, to town, to school or any where on Monday. . . . If you work, take a cab, or share a ride, or walk. Come to a mass meeting on Monday at 7:00 p.m., at the Holt Street Baptist Church for further instruction."

Eager volunteers distributed the leaflets. The next day, King and Abernathy went around Montgomery, informing people about the boycott, telling them not to ride the buses to work, urging them to be orderly and calm. There was to be no violence.

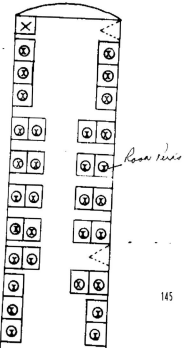

Seat layout on the bus showing where Rosa Parks sat, December 1, 1955

Rosa sia

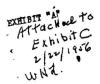

EXHIBIT "A" attached to Exhibit C 2/22/1956 WND.

145

Soon after King went to bed that night, baby Yolanda woke up and began to cry. Now Martin and Coretta were awake. They talked about the protest. Would it succeed? How would they know? They decided that if 60 percent of Black people cooperated with the movement, it would be a success. Perhaps the next meeting would encourage more protesters.

Around midnight came a most welcome call. Every Black taxi company in Montgomery had agreed to support the protest on Monday morning. They would carry passengers to their destinations for an emergency ten-cent fare. Exhausted, the King family finally slept.

Monday morning arrived. Martin and Coretta awoke by five thirty. They took turns watching the bus stop outside their window. They watched for a long, long half hour and saw nothing. King had gone to the kitchen to get a cup of coffee when Coretta called, "Martin, Martin, come quickly!" He put his cup down and ran to the living room window.

Coretta pointed to a bus moving slowly past. A second. Then a third. Buses drove past in the dark, lighted up on the inside, empty but for a handful of white passengers. No Black people were riding the buses!

King sprang into his car and drove around the city. In the morning chill, hundreds of Black citizens of Montgomery were walking to work. Others caught rides with friends and family. The boycott was a resounding success. And King noticed something about those people walking to work. "They knew why they walked, and the knowledge was evident in the way they carried themselves."

Rev. King would describe December 5, 1955, as a "day of days." As it came to an end, everyone was aware that something momentous had just taken place. It was not just that a message had been sent to the bus companies and the city of Montgomery. That message had gone out to the mass meeting of minds in the Black community. Thousands of people gained the power that day to take a simple action. With that action, they made a difference. A seat on a bus became, to the American civil rights movement, what a fistful of salt had been twenty-five years earlier to Indians seeking independence.

Two white women on an otherwise empty Montgomery bus during the boycott

13

Against the Constitution

That afternoon, the boycott organizers met again in Rev. King's church basement, this time to form a new organization, the Montgomery Improvement Association (MIA), to oversee the continued boycott. They assigned tasks. Rides had to be arranged to get people around the city while they were boycotting the buses. A fundraising committee sought donations. A program committee planned mass meetings.

To King's surprise, the group elected him its president. It was a risky job—white reprisals were almost certain. He accepted, then went home as quickly as he could. He had twenty minutes to write a speech for that evening's event at the Holt Street Baptist Church—his very first political speech! He wasted five minutes working himself into a panic over it, then settled down to scribble notes. He had hardly collected his thoughts when a friend arrived to drive him to the first mass rally of the movement.

Within a couple of blocks of Holt Street, traffic slowed to a crawl. The car inched forward, then stopped amid a sea of jostling bodies. King mused, "This could turn into something big."

He got out of the car and pushed through the crowd for fifteen minutes before he reached the church door. Church members were hurriedly rigging up loudspeakers so all those who would have to stand outside could hear the speech.

As soon as King got inside, the pastor called him to the pulpit. He stood there for a moment, taken aback at the crowd. People crammed into aisles and balconies, sat on the floor, peered in through the windows.

King began to speak, his mind still searching for answers to his own doubts. He talked about Rosa Parks refusing to give up her seat. He talked about the law that segregated the buses. The crowd listened, murmured in agreement and approval. As he talked, he scanned the faces, seeking reactions. With every turn of phrase, every lilt and pause, he called for their response. "You know, my friends, there comes a time . . ."

Scattered cries floated up: "Yes!" "Amen."

". . . when people get tired of being trampled over by the iron feet of oppression."

Cheers broke out, swelling into a thunderous wave. Applause rolled in from the outside and rose up to the ceiling. The floorboards vibrated to the thumping of feet. Awash in loving faith, King found his voice—and his conviction. "And we are not wrong," he said. "We are not wrong in what we are doing . . . we are only using the tools of justice." His voice rode on the surging tide of acclamation. "If we are wrong, God Almighty is wrong."

"Yes!" cried the audience.

"And we are determined here in Montgomery to work and fight until justice runs down like water . . ."

"Yes!"

"And righteousness like a mighty stream." That was a line from the Bible, one of his favorites. Poetic and grand, it gave power to the speaker and, in turn, to those who listened.

As King finished and left the church, people reached out to touch him.

The hopeful start gave way to a long struggle. The police commissioner sent a notice out to taxi drivers—the city had made it illegal for taxi drivers to give pedestrians free or cheap rides. Customers must pay at least forty-five cents a ride, or the drivers would face charges of breaking the law.

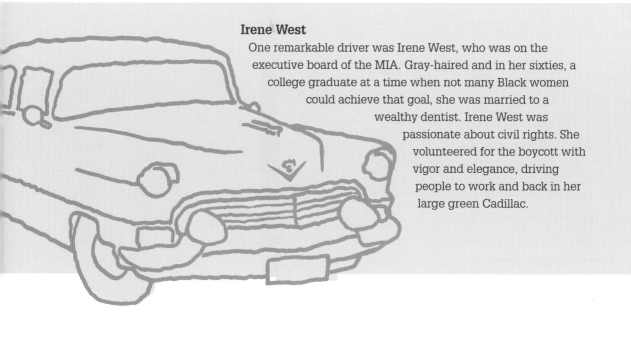

Irene West

One remarkable driver was Irene West, who was on the executive board of the MIA. Gray-haired and in her sixties, a college graduate at a time when not many Black women could achieve that goal, she was married to a wealthy dentist. Irene West was passionate about civil rights. She volunteered for the boycott with vigor and elegance, driving people to work and back in her large green Cadillac.

In response, the MIA quickly organized volunteers with cars—150 signed up the very first night. They collected passengers from forty-two stations. Many volunteer drivers were ministers. Others were teachers, housewives, businessmen, laborers. Rides came from unexpected volunteers—wealthy white women who desperately wanted their Black help to arrive on time. Since the household help refused to take the buses, some of these women sallied out to give them rides!

Bus officials and city administrators were confident the protest would fizzle out in a few days. Surely, on the first rainy day, Black workers would go back to riding the buses.

The rain came. The buses remained empty.

A week after the first triumphant boycott day, the city officials agreed to negotiate. The MIA chose twelve people to represent the Black community. Dr. King was their spokesman. They presented a brief list of demands. The first was a guarantee of courteous treatment. The MIA even accepted that Black passengers would get on from the back, but they insisted that all passengers be seated on a first-come, first-served basis. Black bus operators should be employed on routes that served mostly Black communities.

It was only a temporary compromise, and they knew it. It accepted segregation, which none of them wanted. But at least the bus system would be required to treat Black passengers with some dignity.

A meeting was held. King attended. The commissioners and the bus company's lawyer began raising questions. They challenged the MIA's proposal. Not the courtesy part. That was fine. Hiring more Black drivers—well, that was not city business. The bus companies could hire whomever they liked. As for first-come, first-served seating, that was flat-out illegal! How could Black and white people practically rub knees on the bus when segregation was the law in Alabama?

Frustrated, King began to realize that when Black people asked for justice within the law, the white city fathers had the law itself to back them up. Justice was impossible when the law itself was unjust. King decided to close the meeting.

He was angry, and he hated feeling that way. Anger was corrosive, yet how could he endure it from his opponents without getting angry himself? In the days and weeks that followed, he began to think about Jesus. What would he do? And he thought of Gandhi's teachings that he had read and heard about, back in his student days.

The more he thought about it, the more convinced King became that nonviolence was more than the lack of violence. It was the world's most powerful tool to resist unfair laws. Look at the millions who had marched for freedom in India! In Dr. King's words, "Christ furnished the spirit and motivation while Gandhi furnished the method." And the method was nothing less than love—the kind of love that the ancient Greeks called *agape*, a love so wide, it embraced the whole world, urging communities toward fairness and justice.

Christmas 1955 drew near. King called on Black people to take money meant for gifts and divide it into thirds. A third could go to help fund the boycott, a third to charity, and the rest into savings. If Black people refused to buy presents, white shop owners would not make money off them. It worked. Christmas purchases in Montgomery took a sharp dip. Store owners noticed, but they weren't too worried. This wouldn't break them.

The bus companies, however, were in trouble. By early 1956, they demanded (and got) a fare increase to make up for their lost Black ridership.

A local paper, the *Advertiser*, published a full-length interview with King. It was the first time ever that the paper had run a profile of a Black person.

Another *Advertiser* article stirred controversy. It announced that the boycott was about to end. All Blacks would return to the buses on Monday morning! Bus drivers would be courteous. There would be special all-Black seating during rush hours. Otherwise, the seating would remain "normal"—that is to say segregated. King was caught by surprise. His heart sank. The article claimed that the protesters were represented in these talks by "three prominent Negro ministers."

Meanwhile, in India . . .

A teacher in a Methodist missionary school in the town of Nagpur, India, heard commotion outside his classroom. He rushed out to see what it was. An American colleague, James Lawson, was yelling at the top of his voice, stamping his feet, clapping his hands. What was the matter?

Lawson pointed to a story in a local English-language newspaper, the *Nagpur Times*. It was about thousands of Black people refusing to ride the buses in a small, segregated city in the United States. Lawson, a Black man, was so excited, he could hardly speak.

Gandhi had been dead seven years. Independent India was deeply divided. Gandhi's ideas and methods seemed to be disappearing in the land of his birth. Now Lawson saw hope for his own people in America. He knew at once that he would one day meet this Martin Luther King Jr. He would work at his side in the cause of civil rights for Black people in America.

A newspaper article published in India in 1956 said "Gandhi's shadow watches over Alabama."

James Lawson, arrested in Mississippi, 1961, during the Freedom Rides

A little sleuthing revealed that these ministers were three country preachers who had been called by the Montgomery mayor to city hall to discuss "insurance matters." Upon arrival, they were handed a copy of a bus settlement and persuaded to sign it. They weren't representing anyone. In fact, they had been conned into signing!

King joined MIA leaders, driving to possible meeting places—drinking holes, country "dives," anywhere that working people gathered—to quell the rumors that the article set off. And the next day, despite the article, the buses remained empty.

In the meantime, Rosa Parks had been convicted for her act of defiance and fined ten dollars plus four more in court costs. She appealed. That appeal went nowhere in the state court. At the same time, while the MIA discussed legal options, city officials tried to divide the Black community by spreading rumors about its leaders. Prominent white citizens suggested that a young man like King was not fit to lead such an important cause. King began to doubt himself. He offered to resign, but MIA members refused to let him give up.

Police began by harassing carpool drivers, ticketing some for going too fast, others for going too slow or not signaling turns. Still others were charged with purely imaginary traffic violations! The fines they paid funneled precious money away from boycott contributions, into the city coffers.

On January 26, 1956, Rev. King was driving home from his church along with the church secretary, Lillie Thomas, and Robert Williams, a friend from Morehouse. He stopped to pick up passengers from a carpool stop. Police were stopping and questioning the drivers. As he drove on, he heard them scoff, "There's that damn King fellow."

King noticed that two policemen on motorcycles were following him. He drove slowly, keeping an eye on them. When he stopped to let his passengers out, a policeman sputtered his motorbike up to the car window. "Get out, King," he said. "You are under arrest for speeding thirty miles an hour in a twenty-five-mile zone."

Soon King was in the back of a police cruiser heading out of downtown. Visions of lynchings and murders flashed through his mind. He was "trembling within and without." Then he saw a lighted sign: MONTGOMERY CITY JAIL. It was a relief to be thrown in jail!

In the crowded cell, he found other protesters, packed together

Station wagons line up to give rides.

with "vagrants and drunks and serious lawbreakers." The conditions were vile—wooden slats, torn-up mattresses, a toilet in one corner. No privacy at all. King thought that no one, no matter what he'd done, should have to serve time in a place like this.

King was fingerprinted. Abernathy and others scrambled to raise bail money. Word of the arrest spread throughout the Black community. Supporters crowded around the jail. Frightened that the crowd might turn into a mob, the jailer released King even before bail had been posted.

The MIA called mass meetings to calm people who might otherwise become frustrated and turn restless, maybe even violent. Organizers decided that King should not drive anymore. A group of drivers and bodyguards was formed to protect him.

But how could anyone protect a telephone line? The Dexter Avenue Church parsonage number was in the phone book—35197. Anonymous callers harassed the family with curses and threats. Late one night, the phone rang. Dr. King answered it. The voice on the other end uttered a racist slur. Then it went on to say, "[W]e are tired of you and your mess now. And if you aren't out of this town in three days, we're going to blow your brains out and blow up your house."

King hung up. Fear gripped him, not for himself, but for Coretta and his new baby.

In a way, the calls meant that the movement was succeeding. The white supremacists were afraid. Why else were they making abusive, anonymous calls? The calls reinforced the hateful messages King and others involved in the boycott were getting from vigilante groups, including the Ku Klux Klan (KKK). But he had to acknowledge his own fear. And if he was afraid, how could he ask others to look to him for strength?

King got out of bed and began to walk the floor, unable to sleep. He went to the kitchen and made a cup of coffee but could not drink it. He finally sat with his head in his hands, praying aloud, "Lord, I must confess that I'm weak now . . . I'm faltering . . . I'm losing my courage."

Suddenly, a voice spoke to him. "Martin Luther, stand up for righteousness. Stand up for justice. Stand up for truth. And lo, I will be with you. Even until the end of the world." He was stunned. He knew in his heart that this was the voice of God. It was nothing less than an answer to his prayer. He felt flooded through with strength. Whatever lay ahead, he was ready now.

The MIA met, voting to file a federal lawsuit against bus segregation in Montgomery. At the next mass meeting, King explained the plan to two thousand people crowding into Abernathy's church. He tried to sound confident, to boost everyone's courage, but he could tell that his speech lacked fire. Then an elderly woman, whom everyone knew as "Mother Pollard," rose and walked slowly to the front of the church. It was not uncommon for elders to speak up, sharing their experiences. Sometimes they'd ramble, but the younger people always listened politely.

"Come here, son," said Mother Pollard, and she hugged Rev. King. "Something is wrong with you," she said. "You didn't talk strong tonight."

King protested that he felt fine, but she was sure something was wrong. Was it white folks bothering him, or something else? Was it someone in the movement? King smiled. He didn't know what to say.

Mother Pollard put her face close to his. She said, "We is with you all the way. But even if we ain't with you, God's gonna take care of you." And she made her way back to her seat, leaving King teary-eyed. The crowd cheered. It was a moment of connection, rare and precious. Everyone in the struggle needed moments like that.

But danger loomed closer than King could imagine.

The organ played. The service went on. He noticed that people were looking at him and whispering. What was wrong? Finally, someone told him. His house had been bombed! His first thoughts flew to Coretta and little Yoki. Were they safe? Abernathy didn't know.

The cold calm of a sudden shock descended upon King. He gave everyone news of the bombing, told them to go home peacefully, then excused himself. With terrified gasps, the crowd parted for him.

He hurried homeward. Along the way, he saw restless, angry Black people. For self-defense, some carried guns and knives. Small boys toted broken pop bottles like weapons. King overheard a man telling a police officer, "Now you got your .38 and I got mine; so let's battle it out." Dismayed at the movement descending into violence around him, frightened for his loved ones, King rushed home.

Stepping onto the front porch, he had to walk across broken glass, from windows shattered by the bomb blast. Members of the Dexter Avenue Church packed the living room. The mayor and the police commissioner arrived. King pushed through into the back room where Coretta, still in her robe, sat with the baby. King hugged his wife and baby. How calm Coretta was! Overcome with gratitude, he gave prayerful thanks and went back to the living room.

Mayor "Tacky" Gayle and Commissioner Clyde Sellers both condemned the bombing and promised to bring the bombers to justice. No one present was convinced.

King went out to the porch and addressed the gathering crowd. "We believe in law and order," he said. "Don't get panicky. . . . Don't get your weapons. He who lives by the sword will perish by the sword. Remember that is what God said. We are not advocating violence."

Cheers broke out. But when Commissioner Sellers tried to speak, the cheers changed to boos. King raised his hand, reminding people that they needed to hear the commissioner out. Commissioner Sellers promised police protection for the King family. Someone demanded to see Coretta. King called her out. With satisfied murmurs, the crowd dispersed.

Daddy King, worried for his son's safety, urged him to leave Montgomery and come home to Atlanta. King refused. The boycott wasn't over. Since the MIA turned down the city's offer, arrests were likely. How could he leave when his friends might go to jail for the cause that he was supposed to be leading? They couldn't just depend on the pending lawsuit. They had to keep the boycott going.

Sure enough, the city indicted King and eighty-eight other boycott leaders. Instead of waiting to be arrested, they turned themselves in. King was fined $500, refused to pay, and went to jail for two weeks.

The year crawled by. Another bomb exploded, this one in E. D. Nixon's yard. The city offered another settlement that the MIA rejected. Boycott leaders and carpool drivers continued to be arrested.

The buses continued to drive empty.

Meanwhile, a district court lawsuit was headed for the Supreme Court—it involved four Black women who had been mistreated on Montgomery city buses, prior to the arrest of Rosa Parks. One of them was Claudette Colvin.

The press was beginning to pay attention. By midyear 1956, the bus boycott was being covered not just by local and national reporters, but by journalists from England, Japan, Italy, Germany, the Netherlands, Australia—and India.

381 DAYS THAT WAS HOW LONG THE MONTGOMERY BUS BOYCOTT LASTED. DURING THAT TIME, SOME ELDERLY PARTICIPANTS PASSED AWAY. THEIR FUNERALS BECAME PUBLIC GATHERINGS IN CELEBRATION OF THE CAUSE.

A national election came and went. President Dwight D. Eisenhower was reelected in a landslide victory. His party, the Republican Party, had won in Montgomery, Alabama, for the first time in history. Black residents were encouraged, yet baffled. The Republicans were known to be sympathetic to the civil rights movement. White people in Montgomery had voted Republican in sufficient numbers to make this win possible. Was the tide turning?

But the week after the election, on November 13, 1956, Montgomery city lawyers still argued to ban carpooling and fine the MIA $15,000 to make up for the city's lost tax revenues. Arrested once more, King sat at his trial, his face drawn with worry.

The arguments mounted. At the recess, a reporter handed King a note—a bulletin from the Associated Press: "The United States Supreme Court today affirmed a decision of a special three-judge panel in declaring Alabama's state and local laws requiring segregation on buses unconstitutional."

Unconstitutional! King was jubilant. The Supreme Court had declared the Alabama bus segregation laws to be against the Constitution of the United States. The Montgomery bus boycott was over. And it had worked.

A plaque marks the spot on Dexter Avenue where Rosa Parks waited for a bus.

14

Actions Louder
Than Words

The boycott was over; the protesters had won. Yet questions remained. What would happen to Black passengers on the first day that they boarded one of these newly integrated buses? Would white passengers be angry? Would there be backlash against the protesters? King decided that actions would speak louder than words.

Action lay at the heart of Gandhi's methods of resistance. You could speak out against injustice, but until you acted on your words, no one would pay attention. Gandhi had broken the law by picking up salt. King decided to celebrate integration by stepping up onto a bus and inviting colleagues, both Black and white, to join him.

Three men—Ralph Abernathy, local NAACP president E. D. Nixon, and Glenn Smiley, a white civil rights leader—met at King's house on the morning of Friday, December 21, 1956. They walked to the bus stop. Reporters and photographers milled around. Questions flew. Cameras clicked. Then a bus pulled up.

The doors opened. Martin Luther King stepped on from the front. He put his fare into the box. The driver greeted him. "I believe you are Reverend King, aren't you?"

King said he was. It was a moment in history, a moment thousands of people had been waiting for.

"We are glad to have you this morning," said the driver.

As the new year ticked on, it became clear that integration wasn't all a smooth ride. Many Southern cities reacted with violence to the Supreme Court ruling. Someone blew in the front door of King's home with shotgun fire. Buses were fired at. Churches were bombed.

King and associates ride an integrated bus.

What Became of Rosa Parks?

Rosa Parks appealed her conviction, but she lost her job. Her husband quit his job when he was told he could not talk about Rosa and her legal case at work. The family had to move.

Parks continued to be an active, outspoken participant in the civil rights movement. She became a friend to Malcolm X. In years to come, she would be honored as the "first lady of civil rights" and the "mother of the freedom movement." She would receive the Congressional Gold Medal.

So was a Jewish center in Nashville, where the rabbi of the local synagogue supported integration. The Ku Klux Klan was incensed, bent on vengeance.

As the news of violent reprisals poured in, King's heart was stricken with grief and guilt. Had he not encouraged innocent people to protest, only to bring hatred down upon their heads? Was he not then responsible for all this violence? At a mass meeting, he blurted out his fears. "Lord, I hope no one will have to die as a result of our struggle for freedom here in Montgomery." He gripped the pulpit. "But if anyone should be killed, let it be me!" His words dissolved into sobs.

Shocked, the audience cried, "No, no!" King clutched the podium, frozen, unable to say more. Two ministers led him to a seat to recover.

Despite setbacks, the work had to go on. King joined with fellow ministers C. K. Steele and Fred Shuttlesworth to announce the formation of a new organization, the Southern Christian Leadership Conference (SCLC). In the press release, they wrote, "This conference is called because we have no moral choice, before God, but to delve deeper into the struggle—and to do so with greater reliance on non-violence and with greater unity, coordination, sharing, and Christian understanding."

Allies showed up. In February 1957, when King spoke at Oberlin College in Ohio, a student introduced himself. His name, he said, was James Lawson. He had been looking forward to this moment ever since he'd read King's name in the *Nagpur Times* more than a year earlier.

King was fascinated. He talked to Lawson at length. He said he meant to go to India, the land of Gandhi, as soon as he could. He invited Lawson to join the nonviolent civil rights movement in the American South. Yet in his own heart, he worried. This road was so long and the obstacles so many.

A Jewish Rabbi and Civil Rights

In the 1950s, Joel Silverman was a young teen living in Nashville, Tennessee, with his parents and brother. One Sunday evening, his family was watching TV. Joel got up to go to the bathroom. On the way back, as he passed the telephone, it rang. "And so," he says, "I did the natural thing. I answered it. The guy at the other end announced that they had just blown up the Jewish center and that their next intention was to kill my father."

Joel's father was a Jewish rabbi. Rabbi William Silverman led the Temple Congregation Ohabai Sholom, known to all as the Vine Street Temple. Over time, Silverman became more and more involved in the civil rights movement. When a local elementary school was bombed for opening its doors to Black first graders in 1957, Silverman blamed the White Citizens' Council for inciting such acts with its opposition to desegregation. Death threats became a fact of life. Dead animals were thrown onto the family's lawn, with anonymous notes attached to them. The state of Tennessee provided the Silvermans with police protection. "But back then," Joel says, "a lot of the police belonged to the Klan, so you didn't know who was protecting you and who wasn't."

The family had a dog, an Irish setter named Rusty, who barked constantly at trespassers, police, and passersby. One morning, Joel awoke to silence. The dog wasn't barking. He assumed at once that Rusty had been killed, so he went outside to look. The dog had developed laryngitis—from barking too much!

Joel Silverman is now in his seventies. Even when he was young, he knew that his father was involved in something both important and dangerous. He remembers being told not to stand in front of glass windows in case a rock or a bullet came flying through. He also remembers hurrying out of the house early in the morning to do something he was forbidden to do—check the underside of the car for bombs!

Some who demanded civil rights sought other avenues. Malcolm X, an outspoken and charismatic Black leader in New York, was now a spokesman of a growing religious group—the Nation of Islam. The group rejected Christian churches in favor of Muslim teachings. They also advocated armed self-defense. They believed that Black and white people could never be allies. Malcolm X invited King to come hear the message of the Nation of Islam's leader, Elijah Muhammad. King never responded.

Meanwhile, the story of the Montgomery bus boycott continued to spread. It made national, even international, news. Clare Boothe Luce, the first U.S. woman ambassador and the wife of *Time* magazine founder Henry Luce, wrote to King: "No man has ever waged a battle for equality under our law in a more lawful and Christian way than you have." A few weeks later, a *Time* correspondent was assigned to write a full-length profile of Martin Luther King Jr.

An imposing portrait of King graced the red-bordered cover of *Time*. Behind the portrait was a sketch of King speaking at a podium. In the foreground was a bus, with a group of Black people boarding through the front door. That image was on every newsstand and grocery store checkout line in America. The profile stated, "Above all, he read and reread everything he could find about India's Gandhi."

The *Time* article brought King and the larger cause of civil rights legislation to the awareness of more than two hundred thousand Americans. But the man who occupied the highest office in the land was unconvinced. President Eisenhower was less than enthusiastic about reforming the law to make it fairer to people of all races. Ahead of a hunting vacation, stopping to attend church, the president heard a sermon on the need for new civil rights laws. Eisenhower remarked, "You can't legislate morality."

King was dismayed by the president's lack of support. In the months that followed, he spoke about it from the pulpit. Perhaps, he suggested, the president did not understand what the laws were meant for. They were meant to make people behave in acceptable ways to each other, no matter what they thought or believed. As King said on more than one occasion, "It may be true that the law cannot make a man love me, but it can keep him from lynching me, and I think that's pretty important also."

Publicly, the president supported citizenship rights for minorities. Privately, he was uncomfortable around Black people. He was even known to make racist jokes. King sent Eisenhower a telegram seeking to meet him and make his case personally. The president had never hosted a Black delegation at the White House. He did not reply to the telegram.

Meanwhile, King's young family was growing. While he was addressing a business meeting of the Dexter congregation, a courier arrived, bringing news from the hospital. Coretta had just given birth to their second child, a boy, Martin Luther King III. King stopped the meeting to announce the birth. Everyone clapped and cheered. People began to mingle and talk in an impromptu celebration. Good news was hard to come by, and a new baby was good news.

President Eisenhower, glasses in hand

King's audience fully expected him to wrap up the meeting and rush to the hospital. They would have cheered him out the door. Instead, he resumed his interrupted discussion of the church's programs and committees.

Several senior churchwomen huddled outside the door, frowning and talking in whispers. They couldn't interrupt their pastor, even though they really thought his place was with his wife and new baby. Finally, one of them called the hospital to say that Dr. King would be late.

King had always tried to make time for his family. But pulled in so many directions, he could no longer see what really mattered at that moment.

15

In Gandhi's Footsteps

Martin Luther King had long wanted to visit India. He had begun working on a book about the Montgomery bus boycott, *Stride Toward Freedom*, and the methods of Gandhi were much on his mind. The Indian government and the Gandhi Peace Foundation in India had invited him. Activists in the United States urged King to continue employing Gandhi's methods. Those methods had succeeded spectacularly in the bus boycott. Why not use them again, this time to combat other forms of segregation and discrimination? Jesus Christ, King felt, had led him to Gandhi, so he was eager to see the land of Gandhi's birth.

A lawyer who knew of King's work, Harris Wofford, wrote to him: "Isn't this the time for some straight Gandhian civil disobedience?" Wofford urged King to go to India to meet people who had worked with Gandhi. So did Bayard Rustin, a dedicated follower of Gandhi, who helped raise travel funds.

HARRIS WOFFORD AS A BOY OF ELEVEN, HARRIS WOFFORD HAD VISITED INDIA. EVEN AT THAT YOUNG AGE, HE HAD BECOME FASCINATED WITH MAHATMA GANDHI. HE WAS ONE OF THE EARLY WHITE SUPPORTERS OF THE CIVIL RIGHTS MOVEMENT.

BAYARD RUSTIN BAYARD RUSTIN WAS AN OUTSPOKEN BLACK PACIFIST, SOCIALIST, CIVIL RIGHTS LEADER, MUSICIAN, PHILOSOPHER, WORLD TRAVELER, AND ART COLLECTOR. HE WAS ALSO GAY. HE WAS AN ADVOCATE FOR GAY RIGHTS AT A TIME WHEN NO GAY RIGHTS MOVEMENT EVEN EXISTED!

Still, every time King was ready to make the trip, something got in the way. First came a travel commitment. The Gold Coast, once a British colony in Africa, was now independent—a new nation, renamed Ghana. The Kings had been invited to an Independence Day celebration in the capital, Accra.

In Accra, the British flag, the Union Jack, was lowered and replaced by the Ghanaian flag, with red, yellow, and green horizontal stripes and a star in the middle. The new Ghanaian president, Kwame Nkrumah, entered the hall, along with other ministers who had been in prison with him during their struggle for independence. Instead of formal clothes, they wore their prison caps and coats with pride. Later, Nkrumah danced with the Duchess of Kent, who represented the British Crown—a Black man, as King said later, "dancing with the lord on an equal plane." The sight gave King much to think about.

In Ghana, Dr. King also met U.S. Vice President Richard Nixon for the first time. Earlier, he had sent Nixon telegrams, but Nixon had never responded. After they were introduced, King said, "I'm very glad to meet you here but I want you to come visit us down in Alabama where we are seeking the same kind of freedom." In turn, Nixon invited King to come to Washington to speak privately about civil rights.

The birth of the new nation of Ghana made King feel that there was hope for the Black people of America. American media, especially Black journalists, were paying close attention to events in Africa. Radio host Etta Moten Barnett interviewed Dr. King, who said, "I think this event, the birth of this new nation, will give impetus to oppressed peoples all over the world." King was reinvigorated, ready for sweeping change for his own people back in America.

The next time King thought of visiting India, his publishers urged him to finish writing his book first. When that was finally completed, violence prevented him from traveling.

King was in Blumstein's, a department store in Harlem, New York, where crowds of people had gathered to buy copies of his book. He was signing one for a customer when a woman came up to him and asked, "Are you Martin Luther King?"

King said he was. The woman reached into her purse. Something flashed in her hand. King threw his left hand up to block the blow. A blade sliced his hand as the woman plunged it into his chest. He fell forward, clutching at the wound. His attacker shouted, "I've been after him for six years!"

The attacker was named Izola Ware Curry. Her weapon was a sharp-edged steel letter opener with a carved ivory handle. Immediately arrested, Curry was also found to have a gun on her.

Dr. King was rushed by ambulance to

Izola Ware Curry

A Black woman from Georgia who was in her forties when she stabbed Dr. King, Izola Ware Curry was diagnosed with paranoid schizophrenia and committed to a state mental hospital. She was deemed to be incapable of standing trial for her criminal action.

King said, "I bear no bitterness toward her . . . I know that we want her to receive the necessary treatment so that she may become a constructive citizen in an integrated society where a disorganized personality need not become a menace to any man."

She never did become that "constructive citizen." Izola Ware Curry spent most of her life in a series of residential care homes for the mentally ill. She died in a nursing home in 2015, at the age of ninety-eight.

King and Coretta at Harlem Hospital

Harlem Hospital with the weapon still stuck in his body. He was in surgery for two and a quarter hours, because the blade was lodged dangerously close to a major artery. Doctors had to remove two ribs and part of King's breastbone before they could take out the blade. They reported that if he had "sneezed or coughed the weapon would have penetrated the aorta. . . . He was just a sneeze away from death."

Despite all these setbacks, in February 1959, leaving their two young children in the care of family, the Kings finally got ready to travel to India. With them was writer Lawrence Reddick, who had just published a new biography of Dr. King, *Crusader Without Violence*. King joked about all the luggage they had. Surely it was far too much for people who were going to visit the land of Gandhi. Gandhi himself, by the end of his life, had given away almost everything he possessed. In contrast, the first payment the Kings made at the airport in New York was a stiff charge for excess baggage!

They were an excited party of three. Dr. King looked forward to this historic visit. Coretta Scott King was interested in the women of India, Dr. Reddick in its history and government. King wrote that they "made up a sort of three-headed team with six eyes and six ears for looking and listening."

A brief stop in London, a quick detour to Paris, and dense fog over the Alps delayed their arrival in India by two whole days. Hundreds who had gathered in the capital, New Delhi, to welcome them went home, disappointed.

At last, the party arrived "down out of the clouds at Bombay." King and his companions found themselves on a tourist bus, heading to a hotel in Bombay. Wide-eyed and sleepless, they were shocked by the great numbers of poor, homeless people sleeping on the sidewalks and in the alleys of India's largest city. They passed a restless night in Bombay, then caught a flight to New Delhi the following morning.

A crowd had gathered to meet them at New Delhi's Palam Airport. Many bore garlands of marigolds and roses, a traditional way to greet honored guests. Music played. Martin Luther King said, "The people showered upon us the most generous hospitality imaginable." He spoke to a group of reporters. "To other countries I go as a tourist. To India I come as a pilgrim."

Indira Gandhi

Nehru's daughter was married to a man who bore the same last name as Mohandas K. Gandhi, but was not related to him.

Indira Gandhi herself would later become famous as India's first woman prime minister.

. To King's great astonishment, the prime minister had rescheduled the dinner they'd missed for that very night. A head of state reorganizing his entire day to honor a man who was not even a U.S. government official? It was mind-boggling.

Prime Minister Jawaharlal Nehru greeted the party along with his daughter, Indira Gandhi, who served as hostess. The other guests at dinner that night were Edwina and Pamela Mountbatten, the wife and daughter of the last British viceroy of India. Only a dozen years before, Nehru and Mahatma Gandhi had worked through all the complicated details of independence with Lord Mountbatten. And now here were these British guests, friends over dinner! King marveled at such a transition.

INDIA AND BRITAIN: FRIENDS? INDIAN INDEPENDENCE HAD BEEN BLIGHTED BY HASTILY DRAWN BORDERS AND THE CREATION OF MILLIONS OF REFUGEES. BY SOME ESTIMATES, UP TO TWO MILLION PEOPLE DIED IN HINDU-MUSLIM RIOTS. YET IN 1959, INDIA AND THE UNITED KINGDOM BOTH BELONGED TO THE UNITED NATIONS AND MAINTAINED FRIENDLY DIPLOMATIC RELATIONS.

The King party
being received
in Delhi

Would it ever be possible in America for Black and white people to gather together similarly, as friends?

King was eager to talk to the Indian prime minister about Gandhi and the success of the nonviolent movement in India. To his surprise, the prime minister's reply was short. He pointed out that he and Gandhi had not always agreed. Still, King was pleased to find that Nehru knew all about the Montgomery bus boycott and the American civil rights movement. Over the course of the evening, they spoke for nearly four hours about Gandhi, race, colonialism, communism, and more.

Who Was Right: Nehru or Gandhi?

Prime Minister Nehru believed in modern technology and industrial development. In contrast, Gandhi had wanted to return India to its villages. He did not think India should follow European models of development.

Gandhi was once asked whether free India would achieve the same standard of living as colonial Britain. He replied that if a country as big as India grew its economy the way the West had done, it would "strip the world bare like locusts."

Today, Gandhi's musings seem ahead of his time. Scientists estimate that if the rest of the world lived like Europeans and North Americans, humankind would need more than two and a half planets like Earth.

The other guests, including Coretta, listened politely. Later, Coretta wrote that she was glad this long meeting had taken place early in the trip and not later, when everyone was exhausted.

Nehru was not the only one familiar with the Montgomery bus boycott. Indian papers had covered it with interest, and many people offered King congratulations on its success. King remarked that the Indian publications perhaps gave "a better continuity of our 381-day bus strike than did most of the papers in the United States." It was clear that to Indians, the boycott in Montgomery validated Gandhi's techniques.

The morning after the official dinner, the party visited Rajghat, a memorial to Gandhi on the outskirts of the city. King laid a wreath there. Deeply moved, he knelt and prayed.

In Delhi, the Kings met the Indian president, Rajendra Prasad, who had long ago worked with Gandhi on behalf of indigo farmers, and the vice president, Sarvepalli Radhakrishnan, an eminent philosopher who admired Gandhi. King felt as if he'd met the founding

King removing his shoes as a mark of respect at the Gandhi memorial

fathers of the country. It was like meeting George Washington, Thomas Jefferson, and James Madison, all in one day.

King was invited to speak at public meetings and universities. Coretta went with him. At a dinner party, she surprised everyone by wearing an Indian sari. She often sang as much as he lectured. Some Black spirituals had been translated into Indian languages, and audiences often requested these songs dating back to the years of slavery.

After what felt like endless teas and speeches, the "pilgrims of peace" left New Delhi for the north-central city of Patna. They had

The Kings in India, with Coretta wearing a sari

met many distinguished politicians; now King was eager to meet followers of Gandhi who did not hold official positions. Outside Patna, the party met with a man named Jayaprakash Narayan, who lived in a remote rural area.

Narayan believed that industrialization was bad for India and that all factories and central government organizations should be abolished. Narayan wanted India to return to a rural way of life that he saw as purer and better than anything the modern world had to offer.

At the same time, King observed that Narayan traveled by jeep to get to the end of the road where his ashram stood. Surely the jeep had been made in a factory. Life itself, King thought, demanded compromises. It felt impractical, even unwise, to insist on old principles while the world around you was changing so fast.

King also met Gandhi's son, his grandsons, his relatives, and countless people who had taken part in the Indian independence struggle. The retired ruler of the former princely state of Mysore took him to a cattle auction. He attended a labor meeting, held discussions with the chief ministers and governors of states. He met students, teachers, industrialists, holy men, communists. He met Hindus, Muslims, Christians, and others from the many faiths of India. He even met with a group of students from Africa. They argued with him that Ghanaian President Nkrumah's peaceful protest may have worked for him, but it did not stand a chance in other parts of Africa. It would be useless against the violent Belgian rulers of the Congo, or even the whites in South Africa with whom Gandhi had struggled.

In Bombay, the party stayed in a house with no shower and no running hot water. The toilets were holes in the ground. King endured the discomfort without complaint. He was disturbed as well by the number of beggars in the city. It pained him to see people so poor that they were forced to beg for money.

On March 1, the Kings stopped at Sabarmati Ashram in the western state of Gujarat, from where Gandhi had begun his twenty-four-day Salt March to the flats of Dandi. Next, they journeyed to a remote village to meet another famous Gandhian, a man named Vinoba Bhave. To talk at any length with Bhave, King was told he would have to join him on his "morning" walk—at 3:30 a.m.! Bhave walked a nearly ten-mile stretch daily, before his routine of prayers and meetings began.

King was tired. The travel and the unfamiliar, spicy food had upset his stomach. He begged permission for an "Americanized" option. He and Reddick got a ride in a car and caught up with Vinoba on his walk. King had to think fast so he could put the right questions to his walking audience. Their talk ranged over many topics.

Vinoba suggested that countries needed to disarm. King was struck by this radical vision. The United States and the Soviet Union were in a mad race to develop ever more powerful weapons—nuclear bombs, the most destructive known to humankind. What if that arms race could be stopped? he thought. What if India and Pakistan could cease their endless fighting over Kashmir? Did peace within a country not also mean peace between nations? King had once doubted peaceful protest could ever bring rights to his people. Now he embraced the concept of world peace.

Another Gandhi follower who made an impression on King was a young woman named Krishnammal. She was born to a landless

family, in a group of people who had been discriminated against for centuries, India's so-called untouchables. They were peasants and laborers. They tilled the land and did work that others considered unclean. Krishnammal told Dr. King that he should visit a village and see for himself the plight of her people. "Just outside the village they are living," she said, referring to the fact that Dalits were not allowed near the dwellings of upper-caste Hindus, "and they are bonded laborers to the landlords. You go."

He did. The visit confirmed what King had already begun to believe. Oppressed people everywhere want the same things: freedom, justice, equality, peace.

By the time they left India, King and his party had crisscrossed the Indian subcontinent. They flew over long stretches from north to south, traveled by train for shorter distances, reached remote places by car and jeep. They went to the southernmost tip of India, where some of Gandhi's ashes had been scattered in the sea. Everywhere they went, they were besieged by reporters. Photographs of them were splashed across the front pages of India's newspapers. Autograph seekers mobbed the group. When they traveled by plane, even the pilots came out from the cockpit into the cabin, wanting autographs.

Speaking for Coretta and Lawrence as well as for himself, King called the trip "one of the most concentrated and eye-opening experiences of our lives."

On his return to the United States, King spoke and wrote about his travels in India. On Palm Sunday, back in his pulpit at Dexter Avenue Baptist Church, he gave a sermon. On this holy day, the start of Easter, he would usually have spoken about Jesus Christ entering Jerusalem, riding a donkey, with people scattering palm fronds in his path. But India was still on King's mind. He said, "I beg of you to indulge me this morning to talk about the life of a man who lived in India. And I think I'm justified in doing this because I believe this man, more than anybody else in the modern world, caught the spirit of Jesus Christ and lived it more completely in his life."

He quoted Gandhi, saying, "If you are hit, don't hit back; even if they shoot at you, don't shoot back; if they curse you, don't curse back, but just keep moving. Some of us might have to die before we get there; some of us might be thrown in jail before we get there, but let us just keep moving." As a youngster, he'd longed to put his body where his mind was. Now his words combined the powers of mind, body, and soul.

The congregation murmured and sighed and cried, "Yes, yes!" as King wove his words around those other words from the man in whose footsteps he had made this pilgrimage to India. Martin Luther King Jr. was only thirty years old.

16

After India

The visit to Gandhi's homeland had touched King's heart and his conscience. It had filled his mind with contradictory ideas and his heart with competing emotions. He pondered over the great gap between the modern American lifestyle and the ancient ways of India's villages. He yearned for equality among the races in the United States. The teachings of Jesus were a bedrock in his life. Now the example of Gandhi's life also inspired him.

Every chance he had, he tried to pass this inspiration on to others. John Lewis, an eighteen-year-old introduced to King by his good friend Ralph Abernathy, drank in every word. Lewis was a country boy. Starstruck by King, he stammered out his request. He wanted to sue for the right to enter Troy State, an all-white college in his home county. He said he'd learned about Gandhi and nonviolent resistance from James Lawson. He'd die for the right to go to college if he had to, but he figured nonviolent protest could

How Should a Man of Peace Dress?

King wondered if he should change to a simpler dress and lifestyle, as Gandhi had. For practical reasons, he decided to give up that idea. In mid-twentieth-century America, dressing in an unusual way might drive people from his cause rather than attract them to it.

Could he live more simply? It was hard to see how. He needed a car and a telephone to do his work. He decided he would try to be like Gandhi spiritually. He would take what worked from Gandhi's philosophy and methods. He would change what did not.

get him there instead. King agreed to help "the boy from Troy."

Encouraged by determined young people like Lewis and inspired by his trip to India, King felt torn. His church needed him, but so did the SCLC in Atlanta, the group he had founded along with fellow ministers. Also, his father was getting older and could use his help. After three years of traveling back and forth between Montgomery and Atlanta, when the board of deacons at Daddy King's Ebenezer Baptist Church offered Martin Luther King Jr. the position of co-pastor, he accepted.

On February 1, 1960, the congregation at Dexter bade the King family an emotional good-bye. The church filled with the faces and voices of people who knew and loved the Kings. Ralph Abernathy welcomed everyone. He called the event a "Testimonial of Love and Loyalty." A wooden box sat on a table. At the end of the gathering, Abernathy gave it to King. It was filled with money.

King was touched. But he hesitated. He couldn't take it. It wasn't his to keep. He decided to divide the cash between the MIA and the SCLC, the one group in Montgomery and the other in Atlanta, both working for the rights of Black people. Gandhi would have approved.

On the very day that King was bidding farewell to friends, colleagues, and well-wishers in Montgomery, dramatic events were unfolding in Greensboro, North Carolina. Four Black freshmen from

North Carolina A&T had gone down to the Woolworth's store and quietly taken seats at the whites-only lunch counter. It was a "sit-down protest."

The waitress was Black herself, but she refused to serve them. They remained seated. Flustered, the management tried to ignore them. At the end of the day, the students said they'd be back the following morning.

That was on a Monday. On Tuesday, the group was joined by nineteen more. By Thursday, there were eighty-five protesters. Somebody phoned James Lawson with more news. More sit-ins were about to begin in Durham, Raleigh, and other cities in the state.

Lunch Counter Sit-in Instructions
"Do not strike back or curse if abused. Do not laugh out. Do not hold conversations with the floor walker. Do not leave your seat until your leader has given you permission to do so. Do not block entrances to stores outside nor the aisles inside. Do show yourself courteous and friendly at all times. Do sit straight; always face the counter. Do report all serious incidents to your leader. Do refer information seekers to your leader in a polite manner. Remember the teachings of Jesus, Gandhi, Martin Luther King. Love and nonviolence is the way." (Written by John Lewis. Five hundred copies were made on a mimeograph machine.)

Fred Shuttlesworth, co-founder of the SCLC, believed that the sit-ins could "shake up the world." He told King they should support the young people making this powerful statement. James Lawson spoke to a group of five hundred in Nashville, teaching them how to conduct themselves at a sit-in.

As the number of protesters swelled, the sit-ins grew into a movement, spreading to other Southern cities. Angry counterprotests turned violent. Groups of white people armed with baseball bats randomly attacked Black shoppers in Montgomery.

Meanwhile, the state of Alabama was after Dr. King—for back taxes. King himself admitted he was paying less attention to bookkeeping than to the tough work ahead. He had already paid more than $2,000 in back taxes to both the federal government and the state of Alabama. He traveled to New York to meet with lawyers regarding his case.

On his way home, King stopped at Durham, North Carolina, where the Woolworth's lunch counter had closed in hopes of averting a sit-in by Black students. That night, he spoke at a rally in support of the sit-ins.

He praised the young people who were daring to speak with their actions, to ask for change. What was fresh and new was the fact that this movement was "initiated, led, and sustained by students. What is new is that American students have come of age. You now take your honored places in the world-wide struggle for freedom."

The young people sitting peacefully at lunch counters, refusing to leave, had taken a Gandhian action. King urged them not to fear going to jail. "If the officials threaten to arrest us for standing up for our rights, we must answer by saying that we are willing to fill up the jails of the South."

Fill up the jails. The exhortation became a rallying cry. The hymn "We Shall Overcome" became a rallying song.

Legal problems continued. Georgia sheriff's deputies served King with an arrest warrant. He had been indicted for perjury in Alabama. The attack on his honesty disheartened King. He did not have the money to fight these charges in court. When legal fees began to mount, a group of friends, including Stanley Levison and Bayard Rustin, formed a Committee to Defend Martin Luther King and the Struggle for Freedom in the South. They took out a full-page advertisement in the *New York Times* asking for support—and contributions.

In the end, the case went to trial. A jury of twelve men, all white, acquitted King. When the verdict of "Not guilty" was pronounced, the elder Kings and Coretta all burst into tears. In her autobiography, Coretta Scott King described it as "a triumph of justice, a miracle that restored your faith in human good."

Triumph and trouble took turns. A cross was burned on the lawn of King's house—a signature act of the Klan. Intended to intimidate everyone within, it was a frightening reminder that desegregation would not be won without a fight from those who opposed it.

Across the South, the lunch counter sit-ins spread, organized by student leaders, including John Lewis and his friend James Bevel. Lewis, Chicago native Diane Nash, and fourteen others were the first to be arrested. They chose to go to jail instead of paying a fine. As the protests increased, so did the arrests.

perjury | *noun* (plural perjuries) is the offense of knowingly telling an untruth in a court of law.

The state of Alabama alleged that King had perjured himself by falsifying his taxes for the years of 1956 and 1958.

King and his son inspecting a burned cross on their lawn

Because of his work in the movement, James Lawson was expelled from the Divinity School at Nashville's Vanderbilt University. Four hundred Vanderbilt teachers threatened to resign in protest. The university relented, but Lawson chose to complete his degree at Boston University.

The Nashville mayor called a truce. He promised to appoint a committee with Black and white members to discuss segregation in downtown stores. Diane Nash led a protest at the Greyhound bus terminal lunch counter. To everyone's surprise, the students were served. No one was told to leave. No one was arrested.

Elsewhere, however, protests were met with force. In Orangeburg, South Carolina, four hundred students marching to sit-ins were met with tear gas and water hoses. Despite being battered by the force of water from the hoses and choking up from tear gas, the students remained admirably calm.

MEMORY, 1960 CHARLES MCDEW, A LEADER OF THE MARCH, RECALLED SEEING A DISABLED WOMAN KNOCKED DOWN BY THE FORCE OF THE WATER FROM A FIRE HOSE. A COLLEGE FOOTBALL STAR HELD HER IN HIS ARMS. ON HIS FACE WAS A LOOK NOT OF ANGER BUT OF SADNESS. MCDEW WOULD NEVER FORGET THAT SIGHT.

Wherever protesters gathered, they organized. They discussed strategies. They vowed to stay peaceful. King contributed money to the cause, making a donation to the SCLC even though his personal budget was stretched at the time. In April 1960, he spoke at the opening conference of a new organization, the Student Nonviolent Coordinating Committee (SNCC, pronounced "snick"). In his speech, he urged the student leaders of sit-ins from ten states and forty communities to think deeply about the idea of nonviolence. They should not simply join the cause and follow blindly:

"It must be made palpably clear that resistance and nonviolence are not in themselves good. There is another element that must be present in our struggle that then makes our resistance and nonviolence truly meaningful. That element is reconciliation. Our ultimate end must be the creation of the beloved community."

The beloved community. King really believed that it was possible to oppose injustice and then make peace with your opponents, as the Indians had with the British. He sought allies wherever he could find them. He tried to use language that would bring people closer together, help them understand one another. He was always trying to widen the reach of the movement, all the way to the highest offices of the land.

For months, King had tried, without success, to meet with Senator John F. Kennedy. Kennedy was seeking the Democratic Party's nomination for president of the United States. Finally, in the summer of 1960, the two men met in Kennedy's apartment in New York. They talked for an hour over breakfast—about discrimination in federally assisted housing, the enforcement of voting rights, and the need to pass strong civil rights laws.

Kennedy seemed to understand what King was saying, but did he fully grasp the meaning of the cause? It was hard to tell. King found himself wondering if Kennedy had any Black friends. Meeting with Kennedy a second time, after his nomination for the presidency, King saw that Kennedy had taken the trouble to speak to

Black leaders and educate himself about the civil rights movement. He became convinced that Kennedy was on the side of Black people in America. That, as president, he would do more for them than Eisenhower had.

Meanwhile, the lunch counter sit-ins continued. In October 1960, Georgia students begged King to join them at the snack bar in Rich's, a downtown Atlanta department store. He did, and he was arrested right along with them for trespassing. He refused to pay the $500 bond, saying he'd rather stay in jail for ten years.

Refusing Bail

Refusing bail was a common practice in the civil rights movement. In an interview with *Life* magazine days before, King had said: "You don't pay the fine and you don't pay the bail. You are not to subvert or disrespect the law.

You have broken a law which is out of line with the moral law and you are willing to suffer the consequences by serving the time."

It was exactly what Gandhi had first taught his followers to do in South Africa, half a century earlier.

The students shared King's prison cell for three nights. They talked about Gandhi, about Christianity, Jesus, love, and the Montgomery bus boycott. He lifted their spirits in the dismal surroundings, singing, meditating, playing games with them.

Troubled by King's arrest, Senator Kennedy called Mayor Hartsfield of Atlanta, asking about King's constitutional rights. The mayor quickly ordered the release of Martin Luther King and "all other incarcerated Negroes," claiming this was on the recommendation of Senator Kennedy. But perhaps the mayor had just panicked or was trying to avoid bad press.

The released students agreed to a temporary halt to the sit-ins. King, however, was arrested again, this time on an old traffic violation charge. He had paid that fine months before, but the county argued that his probation required that he stay out of trouble for a year. By being jailed again so soon, he had violated these terms. The judge found him guilty and sentenced him to serve four months of hard labor in Georgia's public-works camp.

What a severe ruling that was! No bail was allowed. He would go from Fulton County Jail to prison in neighboring DeKalb County. King told Coretta he'd have to serve his time. She was terrified. DeKalb County was Ku Klux Klan country. Black people had gone to jail there and simply disappeared—no release, no explanation, not even their bodies found.

On the night of his detention at DeKalb, King was awakened by shouts. "King! Get up!" A flashlight shone in his face. He could see figures standing over him. Fear gripped him. They made him get up and get dressed. He was handcuffed, his feet shackled with chains. They dragged him to the sheriff's car and tied his legs to something on the floor so he could not escape. When he asked where they were taking him, no one answered. The car drove through the night along empty highways. With each bump on the road, King's body tensed. Where were they taking him? The whole thing may have reminded him of a similar ride back in 1956 when he was arrested during the bus boycott, only now the stakes were higher.

At last, the car stopped at the gates of a prison. The sign read: REIDSVILLE PENITENTIARY. They had driven two hundred and twenty miles from Atlanta to Reidsville! It was a notorious prison, deep within Klan country. The wardens were known to be brutal. King was given a uniform with striped pants, housed in a cellblock for psychotic and violent inmates.

Allowed one phone call, he spoke quickly to Coretta, knowing the call had thrown her into panic. Then he steeled himself to face his wretched surroundings. Cockroaches infested his cell. The food was vile. The cold was numbing.

As word spread about Reidsville's new inmate, King received notes from other prisoners. Some expressed support. Some offered to go on hunger strike in his honor. Some were criminals who wanted advice on how to get out of jail. King did not encourage them. He wrote to Coretta, telling her he had faith that this suffering would not be in vain. He asked her to bring books when she came to visit.

Coretta tried to stay calm. The children were asking where Daddy was. A family friend overheard a conversation between Yoki and a white classmate. The classmate remarked that Yoki's daddy was always going to jail. She replied, "Yes, he goes to jail to help people."

Coretta was now expecting a third baby. She was not sure she could make the long drive to Reidsville. She was getting ready to see a lawyer about her husband's case when the phone rang. It was Senator Kennedy. He said he wanted to express his concern. He said she should call on him if there was anything he could do.

Robert Kennedy, JFK's brother, had a temper, and he wasn't pleased about the senator's call to Mrs. King. As his brother's campaign manager, thirteen days before the election, sudden news in the media made him nervous. News stories could shift votes, and a shift in the wrong direction could lose Kennedy the election. But then a campaign worker told Robert Kennedy about the flimsy grounds for this latest imprisonment. Kennedy was indignant. "How could they do that?" he demanded. "Who's the judge? You can't deny bail on a misdemeanor." Perhaps Kennedy was unaware that Southern judges could, and often did, flout the rules when they dealt with Black people.

Fuming, Robert Kennedy called Oscar Mitchell, the Georgia judge who had sentenced Martin Luther King Jr. He said that, in his opinion, any decent American judge would release King on bond by sundown. Judge Mitchell, in a sudden change of heart, declared his famous prisoner would be out on bail soon.

In the ranks of the Kennedy campaign, panic spread. Should they deny the second call had ever been made? Would it hurt JFK that his brother and campaign manager, a qualified lawyer, had called a sitting judge about a current case?

Regardless, King was released and warmly received by crowds of delighted supporters.

To the mainstream press, Kennedy's possible involvement in King's release was a minor election-related story. To the Black press, it was huge. In his church, Daddy King said he'd expected to vote against Senator Kennedy, but now he was ready to take a suitcase full of votes and dump them in Kennedy's lap!

Dr. King himself did not want to back either presidential candidate, neither Kennedy nor Nixon. He felt that his work for civil rights for Black people should be beyond politics. But Daddy King's declaration carried weight. A century earlier, in the racially divided South, Democrats had backed slavery. Now Black voters began to think of a

King greeted by
his family upon
his release from
Reidsville

Democrat as a possible president. In the end, John F. Kennedy carried around 70 percent of the Black vote.

Among the masses of mail that Kennedy received congratulating him on his election was a telegram from Sir Winston Churchill, the elderly, retired British prime minister who had opposed Gandhi's satyagraha in both South Africa and India.

17

Knowing the Enemy

King was released from Reidsville only a few months before the birth of his third child in 1961. The baby boy was named Dexter after his father's beloved church in Montgomery. The new baby brought joy and hope.

Black America, too, was hopeful. Voting for Kennedy in vast numbers, Black people had placed their faith in him. They expected swift changes. The previous year, the Supreme Court had ruled segregation at interstate bus terminals and train stations to be unconstitutional. But the signs stayed up at those terminals—there were "white" and "colored" restrooms, water fountains, restaurants, waiting rooms. Small towns in the South were bent on disobeying the law.

In the summer of 1961, a group of young people began a new kind of protest. They rode the interstate buses. They planned to get off at the terminals and use the whites-only facilities—bathrooms and waiting rooms. If they were stopped, they'd let themselves be arrested.

CORE and Gandhi

King's friend and advisor Bayard Rustin worked for CORE, as did a man named James Farmer. Rustin and Farmer had learned lessons in peaceful protest from a follower of Gandhi, poet and playwright Krishnalal Shridharani. King had studied Shridharani's book *War Without Violence* during the Montgomery bus boycott.

These "Freedom Riders" were trained by a group called the Congress of Racial Equality (CORE) and SNCC. Young people from all over the country flocked to a meeting in Washington, DC. Among them was John Lewis, the "boy from Troy" who said he'd die for the right to go to the college of his choice. At twenty, he was the youngest in the group.

In growing numbers, young people rode the buses. They got off at the terminals—and were met by angry mobs. Fists and bats and broken bottles in hand, the mobs were gathered and egged on by the Ku Klux Klan. In Anniston, Alabama, attackers stopped a bus and set fire to it. Terrified passengers huddled by the road. Journalists quickly arrived on the scene. The image of the burning bus made it into the world's newspapers.

Dr. King's friend Fred Shuttlesworth warned that the Ku Klux Klan was waiting in Birmingham to ambush Freedom Riders. The commissioner of public safety in Birmingham was a man named Eugene ("Bull") Connor. He was a friend of the Klan.

The Klan was indeed waiting. The police stayed away for fifteen minutes while Klansmen swarmed the integrated bus, bruising and bloodying the riders getting off. Black or white, the riders were met

with clubs, fists, pipes, and other homemade weapons. By the time the police arrived, the Klansmen had dispersed. A reporter asked Bull Connor why it took the police so long to respond. He replied that it was Mother's Day, so they were visiting their mothers.

The number of rides increased through the summer. So did the violence. In Atlanta, King met with the Freedom Riders. He warned that the mood in Alabama was ugly.

Freedom Riders watch the bus they were riding burn after a white mob set it on fire. Anniston, Alabama, 1961

In November 1961, the Interstate Commerce Commission banned racial segregation in bus terminals, yet many local terminals refused to comply. Three high school students were the first to be arrested for entering the white section of the bus terminal in Albany, Georgia. They were bailed out, but word got around. A couple of college students followed suit. They spent Thanksgiving in jail.

As the momentum picked up, more and more protesters arrived to be arrested. Like the marchers in Gandhi's satyagraha, they were unarmed and unstoppable. The city of Albany arrested hundreds, packing them into cells in hellish conditions. An organizer sent a telegram to Dr. King, inviting him to support the movement with his presence.

Along with Ralph Abernathy, King traveled to Albany, where more than fifteen hundred people packed two churches, with loudspeaker systems rigged up in between. The crowd began to sing, "Free-dom! Free-dom!" Great waves of song rippled out into the street, the words echoing back and forth between the two buildings. The call for freedom was, quite literally, in the air. It quivered through the bodies of the waiting people. The very ground trembled with the sound.

As King entered Shiloh Baptist Church, the voices burst into a spontaneous chorus: "Martin King says freedom! Martin King says freedom!"

King began to speak. He told the crowd that they could not sit back and wait for progress. It was time to act—even if that meant being willing to die. The crowd grew somber. He picked up his pace. He talked about going to jail without hating the white folks who put you there. People clapped loudly. He talked about the power of saying no. They clapped again.

As he stopped, someone began singing "We Shall Overcome." The crowd picked it up until a mighty chorus poured out into the night.

On December 16, 1961, King led a group of more than two hundred people toward city hall. Troopers blocked their way. The marchers turned onto alternate streets. The troopers caught up with them. The police chief, a man named Laurie Pritchett, ordered the marchers to disperse. They kept walking. Motorcycle officers stopped them at every turn, until finally the column, singing "We Shall Overcome" all the way, ended up in an alley. A line of policemen stood ready with paddy wagons behind them, sealing off the exit. King knelt. The entire group knelt. They prayed. They got up again and moved forward. Police arrested them all. King refused bond. He expected to spend Christmas in jail. He hoped thousands would join him.

But the will of the movement was flagging. Protesters were jail-weary and the local leadership was fragmenting, split by differing opinions on what steps to take next. Leaders reached an agreement with the city. The authorities would release all local movement prisoners without bond if King left and the demonstrations stopped. King felt the agreement was premature, but there was nothing he could do. His trial was postponed by sixty days, and he, too, was released. City officials were delighted to see the movement's energy dissipate.

We shall Overcome

We shall overcome, we shall overcome
We shall overcome some day
Oh, deep in my heart, I do believe
We shall overcome some day

The Lord will see us through, the Lord will see us through
The Lord will see us through some day
Oh, deep in my heart, I do believe
The Lord will see us some day

were on to victory, were on to victory

When King returned to Albany six months later for sentencing, he was fined $178. If he did not pay, he would have to spend seventy-five days in jail. King and Abernathy chose jail. A week later, they were released—Pritchett had quietly arranged for the fines to be paid, crediting an anonymous city resident. King protested, but it was no use. If it hadn't been so frustrating, it would have been funny. Abernathy joked that he'd been thrown out of lots of places in his day, but never before had he been thrown out of a jail.

King decided to stay and fight in Albany. He tried to mount a nonviolent campaign in the community, seeking to desegregate all the city facilities. He gathered supporters. They marched. They listened to his sermons. But city officials ignored him.

Police Chief Pritchett may have been part of the reason behind the struggles of the movement in Albany. Here was an enemy armed and ready, not only with the forces at his command, but with knowledge of King's methods. Pritchett had done his homework. He had read King's Gandhian speeches, and he knew how to react to nonviolent tactics.

In public, the police chief used no violence. He was never rude or offensive. When protesters prayed, he bowed his own head. Then he arrested them and sent them to jails all over the state, where the treatment was predictably brutal. He gave King round-the-clock police protection, which King found annoying. But he never lost his cool. The two men grew to have a wary respect for each other. Once, King even canceled a demonstration so that Pritchett and his wife could spend their wedding anniversary day together.

Demonstrations in the summer of 1962, however, degenerated into violence. A pregnant protester was knocked unconscious by a policeman. Black Albany erupted in rage. Two thousand rioters fought the police with rocks and bottles. "[S]ee them nonviolent rocks?" Pritchett chortled to reporters.

King was devastated. He canceled further marches, calling for a "Day of Penance." He prayed. He toured the city. He asked people for their peaceful support. He tried without success to get President Kennedy to pressure the city of Albany to desegregate its buses, public spaces, and schools. He led one last demonstration and was arrested yet again. Chief Pritchett treated his famous prisoner well, even allowing Coretta and the children to visit.

King and Abernathy expected to be sentenced, but the court ordered their release. And Albany remained segregated.

King being arrested by Laurie Pritchett

Why was the federal government doing nothing? The president had not come to King's aid. Robert Kennedy, now the U.S. attorney general, had even congratulated the mayor of Albany for "keeping the peace." Agents from the Federal Bureau of Investigation (FBI) arrived in Albany, but they seemed to be investigating the protesters. When whites were injured, FBI agents supported them. But when Blacks filed complaints about violations of their civil rights, the agents did nothing. Interviewed in the robing room of Riverside Church in New York, just after he had preached a sermon there, King said, "Every time I saw FBI men in Albany, they were with the local police." Many FBI agents came from Southern white backgrounds. How could they see the point of view of people whom they had been raised to despise? And what about segregationist judges in the state and federal courts? Would they rule in favor of civil rights, or would they serve their own political biases?

The FBI director, J. Edgar Hoover, was irritated by that *New York Times* interview. He already considered Martin Luther King Jr. to be a communist. And in Hoover's opinion, communism was the number one enemy of the United States of America. Hoover began to send memos about King to Robert Kennedy. He placed King's name on a master list of dangerous people who, in Hoover's opinion, should be rounded up if there were ever a national emergency. Eventually, he even obtained permission from Robert Kennedy to tap King's telephone lines at home and at the SCLC office in Atlanta. Worried, Andrew Young wondered if the group should suspend its work in the South.

King had made a powerful enemy.

18

Bombingham

The movement in Albany, Georgia, left the Black community exhausted. Ninety-five percent of the Black population had taken part in marches and boycotts, and 5 percent had gone to jail. When months went by with no change, the press declared the movement a failure. King disagreed. He wrote, "The people of Albany had straightened their backs, and, as Gandhi had said, no one can ride on the back of a man unless it is bent." Indeed, the city added thousands of Black voters to the rolls. A segregationist candidate lost the council election. A year later, Albany removed the segregation ordinances from its city code.

In the neighboring state of Alabama, the governor, George Wallace, had vowed to continue "segregation now, segregation tomorrow, segregation forever!" White churches, stores, and parks were off-limits to Black people. Black children went to Jim Crow schools. They could play only in the streets, because there were no playgrounds for them. Their parents could only hope to get the most menial jobs.

Yet here, in this most segregated of cities, the protest movement had managed to take root. Fred Shuttlesworth had been leading civil rights protests here for seven years. His home had been bombed, his church attacked. He and his wife had been beaten with chains and stabbed when they tried to enroll their children in a white school. Now Shuttlesworth planned a boycott of white merchants, similar to the Christmas boycott that King had led in Montgomery in 1955. He invited Martin Luther King to Birmingham.

King spoke at a meeting of the SCLC. As he talked, a young white man sitting in the audience leaped up onto the stage, drew his clenched fist back, and punched King squarely on the mouth. King staggered from the blow, but he did not try to defend himself. The man hit him again and yet again. People in the audience rushed to help. Finally, the police and a couple of SCLC members managed to pull the attacker away. They were about to haul him out, but King asked them to let the young man sit back down.

After the meeting, King said that it was the system that created young men like this. He didn't want to press charges. He wanted to change the system. Coretta asked her husband why on earth he had let the man remain. What if he'd had a gun? King replied that if he had, he'd have used it before then.

Change was slow and elusive. In Mississippi, Diane Nash organized literacy and citizenship classes for Black people. Yet, as King watched on television, the University of Mississippi blocked the path of a Black applicant, James Meredith. White students rioted, protesting Meredith's enrollment.

President Kennedy sent federal troops in to halt the riot.

Along with Ralph Abernathy and Dr. W. G. Anderson, the president of the Albany Nonviolent Movement, King sent a telegram urging President Kennedy to issue a "second Emancipation Proclamation to free all Negroes from second-class citizenship." Instead, Kennedy issued an executive order ending discrimination in federally funded housing—a necessary action, but hardly enough. In February 1963, he sent a new civil rights bill to Congress. It was mostly limited to protecting the right to vote. And it did not pass.

✮✮✮✮✮✮✮✮✮✮✮✮✮✮✮✮✮✮✮✮✮✮✮✮✮✮✮✮✮✮✮✮✮✮✮✮✮

Kennedy and the Promise of Liberty

Why did President Kennedy ignore Dr. King's reminder? He had many other problems to deal with.

The United States and the Soviet Union were in an arms race, each country trying to build and maintain superior weapons, including nuclear weapons. In 1962, the Soviets decided to arm Cuba—a crisis that came close to plunging the world into nuclear war!

Across the South, resistance continued into 1963. By then, Birmingham's Black neighborhoods were so gutted by bombs and vandalized by armed bands of hostile whites that the city itself began to be known as "Bombingham." Nonetheless, Birmingham was the place where the SCLC decided to wage its next struggle. It was called Project C, for "confrontation." Members would target the city's commercial district. They would march. They would boycott the downtown shops and services that needed Black business.

The local Black community lent ample support. A wealthy Black businessman, A. G. Gaston, let King use his motel for his headquarters. The motel was across from the Sixteenth Street

Baptist Church, which hosted large meetings. By March 1963, 250 people had pledged to take part in demonstrations and spend at least five days apiece in jail.

King worried that wouldn't be enough. He traveled to Washington, DC, to recruit additional volunteers, in case backups were needed—to march, to get arrested, to fill the jails. King's family needed him as well. He returned home just in time to take Coretta to the hospital for the birth of their fourth child, Bernice Albertine, whom they called "Bunny." Then it was back to Birmingham, followed by a quick trip to New York with Shuttlesworth to rally more support. In New York, King joked about being arrested. He said Shuttlesworth snored so loudly, it was torture being his jail cellmate! Jokes apart, his friend could see that King was on edge.

Project C protesters, too, had reason to feel edgy. They had to face not Laurie Pritchett, whose racism was masked with courtesy, but the openly bigoted Bull Connor, who was now running for mayor of Birmingham. Would the demonstrations push scared white voters to elect him?

As it turned out, Connor lost the election. But now the movement was flagging.

When King put the call out for the next protest, to his disappointment, only sixty-five people responded.

When the small group of protesters showed up to sit at lunch counters downtown, Connor had them all hauled to jail.

The new mayor, Albert Boutwell, drew on the lessons of Albany. He ordered the police to be courteous, so there were no incidents for the press to cover. Project C looked about to fizzle out. Those whom

King was trying to confront were simply refusing to play.

In the meantime, a growing group of volunteers needed training. Nightly meetings brought in new recruits to serve in this nonviolent army. Some arrived angry, ready to beat up white people. SCLC staffers ran role-playing sessions on how to resist without violence, how to receive anger without generating more anger, how to be beaten without striking back. The group sang, talked, listened. Slowly, they grew into a nonviolent army.

The protests grew, and so did the arrests. The state court banned

Student waiting for lunch counter service that never came

A Story Worth Scooping
Word got around that Dr. King was waiting for the right time to show up at the Birmingham protests, so he could be arrested. The press paid attention. "Go where the Mahatma goes," news editors told their reporters. "He might get killed."

An assassination would be a story worth scooping.

King and other leaders from demonstrating. If King disobeyed, he would certainly be arrested. Some SCLC members objected. King had connections. He could raise money that the movement badly needed. Who would fund-raise if he went to jail?

In the end, he decided to join the demonstration. It was what he called a "faith act."

On Good Friday, 1963, around fifty marchers, ranging in age from fifteen to eighty-one, set out for city hall. When they spotted Martin Luther King Jr. in the group, the policemen forgot their newfound courtesy. They grabbed King by the belt and threw him into a paddy wagon. He ended up in a small cell with no windows. It had a cot with metal slats and no mattress. No calls were allowed and no visits. It was like being in a dungeon.

King did have newspapers to read. A copy of the *Birmingham News* ran a story with the headline WHITE CLERGYMEN URGE LOCAL NEGROES TO WITHDRAW FROM DEMONSTRATIONS. A group of eight clergy wrote that "our Negro citizens" were being incited by "outsiders" to take "extreme measures." Even though their own congregations were all white, the ministers agreed that segregation should end. Still, they reproached the protesters:

"We further strongly urge our own Negro community to withdraw support from these demonstrations, and to unite locally in working peacefully for a better Birmingham. When rights are consistently denied, a cause should be pressed in the courts and in negotiations among local leaders, and not in the streets."

The ministers meant well. But here again were calls to wait. To be patient. For how long? How long were Black people in America supposed to wait?

In the margins of the paper, King began to scribble his reply. He wrote and wrote. He could not stop. When his lawyer and occasional speechwriter, Clarence Jones, was finally allowed to meet with him in jail, King gave the newspaper to Jones, every inch of it filled with his reply to that letter. He gave him other scraps of paper as well—paper towels and napkins, all covered with his writing. Jones had no idea what King was up to, and he had other concerns—terrified parents of the arrested teenagers were demanding to know when their kids were going to get out of jail!

Every time he visited, King asked Jones to bring more paper. Jones did. Then he smuggled out the filled-up pages. Finally, typed, the letter was twenty pages long. It was a reply to everyone who had ever expressed doubts and skepticism about King's strategies—some in the NAACP, the Kennedys, and now these ministers. When Jones eventually read it, he could not believe his eyes.

The letter spoke a clear and ringing truth. King wrote: "I am in Birmingham because injustice is here." He said the ministers were right in calling for negotiation. That, he maintained, was the purpose of the direct action of protest. Freedom was "never voluntarily given by the oppressor; it must be demanded by the oppressed."

Meanwhile, he wrote, "The nations of Asia and Africa are moving with jetlike speed toward gaining political independence, but we still creep at horse and buggy pace toward gaining a cup of coffee at a lunch counter. Perhaps it is easy for those who have never felt the stinging darts of segregation to say, 'Wait.'"

And what about the children? He wrote about his daughter Yoki. All she wanted to do was go to a new amusement park—Funtown. When she was told it was closed to colored children, he could see "clouds of inferiority beginning to form in her little mental sky." He quoted St. Augustine: "an unjust law is no law at all." He quoted saints, poets, philosophers. He said that one day the "sit inners" and demonstrators would be seen for who they were, the real heroes of the South. Everything he knew and felt went into this letter—it was a cry from the heart.

Today, the "Letter from Birmingham Jail" is recognized as a great and profound testament to nonviolence and peaceful change.

After nine days in jail, King agreed to have his bail paid so he could be released. He was needed in the community. The movement was flagging. There weren't enough demonstrators. Maybe people were afraid. Maybe they didn't trust that anything they did would be effective. Once again, King's doubts set in.

Then James Bevel, who had been in Albany and on the Freedom Rides, had a suggestion. Why not call on high school students to join? The SCLC could plot times and distances for the marchers as usual, planning alternate routes when needed. Only one thing would be different: Young people would be invited to join.

It was a bold and shocking idea. Many parents were aghast. Malcolm X spoke out against it. King worried about placing children in danger. In the end, he decided to go ahead. It was another "faith act."

As it turned out, young people were desperate to join. They were already showing up to meetings in such large numbers that special times had to be set up just for them. The SCLC youth meetings run by member Rev. Andrew Young filled to overflowing.

Through speeches, radio announcements, and word of mouth, King and the SCLC called upon Birmingham's Black children to come and join a march on May 2, 1963. From sixteen down to as young as six, they swarmed to the Sixteenth Street Church, from every school in town and some outside. When one teen heard that there were kids from out of town who wanted to join, he drove his shiny new car to the city outskirts to fetch them. He found an entire school empty, with every student outside, ready to march. Dozens of kids clambered onto his car. Eight hundred marched behind.

Clapping and singing, they came. Many brought toothbrushes and toothpaste. They knew they were not going home that night. They were going to be arrested.

James Bevel directed the crowds toward Kelly Ingram Park,

between the church and the Gaston Motel. There, Bull Connor's forces waited to cart the young protesters to jail. When the paddy wagons filled up, school buses were used to imprison children and teenagers. On the very first day of the march, 973 were arrested! When the marchers filled the jails, hundreds more were packed into stock-pens at the fairgrounds.

Connor had been prepared to keep his men polite and courteous, but he had expected a few dozen protesters. Here were hundreds, then thousands. The children kept coming, and Bull Connor snapped. He ordered his men to turn high-pressure water hoses on. Water jetted out of those hoses with so much force that it could rip a person's clothes off. Connor's men aimed for the head, knocking down screaming children.

When the water hoses stopped, most of the crowd had dispersed. Ten young people remained standing. Eyes closed, streaming water, fists clenched against the terror, they sang a single word: "Freedom." With that sight and sound, the crowd came surging back.

Then Connor called in the dogs.

Suddenly, Birmingham was all over the national and international news. The images ricocheted around the world. A police dog with a boy's sweater between his teeth, jerking. Another leaping at a youth to tear into his stomach, yet another ripping the pant leg off a young man. Even skeptics of desegregation flinched at the sight of police dogs lunging for young people's throats.

In the Oval Office at the White House, President Kennedy saw the pictures. The sight made him sick.

Bull Connor, 1963

Throughout, the students remained peaceful. At one point, marchers neared the line dividing Black and white sections of the city. Connor ordered them back. They refused. Some knelt on the ground. Connor directed his men to turn on the hoses. The marchers stared right at the police. Then, slowly, they got up and began to advance. As if hypnotized, the police stepped back. Fire hoses in their hands, they gave the marchers passage.

For eight days, three thousand children marched in Birmingham

Water jets hit protesters.

Police dogs set
on civil rights
marchers

in what came to be called the Children's Crusade. The president sent
a negotiator to speak to King and the other Black leaders, as well
as to the newly elected city mayor and his government. On Friday,
May 10, they reached an agreement. The SCLC would end boycotts
and demonstrations. The city would desegregate downtown stores and
release protesters from jail. It was a quiet triumph for the movement.

Slowly, resistance from all-white schools, libraries, and universities began to crumble. Once, King put out a call for volunteers, and
six small children showed up. Andrew Young told them they were too
young to march, so instead, he sent them to the public library, which
had only just opened its doors to Black patrons. Off they went to the
building in the white district, where, two weeks earlier, they would
have been turned away. "Shyly but doggedly," King wrote, "they went
to the children's room and sat down, and soon they were lost in their

books. In their own way, they had struck a blow for freedom."

Segregationists were furious. Outside town, the Klan met. King's brother's church was bombed. Another bomb went off at the Gaston Motel, injuring several people. President Kennedy sent three thousand federal troops to the area. He threatened to put the Alabama National Guard under federal control. Only then did the attacks cease.

The board of education tried to suspend or expel all the children who had taken part in the Children's Crusade. The SCLC and NAACP went to court and won. The young people stayed in school.

The day the University of Alabama was forced to open its doors to Black students, Kennedy delivered a speech on national television. Civil rights were no longer a legal issue, he said, but a moral one. He said the nation, "for all its hopes and all its boasts, will not be fully free until all its citizens are free."

King sped a telegram off to the White House, calling the speech "one of the most eloquent, profound, and unequivocal pleas for justice and freedom of all men ever made by any president."

On June 19, 1963, President Kennedy sent a sweeping civil rights bill to Congress, calling for the strengthening of voting rights, banning discrimination in public places, supporting school desegregation, and allowing the president to cut off public funds to any local or state program that practiced discrimination. Justice, yearned for by so many, seemed finally within reach.

" Now the time has come for this Nation to fulfill its promise. "

—John F. Kennedy

19

"Free at Last, Free at Last"

Change came in small increments. The city of Atlanta abolished its segregation statutes. Long after his daughter had first asked to go there, King took Yoki to Funtown, which had opened its gates to Black children without a fuss. They went on rides. People stopped him to ask if he wasn't Dr. King and if that wasn't his daughter. The victory was sweeter than the cotton candy they shared.

But the work was far from over. In the summer of 1963, in King's words, "a great shout for freedom reverberated across the land." Black people had marched in cities across the country. Now it was time to take the movement to the nation's capital, Washington, DC. A great civil rights march was scheduled for August, three months after the triumph of the movement in Birmingham. Even in a time before today's instant communications, every civil rights organization in the country was involved in its planning. The march was expected to attract a mightier throng of people than ever before.

Thousands. Hundreds of thousands. People of all colors, from all professions and all walks of life—union members, musicians, politicians, teachers, writers, artists, doctors, lawyers, and more. Mothers with babies in strollers. Fathers with small children perched on their shoulders. Churchwomen in their church hats with pocketbooks and fancy shoes. Working people. Elders. People of all races. Members of white churches in record numbers. They gathered through the chilly night and into the dawn, as the sun burned off the morning mist.

The day grew bright and hot and humid. The sun shone down upon the National Mall. From the giant seat atop the steps of his pillared monument, the marble statue of Abraham Lincoln looked down upon the quarter million people gathered there.

People held hands in giant human chains. Thousands of voices sang together, "We shall overcome." Slowly, the crowd moved along the expanse of green to the steps of the Lincoln Memorial. The proceedings opened with songs and speeches. Then the organizer of the march, A. Philip Randolph, introduced the Rev. Martin Luther King Jr. He called him "the moral leader of our nation." King stood at a thicket of microphones as the murmuring crowd stilled into expectant silence.

In Their Crosshairs

The night Kennedy made his historic declaration on civil rights, a murder took place in Jackson, Mississippi. The murderer, a white man named Byron De La Beckwith, waited in a clump of honeysuckle with a gun in his hand for Medgar Evers.

Evers, the NAACP's state field secretary, was a World War II veteran who had worked on the investigation of Emmett Till's murder back in 1955. He had also helped James Meredith gain admission to Ole Miss.

De La Beckwith gunned Medgar Evers down in his driveway. He died in the hospital. Evers was thirty-seven years old. He left behind a wife and three young children. His killer would not be convicted for another thirty-one years.

Medgar Evers had been a good friend of the Kings. When Coretta heard of his murder, she worried that Martin would be next. He was always out on the street with marchers, speaking to crowds. Would-be assassins surely had him in their crosshairs.

Edith Lee-Payne on her twelfth birthday, March on Washington

The Power of a Photo

For years, Edith Lee-Payne didn't know anyone had taken her picture at the March on Washington on August 28, 1963, a day that also happened to be her birthday. Only in 2008 did she find out that her picture was in a Black history calendar! It took her three years to trace the photo to the National Archives, where it had been credited to "an unknown photographer." That photographer was Rowland Scherman. On his first assignment that day, Scherman didn't realize that he was about to witness one of the most monumental events in U.S. history. Or that his picture would convey to millions the emotions and intensity of the day, captured in the face and eyes of one twelve-year-old.

"Five score years ago," King began, "a great American, in whose symbolic shadow we stand today, signed the Emancipation Proclamation."

As King went on, his attorney and advisor Clarence Jones sat up in surprise. This wasn't the prepared speech King had talked to colleagues about, just the night before! Jones had taken notes at that meeting. Ralph Abernathy and Lawrence Reddick had been there, along with Bayard Rustin and others. King had appeared preoccupied. He said he was going to his room "to counsel with my Lord." Everyone assumed the final version of the speech was already completed.

Now Jones heard King speaking with nothing more than the notes that Jones himself had taken. King was now taking his cues from the audience, speaking from the heart, speaking directly to the teeming multitude gathered. He stood solid as a rock, his voice strong and sure.

Young women at the March on Washington

King talked about Lincoln and the Emancipation Proclamation. About how Black people "languished in the corners of American society." He said the Constitution was a "promissory note" that guaranteed the "unalienable rights of 'Life, Liberty and the pursuit of Happiness.'" America, he said, had defaulted on this promise. As far as Black people were concerned, America had given them a bad check, "a check which has come back marked 'insufficient funds.'" The crowd erupted into applause.

"Now is the time . . . ," King said, and the crowd murmured his words back to him. "Now is the time."

King called upon protesters to "forever conduct our struggles on the high plane of dignity and discipline. We must not allow our creative protest to degenerate into physical violence." He said, "Go back to Mississippi, go back to Alabama, go back to South Carolina, go back to Georgia, go back to Louisiana, go back to the slums and ghettos of our northern cities, knowing that somehow this situation can and will be changed. Let us not wallow in the valley of despair."

Then something happened that changed the speech and the day and pulled them both right into history. King said, "I have a dream."

Jones heard a voice call out, "Yes! Tell 'em about the dream." It was Mahalia Jackson, King's favorite gospel singer.

For a second, King turned toward Mahalia. Then he took the prepared notes before him and slid them to the left of the lectern. He grabbed the lectern and looked out at the crowd.

Jones turned to the person standing next to him. "These people out there," he said. "They don't know it, but they're about ready to go to church."

King stood up straighter. His voice grew deeper. "I have a dream," he repeated. His voice rang out in sonorous rhythms, the words circling back around in glorious repetition.

Those words, "I have a dream," have come to define not only the entire speech, but the day, and perhaps even King himself. His soul was in those words.

As he spoke, King wove together the hopes of the nation and his own dreams, a father's dreams for his children. They were inseparable. He rolled to a finish with a rousing cry "to speed up that day when all of God's children, black men and white men, Jews and Gentiles, Protestants and Catholics, will be able to join hands and sing in the words of the old Negro spiritual, 'Free at last, free at last. Thank God Almighty, we are free at last.'"

A shiver ran through the masses assembled on the National Mall. Then the applause thundered out. Here it was, King's vision of the "blessed community," a sacred gathering in the beating heart of the nation's capital.

A toddler in a stroller, March on Washington

Jackie Robinson and son at the March on Washington

Crowds, including
a man in a
tree, March on
Washington.

King at the
mic, March on
Washington.

King and others
at the March on
Washington

White Hats

In the film footage of King's famous speech, we can see many men in the crowd wearing a *topi*, a white hat. In India, this was known as the "Gandhi topi." Gandhi himself rarely wore one, but many who were part of the Indian independence movement did. In the footage, King does not wear the Gandhi topi, but many of those around him do. It is yet another small link of image and story, event and sequel, idea and action, between the lives of these two men.

King was the orator that Gandhi never became. As the civil rights movement went on, King came to rely less on Gandhi's writing and philosophy and more on his own interpretations and his conscience. Still, one thing is clear. It fell to King to help fulfill Gandhi's prophecy, made to Howard Thurman and his group, long ago in a tent in India: Black Americans would deliver "the unadulterated message of non-violence" to the world.

The March on Washington was covered enthusiastically by media around the world. CBS was the only American television company to broadcast it live. For Black people seeking equality and justice, it turned the anguish of generations into hope.

Gandhi topis in India

Gandhi topis at the March on Washington

The optimism would not last. Less than a month later, the many hopes raised on the Mall were dashed by a blood-soaked tragedy. It happened at the Sixteenth Street Church in Birmingham. King called it a "horror-filled September morning."

It was Sunday. Four hundred worshippers had gathered. Among them were Denise McNair, eleven years old, and Cynthia Wesley, Carole Robertson, and Addie Mae Collins, all fourteen. The girls were in the back, putting on their choir robes, when an explosion rocked the church. It blew a hole in the wall and scattered the screaming crowd. Someone had placed a bomb made of dynamite beneath the steps on the east side of the building. All four girls died.

Poison continued to spew from a bottomless well of hate. Police killed another Black youth in the streets. A white gang murdered yet another as he rode by on his bicycle.

Some in the movement thought that events like the Sixteenth Street Church bombing meant the end of nonviolence. Some suggested that only an armed revolution would gain Black people the rights they deserved. But Chris McNair, Denise's grief-stricken father, said, "I'm not for that. What good would Denise have done with a machine gun in her hand?"

King delivered the eulogy at a joint funeral service held for three of the girls. The mayor had expressed sympathy, had even shed tears on television, but not a single city official came to the service. The only white faces were those of a few ministers.

King was convinced that out of the horror of the Birmingham bombing, some hope and good must come. He wrote a fiery article that was published in the *New York Times Magazine*, titled "In a Word—*Now*." In it, he demanded everything listed in Kennedy's civil rights bill. Everything. Immediately.

He undertook a brutal travel schedule—New York to speak to labor unions, Birmingham to support the movement there, back to Washington, DC, to the White House to meet with the president, then back to Atlanta to work on his book about Birmingham.

On November 22, 1963, King had the television on while he got ready for his next trip. Suddenly, a special bulletin interrupted the program. In Dallas, Texas, President Kennedy had been shot. The first reports stated that he was "seriously wounded." Within the hour came news that the president of the United States had died. King was stunned. He said to Coretta, "This is what is going to happen to me also. I keep telling you, this is a sick society."

She had no words to comfort him.

King knew all too well the sounds of assassinations: "the whine of the bullet from ambush, the roar of the bomb." He was keenly aware that Gandhi, who had called racial segregation "a negation of civilization," had fallen to an assassin's gun. Now more than ever, King knew he himself was in danger.

Later he wrote: "The assassination of President Kennedy killed not only a man but a complex of illusions. It demolished the myth

that hate and violence can be confined to an airtight chamber to be employed against but a few. Suddenly the truth was revealed that hate was a contagion; that it grows and spreads as a disease."

The country mourned the loss of its young president. King thought it also mourned for itself. America, he began to believe, was a nation that tolerated hatred. America allowed a person to take a gun and shoot a president with whom he disagreed.

Martin Luther King was not invited to Kennedy's funeral Mass at St. Matthew's Cathedral. But in his heart, he knew he had to go. He traveled alone to Washington and stood on the street, watching with a heavy heart as the funeral cortege passed by.

Days earlier, on board *Air Force One*, as the dead president's body

was being flown back to Washington, Lyndon B. Johnson had been sworn in as president. Johnson was a man with a terrible temper. He swore and cursed. He worked his staff hard and demanded complete loyalty.

In three decades in politics, Johnson had voted against many civil rights measures. It was not that he didn't feel compassion for the poor. As a young man, he had spent time teaching disadvantaged Mexican Americans in Texas. That experience shaped his heart, but his compassion didn't immediately extend to Black people. He worried that moving too quickly on civil rights issues would alienate Southern states. But after Kennedy's death, King suggested that the new administration might best honor the fallen president by enacting the policies he had initiated. Johnson began to feel pressure to ensure that Kennedy's hopes for equality had not died with him. He began to revive the civil rights bill that Kennedy had sent to Congress.

That bill—stuck at the time in a House committee—would eventually outlaw discrimination based on race, color, religion, sex, or national origin, in public accommodations and in publicly owned facilities. It would require schools to develop plans for desegregation and ban discrimination in employment. It would also offer limited voter protection. Despite reservations, Johnson pushed for a law that aimed to do what no other piece of legislation had done: force the dismantling of the Jim Crow traditions of the South. With the federal government on the side of Black Americans, Southern states would have to comply with the law, even if they did so grudgingly.

The new year brought unexpected fame when Dr. King was named Man of the Year by *Time* magazine. It was his second appearance on the cover of the magazine—and the first time an African American was judged the most influential person in the world.

But trouble continued to brew. By this time, the FBI was actively snooping on King. His travel was exhausting. His health was suffering. There were still cities in America where Black people were terrorized. And he feared for his own children.

In St. Augustine, Florida, carloads of KKK sympathizers drove through Black neighborhoods, shooting at random. A local Black dentist, Robert Hayling, who had led protests to desegregate white shops and restaurants, had the windows of his house shattered by gunfire. Then he was kidnapped, beaten unconscious, doused with kerosene. Only the arrival of the local sheriff saved him from being burned alive. Hayling appealed to the SCLC for help. At the same time, he invited college students, mostly white, from the North to visit the city—not for spring break, but to demonstrate against segregation.

King arrived in May 1964, along with other SCLC activists. The streets—and the jails— were filled with protesters. King's rental house was shot at. He and Ralph Abernathy tried to enter a whites-only restaurant and were promptly arrested. Meanwhile,

Martin Luther King Jr. and his son Marty walk up the stairway in front of their house after church

protesters marched daily to whites-only beaches, demanding they be opened. At the site of the city plaza known as the Old Slave Market, they were met by Klan members armed with bricks and rocks, tire chains and broken bottles. King appealed to President Johnson for help in stemming the violence.

A local grand jury claimed that King and the SCLC had destroyed "racial harmony" in the city and ordered them to leave St. Augustine for one month. King replied that St. Augustine had never had racial harmony. What was there to disrupt?

In Washington, the Civil Rights Act, introduced by President Johnson, wended its way through Congress. Johnson took his arguments directly to Southern Democrats, persuading, cajoling, appealing to their consciences.

Small victories in court raised hopes. A Florida judge, Bryan Simpson, heard cases against the Ku Klux Klan and other white supremacist organizations and ruled in favor of the Black citizens represented by the SCLC. It wasn't all settled yet, but King and the national SCLC leaders could leave St. Augustine now.

On July 2, as millions watched on television, 250 people in the East Room of the White House saw President Lyndon Johnson sit down at a polished desk, a forest of a hundred pens bristling against its gleaming wooden surface. He picked a pen to sign a new law passed by Congress—the Civil Rights Act of 1964. Johnson signed a tiny part of his signature, then handed the pen to a well-wisher. The next pen inscribed another fraction of an inch, and the next yet another. To sign the historic bill into law, President Johnson used over seventy of those ceremonial pens. Dr. King received one of them.

20

Champion of Peace

Finally, the scales were tipped toward justice. King called the act "a bright interlude in the long and sometimes turbulent struggle for civil rights." President Johnson had moved slowly—sometimes more slowly than Dr. King wanted—but his hesitation came from "careful practicality."

The law had a personal effect as well. The King children could go to an integrated school. Spring Street Elementary School was known to be one of the best in Atlanta. Until now, it had been all white. Coretta did not want her children to be the only Black students enrolling there, so she asked Juanita Abernathy, Ralph's wife, if their children could change schools together. The Abernathy and King children enrolled at the same time.

This heartening interlude didn't last. Violence struck again, this time in Mississippi. White gangs burned churches and killed Black people. Three civil rights workers, arrested, supposedly for speeding, mysteriously disappeared. King traveled to the state to help SNCC and CORE members register Black voters, in a campaign that came to be known as Freedom Summer.

Those within the movement were divided on how to carry on. The NAACP promoted lawsuits over marches and publicity. SNCC workers began to grumble that King got all the attention. Some said he came to town to speak and attract crowds. Then he'd move on to his next engagement. Behind his back, some SNCC workers sarcastically called him "de Lawd." The caricatured insult arose from their own hurt. They, the foot soldiers in the civil rights battle, felt largely unrecognized, while he got all the headlines.

Echoes of Black frustration resounded across the country. Urban ghettos in Chicago, Philadelphia, and Jersey City were racked by riots. King pleaded with white Americans to pay attention to the frustrations of Black people. So long as they were "smothered by poverty in the midst of an affluent society," there was always a danger of people exploding into violence.

Among the politicians, the Democrats

Mississippi Burning

Of the civil rights workers missing in Mississippi, James Chaney was Black; Michael Schwerner and Andrew Goodman were white. When their station wagon was found abandoned and burned, a massive search began. The FBI investigation was code-named MIBURN, short for "Mississippi Burning."

In August came the news that the young men's bodies had been found. They had been shot and buried in an earthen dam near the town of Philadelphia, Mississippi.

At the time, the director of the FBI, J. Edgar Hoover, was refusing to offer protection to civil rights workers. In fact, he was encouraging his agents to bug King's hotel rooms and increase wiretaps. But when the bodies showed up, even he had to admit these cases should be prosecuted.

Twenty-one Ku Klux Klan members, including the sheriff and deputy in Neshoba County, were eventually arrested. Obtaining their indictments took years of legal wrangling. Their sentences were ridiculously light, ranging from three to ten years. The last accused was not convicted until 2005, forty-one years after the murders. Even then, the charge was reduced from murder to the less serious one of manslaughter. As with so many crimes based on race, justice was served too little, too late.

seemed to be listening. They nominated Lyndon B. Johnson as their next presidential candidate, with Hubert Humphrey for vice president. The Republicans, too, were listening—to the Southern segregationists. They nominated Barry Goldwater, a conservative candidate with a record of voting against civil rights bills in the Senate. King did not officially endorse Johnson, but he made many speeches urging people not to support Goldwater.

The FBI was still after King. J. Edgar Hoover had labeled King and his associates as communists. Hoover's paranoia came in part from his view of world politics. The United States and the Soviet Union were in a race to build bigger and more powerful nuclear weapons aimed against each other. As a result, the fear of communism extended even to the highest levels of government in America. Communists were seen as Soviet agents, a threat to national security. In Hoover's book, someone like King who questioned the American system was undoubtedly a communist. The head of the FBI felt as threatened by the call for equal rights in the Black community as did Southern segregationists and white supremacists.

But international recognition also came, in a most dramatic way. In October 1964, Dr. King fell ill. He checked into an Atlanta hospital, St. Joseph's Infirmary, with a viral infection. He was admitted by Dr. Asa Yancey, the first Black physician to practice at the hospital. That night, King slept.

The following morning, Coretta called. She could hardly speak. Her voice trembled with excitement. The Associated Press had reported that Martin Luther King Jr. had just been awarded the 1964 Nobel Peace Prize.

King was speechless. Was this a dream? He knew he had been nominated for this great honor. He had not thought he stood a chance of winning. He felt humbled. The prize, he believed, was really won by *all* the people in the civil rights movement.

J. Edgar Hoover ranted, "He was the last person in the world who should ever have received it."

Bull Connor, now heading up the Alabama Public Service Commission, protested, "They're scraping the bottom of the barrel."

In contrast, congratulatory telegrams poured in. Jazz composer, pianist, and bandleader Duke Ellington, who had composed special music in honor of the Birmingham demonstrations, called the news "a beautiful bright shining hope." Robert Kennedy, despite the fact that he'd backed Hoover's phone taps, said the honor was "richly deserved."

On his way to attend the Nobel award ceremony in Oslo, Norway, King stopped in London to preach at St. Paul's Cathedral. A London sightseeing tour troubled him, however, reminding him too much of the power of empires. He felt that the grandeur of the city "was built by exploitation of Africans and Indians and other oppressed peoples."

In Oslo, King was swept into a whirlwind of visits and meetings, press conferences and parties. The grand

Dr. King with Dexter

© Flip Schulke

© Flip Schulke

The Kings at Sunday dinner with a portrait of Gandhi overhead

Yolanda (right) and Martin III (left) with their mother, Coretta Scott King (in the front seat) leaving school. At center is Juandalynn Abernathy, daughter of the Rev. Ralph Abernathy and his wife, Juanita.

ceremony was to take place on December 10 at the University of Oslo. Coretta said they had "quite a time getting him ready": striped trousers, a gray tailcoat, and an ascot, a wide tie, which he swore he'd never wear again.

Trumpets heralded King's Nobel speech. He swallowed, wiped

Dr. Martin Luther King Jr. displays his 1964 Nobel Peace Prize medal in Oslo, Norway, December 10, 1964.

his eyes, steadied his nerves. He spoke of "the tortuous road which has led from Montgomery, Alabama, to Oslo." The prize, he said, was really for millions of Black people whom he represented. He spoke of his "abiding faith in America and an audacious faith in the future of mankind." He said that when a plane flies, it is not only the pilots and flight attendants who deserve thanks, but also the ground crew, those anonymous workers who check it, fuel it, maintain it, keep it safe and airworthy. This prize was for the ground crew—the anonymous millions who marched for civil rights.

Outside the auditorium, Oslo University students stood against the backdrop of a giant Christmas tree, bearing torches. When King and Coretta emerged, they chanted, "Freedom now" and "We shall overcome."

In keeping with his gratitude to the many marchers who made up the movement, King decided to donate his prize money, $54,600 in all, to several organizations: the SCLC, SNCC, CORE, the NAACP, the Gandhi Society for Human Rights, the National Council of Negro Women, and the National Urban League.

New York City gave King a returning hero's welcome, presenting him with a Medallion of Honor. Dr. King was fresh from the dazzle and celebration of the last few days. He had often used the metaphor of a mountaintop, drawing it from the prophecy of Isaiah in the Old Testament of the Bible. Never had it felt so true. Never had the mountaintop seemed so marvelous.

He said he wished he could stay in Manhattan, but the valley was calling to him. That valley was Selma, Alabama.

21

Bloody Sunday

Selma, in the south-central part of Alabama, was the county seat of Dallas County. It lay between Montgomery and Birmingham in an area called the Black Belt, a name alluding to its rich, dark, cotton-growing soil. Later, the name came to refer to the enslaved people brought there from Africa to work on the plantations.

The issue that drew Dr. King to Selma was voter registration. Black voters were being registered elsewhere in the South—thirty thousand in Georgia alone in 1963. Yet some Alabama counties had not a single Black voter on the rolls. To ward off protests and keep marchers off the streets, a circuit court judge, James Hare, had issued an injunction forbidding the public discussion of racial issues at any gathering of "three or more persons" sponsored by SNCC, the SCLC, and a hefty list of civil rights leaders. King, not being local, was not on that list.

In January 1965, King went to Selma to defy Hare's injunction. From the pulpit of Brown Chapel AME Church, beneath the

ILLEGAL TO GATHER HALF A CENTURY EARLIER, IN INDIA, A PUNJABI PROVINCIAL ORDINANCE HAD MADE GATHERINGS OF FOUR OR MORE PEOPLE ILLEGAL, CLAIMING SECURITY AS THE REASON. ALABAMA'S JUDGE HARE HAD LIKELY NEVER HEARD OF THIS EVENT IN INDIA'S HISTORY, YET HIS INJUNCTION WAS AN EERIE ECHO OF THE TACTICS OF EMPIRE.

high-vaulted ceiling, with the organ pipes gleaming behind him, King addressed an audience eager for action.

Action was what he called for, a campaign for the right to vote everywhere in Alabama. If they were refused, they should appeal to Governor Wallace. If Wallace turned them down, to the legislature. If the legislators didn't listen, they must appeal to Congress.

The crowd spoke back in reply. "Give us the ballot!" People sprang to their feet, clapping and cheering until the great room, with its high arches intersecting overhead, rang with their cries.

King issued a triple challenge for Monday: a march to the courthouse demanding votes; groups of people applying for whites-only city jobs; and a test of the willingness of restaurants to integrate. As he talked, King noticed that state troopers and deputies sat in the back of the room, taking notes. He carried on.

In addition to Judge Hare's injunction, a Selma ordinance stated that any group wanting to parade in the city must obtain a permit. The Monday march organizers knew that their chances of being granted a permit were slim indeed. Declaring the ordinance was a violation of the protesters' right to free speech under the Constitution, King set out for one restaurant after another, along with a group of marchers, Black and white. Seven out of eight restaurants served them.

Next, King, along with Ralph Abernathy, headed for the Albert, a whites-only hotel, to check in. A gracious old brick-front building with pointed arches and wide columns, built with the labor of enslaved people, it was a perfect place to break Alabama's color bar.

Hecklers lined the street—the sheriff and his deputy, a volunteer posse, as well as members of the local Klan and the American Nazi Party. They yelled insults as the group of Black men entered the hotel.

Someone followed King. A white man who looked on the verge of saying something. He made no threats. He appeared harmless enough.

King and Abernathy went up to the counter. They checked in without incident, as did others in the movement, including Fred Shuttlesworth and King's brother, A. D. King.

But the white man stalking King was joined by others. They milled around in the hotel lobby, staring at King, Abernathy, and their fellow guests. Someone in the crowd called out to Dr. King.

King turned and stepped toward the group.

His stalker swung his fist, hitting him once, then twice, so that he collapsed onto the counter. Then he kicked him viciously. A. D. grabbed the attacker. Police Chief Wilson Baker arrested him.

The blow made King's head hurt all day. It was an uneasy reminder of danger lurking in the shadows. How easy it was for an attacker to get close enough to do real harm!

King was well aware of how many people hated him, people who believed

King is attacked by States Rights Party member Jimmy Robinson as he tries to register at the Hotel Albert in Selma, Alabama, January 18, 1965. The woman at left is trying to avoid getting hurt.

that giving rights to one group meant taking them away from another. In Selma, Alabama, in 1965, where more than half of the population was Black, many white people resented the arrival of activists and demonstrators.

Ninety-five years had passed since the Fifteenth Amendment to the U.S. Constitution, which prohibited federal and state governments from denying a citizen the right to vote based on "race, color, or previous condition of servitude." Yet in Alabama, over 80 percent of eligible Black voters remained unregistered. King believed that only a federal law could enforce the Constitution here.

In the past, Congress had heeded the sound of feet marching in the street. The feet of demonstrators were about to sound once more.

The marches began, with participants demanding the right to vote. Teachers headed for the courthouse steps. They had jail kits in hand, complete with toothbrushes. They were pushed back. They kept on coming. The sheriff was ready to throw them all in jail. Others persuaded him that arresting 95 percent of the Black schoolteachers in town might be a bad idea.

Inspired by the teachers, the morticians and barbers planned a march.

On the morning of January 25, 1965, Dr. King led a large group of marchers to the courthouse. U.S. District Judge Daniel Thomas had issued a new ruling that only one hundred people at a time could wait at the courthouse. If there were more, they could be arrested. Many marchers waited to register to vote, and the police began to count heads. When they got to one hundred, they pulled everyone else off the sidewalk. Resisters were arrested.

Sheriff Jim Clark tried to move fifty-four-year-old Annie Lee Cooper. She warned him not to twist her arm. He poked her in the neck with his club. Outraged, Cooper did something that the marchers had been warned not to do. She punched Clark. While three deputies held her down, an infuriated Clark beat Cooper with his nightstick.

Annie Lee Cooper's fellow marchers seethed. The tension boiled. That night, at a meeting at Tabernacle Baptist Church, James Bevel tried to calm the crowd. He warned that it was foolish to hit a white man. "Then they can call you a mob and beat you to death." By "holding their peace," in contrast to those who were supposed to enforce the law, the marchers were shining a spotlight on the violence and cruelty of segregation. King suggested that evildoers could repent and change, and that resisters should meet hatred with love.

The photograph of Annie Lee Cooper being beaten flew worldwide over the newswires.

Mass meetings continued in Selma, as well as in nearby Marion. State troopers rumbled through the streets under the command of Al Lingo, director of the Alabama Department of Public Safety. It was hard to tell if they were keeping an eye out for potential conflict or seeking an opportunity to create it!

In the movement in Selma was a third-grade girl, introduced to Dr. King as "his youngest freedom fighter." Her name was Sheyann Webb. Sometimes King would hold her in his lap as he spoke from the pulpit at Brown Chapel. They'd sing together. At the end of his talk, he'd say, "Sheyann, what do you want?" She'd reply, "Freedom!" When his own children were present, he'd call out the same question to them—and get the same reply.

King, Sheyann
Webb, and
Sheyann's friend
Rachel West

In Selma, on January 31, 1965, seventeen years and a day after Gandhi had fallen to an assassin's bullet, King led 250 marchers in another public call for the freedom to vote. Wilson Baker arrested them all. They had to be housed in a county facility because the Selma city jail was too small. The arrested protesters were in high spirits. While they were waiting to be booked, they laughed and joked and used the restrooms marked WHITE.

The cells were jam-packed, but the prisoners kept one another in good humor. They were sometimes serious, sometimes silly. Newbies to the movement would ask, "How long are we going be here?"

"What's your name again?" an experienced marcher might say. The new recruit would tell them his name.

"Oh, yes," he'd be told. "You're on the B list."

"What's that?"

Then everyone would shout, "You're going to beeeeeeee here for a looooooong time!"

King and Abernathy fasted, prayed, sang hymns, and exercised, wanting to make good use of their time in jail, as Gandhi had done. News arrived of the arrests of hundreds, including schoolchildren. A sheriff's deputy had used a cattle prod on King's assistant, Hosea Williams.

King wrote a "Letter from a Selma Jail," appealing for help from "all decent Americans." He wrote: "This is Selma, Alabama. There are more Negroes in jail with me than there are on the voting rolls." The letter was published as a full-page advertisement in the *New York Times*.

Small victories came. Trying to get around the law, Dallas County voter registration authorities employed a strategy dating back to the end of the Civil War. This was the so-called literacy test, packed with questions that were impossible to answer, their real purpose being to keep Black people from the ballot box. Now Judge Thomas ordered Dallas County to stop using the bogus tests. In response to the favorable ruling, the SCLC temporarily suspended its protest.

LITERACY TESTS OR VOTER SUPPRESSION? SOME STATES HAD EASY TESTS FOR WHITE PEOPLE, AND CONFUSING, COMPLEX TESTS FOR BLACK ONES. SOME INCLUDED DICTATION, WHERE THE PASSAGES WERE DIFFICULT AND THE TESTER DELIBERATELY MUMBLED. SOME REQUIRED "CHARACTER TESTS"— AND FAILED THOSE WHO HAD PROTESTED SEGREGATION! STILL OTHERS LEFT IT ALL UP TO LOCAL POLL WORKERS.

While their husbands were in jail, Coretta and Juanita Abernathy came to Selma to see them and "to participate in the struggle." Speaking to a mass meeting in Brown Chapel, Coretta urged the attendees to stay on the path of nonviolence. At the chapel, she met with Malcolm X, who was in town.

Coretta wrote later that during her short visit with Martin in the jail, she'd told him about the meeting. Malcolm X was not against nonviolence, yet he also believed in the right of people to defend themselves "by any means necessary." But Coretta told King she had spoken to Malcolm. He'd told her that he wasn't in town to make

Martin Luther
King and Malcolm
X in 1964, the
only time they
met

trouble for the protesters. "If the white people realize what the alternative is, perhaps they will be more willing to hear Dr. King." It was a strategic position, meant to send a message to the authorities. Coretta's words calmed King.

King's imprisonment was covered in the national media. From his jail cell, he sent notes to Andrew Young, urging the SCLC to march again. It did. Arrests in Dallas County swelled to three thousand. King and Abernathy were released on bail. Others remained imprisoned in cells overrun by cockroaches, eating foul jail food—salty black-eyed peas and stale, crumbling cornbread, the only meat an occasional boiled chicken neck.

In Selma, young protesters marched, carrying signs that read LET OUR PARENTS VOTE. They faced police clubs and electric cattle prods.

Young Sheyann Webb persuaded her parents to give her a special ninth birthday present: a trip to the voter registration office! She walked between them, holding their hands, singing all the way. But when they got there, they had to stand in line all day long. White women went by, spraying insecticide at them, as if they were nasty bugs. At the end of the day, all Sheyann's parents were allowed to do was take a number, so they could come back the next day to stand in line all over again. Sheyann's mother's eyes got wide. Her mouth set in grim determination. She swore she'd return. She didn't care how long it took—she was

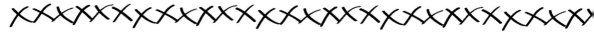

The Assassination of Malcolm X

On February 21, 1965, Malcolm X was about to speak to a packed audience at the Audubon Ballroom in New York. Shots rang out. Malcolm fell to multiple bullets. He was only thirty-nine years old.

Who was responsible? Three members of the Nation of Islam were tried and convicted. Many people believe there was a larger conspiracy behind the killing. The facts remain controversial.

Malcolm X did not always agree with King's approach, but he had devoted his life to action against injustice and was utterly dedicated to human rights. His death hit the movement hard.

going to be there every single day until they registered her. The family raced back home. With no bathroom at hand, not daring to leave their place in line, everyone desperately needed to pee!

Meanwhile, Dr. King visited the next county over, Wilcox County, trying to get Black voters registered there. It turned out that white voters in Wilcox County were kept on the rolls forever—even after they died. These "tombstone voters" routinely appeared to return from the grave to cast their votes for those who were currently in office.

White racists were outraged by the nerve of the marchers. One evening, a group of protesters set out from a church to the jail in Marion, the county seat of Perry County. They were met by police and by Al Lingo's state troopers. Suddenly, the streetlights went out. Police and white mobs charged the crowd, beating and clubbing them. News reporters were particular targets; an NBC reporter was hit in the head until he was bloodied. The mob had even brought spray paint to black out the lenses of cameras.

Marchers trying to escape the blows were followed and beaten. A few took shelter in a nearby café. They included eighty-two-year-old Cager Lee, his daughter Viola Jackson, and her son, twenty-six-year-old Jimmie Lee Jackson. Jimmie had tried five times to register to vote.

Each time, he was turned down. Now the troopers followed the family into the café. They overturned furniture. They shattered the lights. They beat everyone in their path, including the elderly Cager Lee. When his daughter tried to help him, they hit her as well.

Jimmie tried to protect his mother, placing himself in front of her. A trooper threw him up against a cigarette vending machine. Another shot him in the stomach. Jimmie staggered into the street; they clubbed him to the ground.

There was no hospital in Perry County. Jimmie Lee Jackson was rushed by ambulance to Selma, thirty miles away. The public hospital in Selma would not treat Black demonstrators. They turned him away. Jimmie was admitted at last to the Good Samaritan Hospital run by Catholics. Eight days later, on February 26, 1965, he died. As Jimmie was dying, Al Lingo served him with papers charging him with assault and battery.

Jimmie Lee Jackson was buried on a rainy March day. His funeral procession was half a mile long. Dr. King delivered the eulogy at Brown Chapel, saying Jimmie had been murdered by "the brutality of every sheriff who practiced lawlessness in the name of law . . . by every politician who fed his constituency the stale bread of hatred."

SCLC organizers began to plan another march to begin in Selma and end in Montgomery. In Marion, James Bevel urged an attentive congregation, "Be prepared to walk to Montgomery! Be prepared to sleep on the highway!"

Sunday, March 7, 1965, dawned cold and bleak. Hundreds of marchers made their way, by car and on foot, to the Edmund Pettus Bridge on Route 80 eastbound out of Selma (aka Jefferson Davis Highway). Dr. King was not among them—the SCLC was trying to keep its leaders out of jail. If they all got arrested, who would take charge?

Dr. King in Jimmie Lee Jackson's funeral procession

King expected arrests as a result of the march. What he did not expect was the brutality of the police, state troopers, and the sheriff's posse. A deadly wave of troopers and police surged forward to meet the marchers. Truncheons and clubs crunched and thudded in sickening rhythms against the flesh of the marchers, smashing them to the ground. Clouds of tear gas exploded, stinging and burning the marchers' eyes and nostrils. Screams of pain and terror filled the air. Sheyann Webb would never forget the terror of that day. "They had beaten us like we were slaves."

No medical help was at hand for the wounded. By the end of the day, one hundred marchers had suffered broken limbs and teeth, fractured skulls, lashes from the whips, and burns from the tear gas. No one had yet been registered to vote.

The day became known as Bloody Sunday. Like shards of broken glass, its images scattered through the front pages of the nation's newspapers.

22

No Compromise

King decided he could not stay away from the marches any longer. He had to be there in person, and soon. He sent telegrams to religious leaders of all denominations across the country, beseeching them to join him in Selma on Tuesday, March 9, for a "ministers' march to Montgomery." The National Council of Churches passed the word along to its members. Ministers responded. So did Jewish rabbis and students of theology. A young Black student named Jesse Jackson jumped onto a table in the cafeteria at Chicago Theological Seminary, shouting, "Pack your bags!" He talked seven white classmates into driving with him to Alabama.

The Catholic Church had so far discouraged its nuns and priests from joining in civil rights events, preferring to remain on the sidelines in matters of race. But now Catholic bishops were inundated with requests for permission to take part in the Selma march. The Washington diocese granted exceptions, while the bishop of Alabama refused consent. Priests and nuns traveled to Selma anyway.

In Washington, there were sit-ins at the Justice Department in support of the protesters in the South.

In Selma, the movement's lawyers filed a petition in U.S. District Court. They hoped the judge, Frank Johnson, would prevent police and troopers from responding to peaceful protesters with violence. Instead, Judge Johnson suspended the next voting rights march until further notice. It was a blow.

After much soul-searching, King decided to march regardless of the court order. It was past lunchtime on March 9 when he got to the foot of Edmund Pettus Bridge, just south of downtown. A crowd more than two thousand strong waited. A U.S. deputy marshal blocked his way, one hand raised, a bulky document in the other—a six-hundred-word order from Judge Johnson. The deputy marshal began to read aloud, the ponderous legalese of the order scattering in the open air: "This cause is now submitted . . . plaintiffs say they desire . . . enjoined and restrained . . ."

King replied, "I am aware of the order." He requested permission to move ahead. Surprisingly, the deputy marshal backed off. FBI agents stood by, monitoring the proceedings. King began to walk up the wide road sloping up onto the bridge.

The high spans of the bridge arched across the Alabama River. Down below on the other side, on Jefferson Davis Highway, stood rows of state troopers brandishing billy clubs. Major John Cloud boomed at the marchers through his bullhorn, calling on them to stop. King tried to assert the group's right to march.

Cloud only repeated his order. The troopers stood ready, stony-faced.

King asked Cloud to let the marchers pray together. "You can have your prayer," Cloud said. "And then you must return to your church."

The marchers knelt. King motioned to Abernathy to lead them in prayer. "We come to present our bodies as a living sacrifice," Abernathy said.

In the crowd, many prayed out loud. A minister from New York prayed for the people of Selma, the governor of Alabama, and the troopers. He prayed for peace and reconciliation. A rabbi added his voice to the prayerful truce.

Then Major Cloud did something completely unexpected. He turned to his men and ordered them to clear the road. The troopers stood aside. The road to Montgomery lay free and clear before the marchers, an immediate answer to all these heartfelt prayers.

But was it? Or was this a trap? What were the troopers doing? What would they do if the march resumed? Would they move in on unarmed people with clubs and tear gas, as they had done only two days before? Even if they didn't attack, what difference would it make? The marchers would still be violating a federal order. King wavered. He feared that he was leading his people to disaster.

He turned around. "We will go back to the church now!" he shouted. There was stunned silence. Then Abernathy fell in behind him, along with two white women, wives of Congressmen, who had joined the march. Andrew Young waved to oncoming marchers, organizing them into a loop turning around, a giant snaking line of people, murmuring in surprise, groaning in disappointment.

As if in a trance, the marchers went back to Selma. Meanwhile, captured on photographers' film and in reporters' notebooks, the story ran in the papers. There had been no violence, no confrontation. There had also been no march.

Some people felt betrayed. Thousands of clergy, Black and white, had come to Selma for this event. Now there was no event. Others felt the troopers had stood aside only because there were white people in the march. Some SNCC members were angry and disillusioned. How could King just take action without consulting anyone? Who, they demanded, gave him that power? Didn't *their* opinions matter?

King insisted that turning around now did not mean the movement was over. There would be future marches. They would reach Montgomery. But the mood, low on the day that came to be known as Turnaround Tuesday, was about to plunge into despair.

That evening brought terror to the streets. A young white minister from Boston, James Reeb, went out to dinner with a group of marchers. At Walker's Café, one of the few racially integrated restaurants in the area, they dined on fried chicken, turnip greens, and corn bread. Most of the group left by car after dinner, but Reeb and two white friends, Orloff Miller and Clark Olsen, decided to walk to the chapel where Dr. King was about to speak. As they left the café, they heard taunts from across the street. They kept walking. They made for the corner when four white men blocked their way, shouting insults.

One of the men swung at Jim Reeb's head—was that a club in his hand or a pipe? Jim fell instantly. As Miller dropped to the ground in self-protection, two men kicked him. Another punched Olsen with his fists. And then, just like that, it was over. The assailants were gone. Bruised and bleeding themselves, Miller and Olsen scrambled to their feet. They got help as quickly as they could. Jim was incoherent. They took him to an infirmary nearby, from where he was transferred to Birmingham University Hospital. Two days later, Jim Reeb died of massive brain damage.

The news blazed around the nation. "Concerned, perturbed, and frustrated," President Johnson announced that he intended to go before Congress with a new voting rights bill. The law had to step in. This violence had to end.

In Selma, heavyhearted, King got ready to conduct a memorial service for Jim Reeb from the very same pulpit where he'd eulogized Jimmie Lee Jackson. He watched the president's televised appearance. "It is wrong—deadly wrong," Johnson said, "to deny any of your fellow Americans the right to vote." There would be no compromise. He ended with the words of a song, an anthem of the civil rights movement: "We *shall* overcome," stressing the word "shall." By using the words of the civil rights movement's anthem, the president included himself, all of Congress, and, by implication, all the American people among the "we" who had to overcome—overcome prejudice, overcome hatred, overcome bigotry and violence. Johnson, tough-fighting

Southern Democrat that he was, had taken into his heart the meaning, and the language, of civil rights. King wiped a tear from his cheek.

JIM REEB'S MURDERERS THREE MEN WITH PRIOR CRIMINAL RECORDS WERE TRIED FOR JIM REEB'S MURDER BEFORE AN ALL-WHITE JURY, AFTER EVERY POTENTIAL AFRICAN-AMERICAN JUROR HAD BEEN TURNED DOWN. A WELL-KNOWN WHITE BUSINESSMAN COLLECTED MONEY FROM THE COMMUNITY FOR THE DEFENSE OF THE ACCUSED. ALL THREE MEN WERE FOUND NOT GUILTY.

In Montgomery, another Johnson sided unexpectedly with the movement. U.S. District Court Judge Frank Johnson approved the march from Selma to Montgomery. King and his associates were triumphant.

Alabama's Governor Wallace was livid. He claimed he could not protect the marchers. President Johnson called in Alabama units of the National Guard. Protected by the guard, the third march from Selma to Montgomery began. Nearly eight thousand marchers set out on March 21.

King walked much of the way, taking a little time out to have a sore foot treated. He arrived in Montgomery in time to receive those who had walked the entire route. Thousands more had joined the march along the way. On March 25, 1965, King led an exultant twenty-five thousand people through the streets

Dr. King, John Lewis, Ralph Abernathy, and others take a break from marching along Route 80.

The march that made it all the way to Montgomery

of Montgomery to celebrate the impending end of discrimination in voting.

That summer, Johnson's bill was approved by both houses of Congress. In August 1965, the Voting Rights Act was signed into law.

The Voting Rights Act placed all eleven of the former Confederate states under supervision by the federal government. It eliminated the Jim Crow tactics—poll taxes, literacy tests—that had for so long disenfranchised millions of Black Americans. Nationwide, it prohibited the denial or abridgment of the right to vote on account of race or color.

President Johnson signs the Voting Rights Act, 1965.

23

"Precious Lord, Take My Hand"

Beyond the South, elsewhere in the country, segregation was not dictated by the KKK or by local politicians. It was subtler than that. Generations of denying Black people equal jobs, housing, and opportunities had pushed many to the fringes of society. Large numbers of poor people were Black, living in crowded inner cities with high rates of crime and unemployment. The police were, at best, indifferent toward them and often insulting, even brutal. The Voting Rights Act may have given Black people access to votes, but it had not eased their troubles across America.

The summer after the marches in Selma had stirred the nation, a police officer in Los Angeles tried to arrest a Black man for drunk driving. The scene quickly attracted onlookers. They jeered at the officer, who lost his nerve and hit the inebriated driver with a baton. The incident rapidly spiraled out of control. Rumors of police brutality spread throughout Black neighborhoods. Over a thousand people took to the streets, pelting police with bottles and rocks. Residents stoned cars and beat white passersby. They looted stores, many owned by Korean immigrants. They set fires. The state National Guard was called in to restore order. The riots hit the headlines and crackled out through radios and televisions nationwide.

The authorities denied that racial prejudice existed in their city. They claimed that insults and threats from the police were the only language that Black people could understand.

When King visited the scarred neighborhoods, he could feel the anger and despair behind the uprising. Even before the riots, the Watts neighborhood was four times as crowded as the rest of L. A., with few jobs and 30 percent unemployment. Now King saw a burned and blighted cityscape. Later, he would define a riot as "the language of the unheard." He could not excuse the erupting violence. Yet he understood the underlying anger and desperation. The mood in the Black community, he argued, was one of urgency. How many more years would have to go by before the opportunities available to white Americans would be opened to all Americans? He knew well that the more time passed, the angrier people would become. He did not condone their actions, but he expressed compassion for those who saw violent rebellion as the only way to draw attention to their plight.

Before leaving Los Angeles, King called the White House. President Johnson praised him for visiting the riot-torn neighborhood. Johnson agreed that the troubles of urban Blacks came from poverty and unemployment. King urged him to roll out anti-poverty programs in the city, but Johnson complained that he lacked support in Congress. He needed to convince legislators to get on board, and the riots didn't help.

While Los Angeles was still reeling, King was invited to Chicago to support a new campaign there. If Montgomery was about the right to get a seat on a bus and Selma was about the right to vote, the movement in Chicago was about the right to decent housing and an end to racist real estate practices.

When Anger Leads to Violence
When anger consumes a crowd, ordinary people behave in unpredictable ways. During the Watts rebellion, poet Langston Hughes reported seeing a woman rolling a looted sofa down the road. Each time the traffic light turned red, she stopped obediently, then started up again on green. The police escalated the violence by shooting rioters, who in turn fought back. It was war in the streets. The Watts rebellion led to thirty-four deaths, thousands of arrests, and damage and destruction to millions of dollars' worth of property.

In some ways, Chicago was like a Birmingham of the North. Poor housing, discrimination in housing and schools, lack of job opportunities, police brutality—the list of problems for Black people went on and on. Neighborhoods and schools were not segregated by law, but in reality, they were both separate and unequal. King saw the urban ghetto as "an emotional pressure cooker." He decided he needed to be precisely where the pressure was building.

In January 1966, King moved his family to Chicago. Just as Gandhi had moved from place to place to support victims of injustice, King wanted to help the SCLC and other groups organize tenants' unions and demand fair housing for Black people.

Wanting to rent an apartment, he chose a tenement building on

Chicago's West Side. On the National Mall three years before, King had spoken of how Black people lived on an "island of poverty in the midst of a vast ocean of material prosperity." This neighborhood, North Lawndale, was just such an island. Residents called it "Slumdale."

Stepping over the threshold, King felt the chill of the bare dirt floor and the dank hallway, smelled the stench of urine. Up three rickety flights of steps, Coretta found the apartment barely heated, with a faulty gas stove and a broken refrigerator. They unpacked for hours, stopping only when it was time for King to go speak at the Chicago Theological Seminary, where SCLC staffer Jesse Jackson was a student.

Early in the Chicago campaign, King led the takeover of one unheated building, donning work clothes and shoveling out mounds of decayed trash. The residents' collected rent went toward badly needed wiring and heating repairs. Illegal as it was to march into a building and take it over, even in a just cause, Mayor Richard J. Daley refused to charge King. Instead, he slapped the landlord with code violations and announced a program to inspect fifteen thousand buildings on the West Side.

The landlord turned out to be an elderly invalid, who admitted the building was in terrible shape. He said anyone who could take on the mortgage was welcome to it. King saw that the landlords were not necessarily the enemy. They, too, had

Renovating a building in Chicago

their stories. In truth, there were no easy answers.

The sights that King saw during this time in the Black neighborhoods of Chicago broke his heart: hungry children with perpetually runny noses; a baby attacked by rats; a young man murdered by a gang when he was out looking for a job. In the crowded apartment, his own children grew irritable and bad-tempered. There was

© Flip Schulke

Bunny and her father

nowhere to play. He began to see what it meant to live in a ghetto. Meanwhile, Mayor Daley insisted he needed no help from anyone to clean up his city's housing.

In July, riots broke out on Chicago's West Side after police clashed with Black youth following an incident that the young people saw as a harmless prank: opening fire hydrants to play with the water on a hot day, in a segregated neighborhood with no pools. Violence escalated, egged on by gangs roaming the streets. King tried to talk to the gang leaders about peaceful resistance. He didn't have much success getting through.

At home, when the crash of breaking glass sounded in the street below, Coretta hurried the children away from the window.

Mayor Daley asked the Illinois governor to send in the National Guard. Fifteen hundred guardsmen arrived to patrol the neighborhoods, with orders to shoot looters on sight. With violence breeding still more violence, King called on one group of angry young people to set their rage aside and engage peacefully. He said, "Why aren't you all out there tonight? . . . Let us get a movement that the National Guard can't stop. . . . I'm going on with nonviolence . . . I've come to see how far it has brought us. And I'm not going to turn my back on it now." They joined. No bricks, no guns. Just the power of bodies and souls.

King led a massive rally at Soldier Field, where he called for an end to discrimination in housing. Even on this blazing-hot day, with a high of ninety-eight degrees, thirty-five thousand people of all races attended. Mahalia Jackson sang, along with singer-songwriters Stevie Wonder and Peter, Paul and Mary. After the rally, King led a march to city hall, sticking a list of demands on the door with adhesive tape.

Violent Reactions

On a march through a white residential neighborhood, protesters met crowds of white people yelling racist slogans and throwing rocks and bottles. A rock struck King on the side of the head. Someone carried a placard that read KING WOULD LOOK GOOD WITH A KNIFE IN HIS BACK.

Even the police were stunned. Many were second-generation immigrants of Polish, Italian, and German origins. Some had seen hard times in their own families. Now, hearing white people curse out Black protesters, they weren't sure whose side they ought to be on.

King paid little attention to his own safety. He was easily recognizable, and sometimes the marches drew violent reactions. He kept trying to counter hatred with compassion. At one point, King found some Black people spouting anti-Semitic views. He saw their desperation and anger and urged them not to "parrot racial epithets." Many Chicago Blacks resented what they felt was discrimination against

Dr. King (center foreground) walks in a crowd estimated at more than ten thousand people in downtown Chicago on July 26, 1965. The protesters opposed segregation in the city's schools, a result of segregated neighborhoods.

them by Jewish landlords and businesses. Dr. King had long believed that peace was possible between those who distrusted and feared each other. Former enemies could be partners in a journey to reconciliation.

The twists and turns of the Chicago movement only made him work harder to promote these deepest convictions.

By late August, Mayor Daley was eager to find a way to end the demonstrations. Finally, the Chicago Housing Authority agreed to build public housing. The Mortgage Bankers Association agreed to offer mortgages irrespective of race. Although King saw the significance of the agreement, he recognized that it was only "the first step in a 1,000-mile journey."

That journey led him back to the South. In June, James Meredith, whose enrollment at the University of Mississippi in 1962 had forced the integration of the college, had been shot by a white gunman. He had begun a solo march from Memphis, Tennessee, to Jackson, Mississippi, wanting to bring news of the Voting Rights Act to Black voters, to urge them to register. Instead, he was in the hospital with multiple bullet wounds. King flew to Memphis and was relieved to find Meredith recovering. Twenty-five marchers continued on Meredith's behalf, planning to pick up others along the way. When they ran into a hostile highway patrol, King urged calm and managed to deflect a violent confrontation.

In some circles of the civil rights movement, feelings ran high. Some younger activists were angry, unconvinced that nonviolence was working. Some refused to sing the line "black and white together" in the anthem "We Shall Overcome." When King asked why, someone retorted that the whole song should be dumped. It should be "We Shall Overrun," they said. The bitterness of these young people took King aback.

At a mass meeting, Stokely Carmichael, the brilliant, fiery new

SNCC chairman, talked about "Black Power" for the first time. The words disturbed King: They implied a division among the races. They threatened to fracture his vision of "the beloved community." He managed to eke out a compromise. No slogans for the rest of the march. No "Black Power" and no "Freedom Now," either.

Disagreement and debate aside, Meredith's march proceeded, growing in number. It came to be known as the Mississippi Freedom March. Meredith himself rejoined it by the end of the month, as nearly fifteen thousand marchers approached their destination of Jackson. Along the route, more than four thousand Blacks registered to vote.

Meanwhile, American troops marked a year of combat in Vietnam. How, King wondered, could a nation that waged war overseas possibly foster peace at home?

King had not made public statements on this subject, although Coretta had spoken against the war at a rally in Washington just a few months earlier. Now King struggled with his conscience. He was a man of peace. In India, he had dreamed of world disarmament. How could he remain silent while American bombs fell in Vietnam?

The Vietnam War

The Vietnam War, known in Vietnam as the American War, was aimed at stopping the spread of communism in Southeast Asia. The war began in 1954, with the first U.S. combat troops arriving in 1965. Over 58,000 American soldiers died in the Vietnam War. Vietnamese losses are thought to have run into the millions.

The war divided Americans deeply. Anti-war protests eroded public support for American involvement. In the end, the United States lost the war and Vietnam fell to the communists. Today, Vietnam is a socialist country, a fast-growing economy, and a major tourist destination.

One day, he came across a magazine article with photographs of Vietnamese children, their skin burned by American napalm bombs. The images seared themselves upon his soul. He had to speak—now. In April 1967, he gave a speech at Riverside Church in New York. He called for a halt to bombing in Vietnam, saying, "My conscience leaves me no other choice."

King saw the war as "a symptom of a far deeper malady within the American spirit," leading to injustice, inequality, and war. He saw the world as a house for all humanity.

King's critics fell upon the speech with glee. The FBI, which sent the president regular reports on anti-war protests, declared that King was on the side of the communists.

King refused to retract his words. In between lecturing, marching, and explaining his position on the war to the president, he managed to serve another four days in a Birmingham jail for a "crime" that dated back five years: demonstrating without a permit.

Meanwhile, race riots broke out in city after city—Newark, Minneapolis, Detroit, Milwaukee, even Washington, DC. In a speech in Berkeley, California, King called for reforms to help the poor. He launched a Poor People's Campaign, in which thousands would march to major cities. They would meet with government officials. They would demand jobs, unemployment insurance, a fair working wage, and education. People of all races pledged to join. It would be the next frontier in the civil rights journey.

Still, self-doubt tormented King. What did God have in store for him? In private, he spoke often of the fear of assassination.

In March 1968, King's old friend James Lawson invited him back to Memphis, Tennessee, where Black sanitation workers Echol Cole and Robert Walker had been crushed to death by a trash truck compacter. Had they been allowed to ride in the cab with the white driver, they would have lived. Thirteen hundred Black sanitation workers went on strike, demanding better wages and working conditions, wearing signs that read I AM A MAN. In the twentieth century, it was still necessary to remind those in power that Black people are human.

But a protest march in support of the workers turned ugly. Looters smashed shop windows and raided stores. Black Power signs appeared on the sidewalk, suggesting that the violence had been planned. King refused to continue leading a violent march. He urged James Lawson to call it off. As King left the scene, police fired tear gas and clubbed looters and marchers alike. They fired their guns, killing a sixteen-year-old boy. King was horrified. When he regained his composure, he talked to the organizers, to the gang members who had incited the violence, and to the press. He told them he'd be back. He would lead a massive nonviolent march in Memphis. A new, fiery determination replaced his doubts.

He returned on April 3, 1968, despite a crushing schedule, despite a bomb threat on the plane. On his arrival, he sent Coretta flowers—red carnations.

King was not keen to speak that night. He was exhausted, and his spirits were low. He had been worrying that peaceful movements were losing momentum. He'd even been thinking that maybe he ought to fast, as Gandhi had, putting his own life on the line to stir the consciences of the powerful. King tried to get Abernathy to talk for him instead. But Abernathy demurred. The crowds would be disappointed.

They were waiting to hear Reverend Martin Luther King Jr.

King gave in. He made it through pouring rain to the Mason Temple to give his talk. "Something is happening in Memphis," he said, "something is happening in our world." He said people could make change happen. They had done it already in Birmingham, Alabama, and they could do it here. He talked about how he'd been stabbed years before by a troubled woman, and if he'd sneezed, he might have died. And then he wouldn't have been able to do all this work in Albany, in Birmingham, in Selma. He was so happy that he hadn't sneezed. He ended on notes of joy, celebration, commitment, and community. His words echoed through the church. "I've been to the mountaintop." He stirred the hearts of listeners, rallying them to stay on the path of peace and justice.

The next day, King shared lunch with Abernathy, both of them eating from the same plate. Then he went to take a nap at the Lorraine Motel, where he was staying.

While King was napping, someone, wide awake, was stalking him: An escaped convict from Atlanta, following newspaper reports to locate King, had rented a cheap room in a boardinghouse across from the motel. At a store on Main Street, he had bought a pair of Bushnell binoculars. They were so powerful, he could read the room numbers on the motel doors. He tried the scope on his rifle and got a good sighting out the window of a bathroom down the hallway. He waited until his target was in full view.

In his motel room, King shaved and got dressed for the dinner planned at the home of Reverend Samuel Kyles. Kyles arrived and went to King's room to hurry him up, knowing he was tired and easily

distractible. Kyles found King and Abernathy laughing and joking. While Abernathy ducked into the bathroom, Kyles and King stepped out onto the balcony. King chatted with people gathering down in the parking lot. His driver suggested he'd need his coat. King called to Abernathy to bring it for him.

Saxophone player and singer Ben Branch stood below the balcony with James Bevel and Jesse Jackson. Jackson introduced the musician

King and colleagues on the balcony of the Lorraine Motel, April 3, 1968, the day before the assassination

to King, who recalled hearing him play a hymn, "Precious Lord, Take My Hand." He said, "I tell you tonight I want that song, I mean I want you to play it pretty. Don't forget. I mean it."

"Okay, Doc," Ben replied. "I will."

A shot rang out. A bullet tore into King's face. He collapsed to the balcony floor. Abernathy and Andrew Young ran to their beloved friend as he lay in a spreading pool of blood. He was rushed to St. Joseph's Hospital. Doctors tried but were unable to save him.

He died at five minutes past seven.

Later, Coretta wondered if he knew his death was near. The flowers he had sent her were made of silk. He'd never sent her anything but real flowers before. It was as if he meant these to last. Martin Luther King Jr. was thirty-nine years old.

CIVIL RIGHTS ACT THREE MONTHS AFTER KING'S DEATH, PRESIDENT LYNDON JOHNSON SIGNED THE CIVIL RIGHTS ACT OF 1968 INTO LAW. THE LAW IS ALSO KNOWN AS THE FAIR HOUSING ACT. IT WAS A DIRECT RESULT OF THOSE FIRST STEPS TAKEN IN CHICAGO ON WHAT KING CALLED A "1,000-MILE JOURNEY."

The family at
Dr. Martin Luther
King Jr.'s funeral

When the Threads
BREAK

24

The Assassins

Gandhi said, "My life is my message." King said, "I want you to say that I tried to love and serve humanity."

Both men lived by their beliefs. Both struggled to create change through nonviolence. Both tried to win over hatred with love. Both believed in hearing others even in the midst of disagreement. Both worked for solutions that made the world better for everyone. In the end, both fell to the bullets of assassins. In 1948, Nathuram Vinayak Godse fired his semiautomatic pistol point-blank into Gandhi's chest. Two decades later, in 1968, James Earl Ray shot and killed King.

POONA, INDIA
1910

What leads an ordinary boy to become a driven killer? In 1910, Nathuram Godse was born into a high-caste Brahmin family in Uksan village near the city of Poona (now Pune) in western India. His father worked for India's postal service.

The Godses' new baby was the first male child in many years to survive in the family. A soothsayer advised that to distract the evil eye and avert misfortune, they should pierce the baby's nose, a custom commonly followed for little girls. The family obeyed, fitting the baby with a tiny nose ring, called a *nath*. This gave him his name, Nathuram. Nathuram grew up being teased for his pierced nose.

The ring was removed when younger brothers came along. The family decided the curse had worn off, but the name stuck.

Nathuram took part in his religious family's traditional ceremonies. During one of them, a black spot was painted on a metal platter, and onlookers searched the pattern for visions. Nathuram stared so hard, he went into a trance and began speaking in a strange voice. Family members gasped. Surely that was the voice of one of the household gods! They decided Nathuram must be special indeed.

In school, Nathuram was taught in the Marathi language. He had a good memory and learned to recite verses from Hindu scriptures. Each morning, he said his prayers, following custom by saluting the sun. His Hindu faith seemed deeply grounded.

The adults in the family often talked about movements for India's independence from the British, and young Nathuram took it all in. Once, after a lecture about self-rule, he insisted his parents should stop using imported sugar at home.

He was a helpful child. When someone left on a trip, he would carry their bags to the bus stop. A good swimmer, he once jumped into a well to rescue a child who had fallen in.

When he came home, however, he was scolded for not taking a bath. The child was from the untouchable caste. Nathuram should purify himself. The incident troubled him. It showed him how the Hindu caste system divided people, one from another.

Nathuram was not a strong student and never completed his high school examinations. Yet he read poetry and even wrote some in his native Marathi.

When his father retired, Nathuram had to make money to supplement the family's income. Having no qualifications, he set up a tailor's shop, a lowly occupation for a high-caste Brahmin like him. Sewing did not bring in enough money, so he also sold fruit. His parents wanted him to marry, but Nathuram refused.

At nineteen, he met a man named Vinayak Savarkar, who encouraged Nathuram and taught him basic English. Nathuram joined the local chapter of a new militant Hindu group led by Savarkar, the

SAVARKAR AND GANDHI ONCE A LAWYER IN ENGLAND, VINAYAK SAVARKAR HAD BEEN BARRED FROM PRACTICING BECAUSE HE HAD PLOTTED AGAINST THE GOVERNMENT. ALTHOUGH THEY SHARED THE GOAL OF INDEPENDENCE FOR INDIA, SAVARKAR DESPISED GANDHI. HE HOPED TO LEAD A MILITANT FOLLOWING OF HINDUS WHO WOULD FIGHT TO REGAIN A PLACE OF GLORY FOR HINDUISM. HE HATED THE CONGRESS PARTY FOR ITS WILLINGNESS TO COMPROMISE. HE HATED MUSLIMS.

Hindu Mahasabha. *Mahasabha* means "great assembly." Its members wanted a Hindu nation in which Muslims and other non-Hindus were second-class citizens.

The Muslim League's call for a separate Pakistan enraged Hindu nationalists like Savarkar. It proved to them that Muslims were unfit

Nathuram Godse and Narayan Apte

to live in independent India; Gandhi's talk of brotherhood and coexistence was rubbish. Nathuram Godse, now fully immersed in Savarkar's teachings, moved to Poona to prepare for armed revolution. He became friends with a young man named Narayan Apte. They heckled and shouted at Congress meetings, especially when Gandhi spoke.

Before Gandhi's murder in 1948, five attempts had been made on his life—Godse was involved in at least three of them. In 1944, Godse led a protest against Gandhi in Panchgani, a hill town where Gandhi was resting after a bout of illness. Hearing of the protest, Gandhi invited the group to come and speak with him. They refused. That evening, Godse, dagger in hand, rushed toward Gandhi. He was overpowered by onlookers. Gandhi refused to press charges.

Later that year, Godse boasted that he'd stop Gandhi from meeting with Muslim League leader Muhammad Ali Jinnah. As Gandhi was leaving his ashram at Sevagram, Godse tried to get close to him. He was stopped and found to be carrying a dagger. The police took the dagger from him but let him go.

Two years later, while Gandhi was traveling by train, an alert train driver spotted boulders on the tracks ahead. He slowed down. He couldn't avoid hitting the rocks, but his quick thinking averted a tragedy and no lives were lost.

Then on January 30, 1948, Godse came up to his victim, folded his hands in the traditional greeting, namaste. He then gripped his pistol and fired into Gandhi's chest.

Godse was pushed toward the police, who seemed temporarily stunned. A gardener hit the assassin with the blunt edge of his sickle. People grappled Godse to the ground. Forgetting nonviolence, they beat him, bloodying his face before the police finally arrested him.

The trial was held at the Red Fort in Delhi, a towering seventeenth-century sandstone fortress. One hundred forty-seven witnesses testified.

In all, there were nine conspirators. One was pardoned in exchange for cooperating with government prosecutors. Eight were found guilty. When they appealed, two more were acquitted. One was Savarkar, Gandhi's old adversary, deemed not guilty for lack of evidence. Of the rest, four were sentenced to life imprisonment. Only Apte and Godse were found guilty of murder and sentenced to death. Vallabhbhai Patel, who had conversed with Gandhi until minutes before his death, remained convinced

Failed Assassination Attempts
Why was no one arrested for the failed attempts to kill Gandhi? In those days, police departments in different provinces and cities did not always share news with one another.

Moreover, Gandhi himself refused to charge his attackers. He refused additional security. He did not let visitors be searched. Of his would-be assassins, he said, "They are children. They do not understand now. When I am dead then they will remember that what the old man said was right."

Birla House, 2009, the site of Gandhi's assassination

all his life that Savarkar had hatched the plot that killed Mahatma Gandhi.

At the appeals trial, Godse defended his actions in a nine-hour speech. His eloquence moved some, but it did not change the judges' minds about his guilt. The court rejected further appeals.

Gandhi's sons, Manilal and Ramdas Gandhi, asked Prime Minister Jawaharlal Nehru to pardon the men. That was what Gandhi would have wanted. Their requests were ignored. In November 1949, Narayan Apte and Nathuram Godse were executed by hanging.

The Assassin's Ashes

When Hindus die, their bodies are cremated. The ashes are scattered into flowing water. Gandhi's assassin's last wish was that his ashes be immersed in the Indus River. He wanted his ashes scattered only when his dream of an undivided India came true. Decades later, India and Pakistan remain two nations. The silver urn containing Nathuram Vinayak Godse's ashes continues to sit in a realty office owned by a relative, in a crowded area of the city of Pune (previously Poona). Even today, there are people in India who feel that by supporting Muslims, Gandhi betrayed Hindus. In their eyes, Godse was a patriot and a hero.

ILLINOIS, USA
1928

James Earl Ray was born in 1928, in a rented room in the poorest, roughest part of the town of Alton, Illinois. His father, George Ray, was an ex-convict who used many aliases; his father's brother, Earl, spent most of his life in prison. James's mother, Lucille, nicknamed "Ceal," was a quiet woman whose own father had abandoned the family when she was young.

The Rays moved often as George tried unsuccessfully to find work. Then he got arrested for forgery. On his release, they all moved again. Mary Maher, Ceal's mother, had managed to scrape enough together to buy the family a plot of scrubby land near Ewing, Missouri, with no electricity or running water. Poor white people scratched out a living in the area. No Blacks lived in town. It was Ku Klux Klan country.

The Rays now had four children and little money. When James Earl, known as "Jimmy," started school, he arrived barefoot and in torn clothes.

Even as a child, Jimmy had a temper. At recess, he got into fights. He often missed school and flunked first grade. His report card noted a poor "attitude toward regulations . . . violates all of them." Of his appearance, an unsympathetic teacher wrote: "Repulsive."

Two years after the move to Ewing, Jimmy's younger sister Marjorie was playing outside the house, apparently by herself. Suddenly, she ran in, screaming, with her dress, her hair, her whole body on fire. She had been playing with matches and died the next day. The tragedy drove Jimmy's mother to start drinking heavily. Their poverty was desperate. When they needed firewood, the family simply dismantled their house board by board and burned it, patching a one-room shack together to take its place.

By the time Jimmy was in third grade, he had nightmares, stuttered, and wet his bed. He slept poorly, twitching so much that one doctor thought he had epilepsy.

Jimmy had a few friends, none of them close. A teacher, Virgil Graves, found him a "somewhat disturbed child," but felt he had a sensitive side. Graves let Jimmy stay in at recess to listen to the news on the school's only radio. As a result, Jimmy developed an interest in politics. His brother John recalled that Jimmy was sympathetic to Hitler. He believed that Roosevelt was lying when he said that Hitler posed a threat to the world.

Jimmy was fourteen when he had his first encounter with the law. He and his brother John, then eleven, gathered a stack of newspapers that had been tossed off a truck and tried to sell them. They were picked up by the police and released to their mother with a warning. Jimmy traveled back and forth to Quincy, Illinois, a small, segregated town where his paternal grandparents lived. Here, his uncle Earl introduced him to gamblers and criminals. When Earl was jailed for assault, Jimmy lost his mentor in crime.

In May 1944, Jimmy, who now went by his given name, James, dropped out of eighth grade and moved back to Alton. There, he found a job at a shoe company tannery. He worked overtime, saved his seventy-seven cents an hour, and planned to open a gas station. A friend at work, Henry Stumm, told James he owned a picture of Adolf Hitler. He said he knew him personally. James was excited to think that if Hitler won the war, he would make the United States an all-white country, ridding it of Black and Jewish people.

When World War II ended, the company no longer needed to make shoes for the military and James lost his job. He was crushed. It was just before Christmas. All through winter, he tried to find work— and failed.

Though the war was over, the U.S. Army was still recruiting. James joined up, asking to be posted to Germany. His brother Jerry thought he planned to support the defeated Nazis. In the army, James began drinking and using drugs. Within two years, he was discharged for "drunken behavior" and "ineptness and lack of adaptability to military service."

James Earl Ray returned home to a family racked by poverty and alcoholism, with no one to help him pick up the threads of his life. He wandered to Chicago, Colorado, and then Los Angeles, where he threw himself into a life of crime. His first attempts were botched. Surprised during a burglary, he fled the scene, losing his army discharge papers and a bank passbook in a scuffle with a parking lot attendant. When he returned to the scene a few days later, the attendant recognized him and called the police. Ray was charged with robbery and convicted, but released for good behavior after ninety days.

He took off for Las Vegas next, stealing money from a Chinese restaurant on his way. Restless, unable to keep a job, he ended up back in Chicago, where he robbed a cabdriver at gunpoint, stealing a paltry eleven dollars. He was cornered and shot by police. His wounds dressed, he was tried and convicted, and served time in jail. Between arrests, he crisscrossed the states from Illinois to Texas and back, with stints across the border in Mexico and Canada. In 1959, James, along with a couple of ex-con accomplices, took part in a spree of robberies in St. Louis. Following the armed robbery of a supermarket, he was arrested and convicted, and received a twenty-year sentence.

Prison inmates and guards alike noticed that he hated Black people. He talked about moving to another country. Australia was high on his list because he thought there were no Black people there.

A fellow convict talked to James about killing Martin Luther King. After all, businesses affected by the civil rights movement's boycotts might find it worth their while to have King killed. James boasted he'd do the job if the price was right.

James Earl Ray tried repeatedly to escape from prison. His first attempt was right after sentencing, when he tried to jump into a courthouse elevator. Over the next eight years, he tried twice more and was caught. Finally, in 1967, while working in the bakery at the Missouri State Penitentiary, Ray had himself packed into a three-foot-by-four-foot metal box with a false bottom. Loaves of bread were stacked on top, and the box was loaded onto the truck. Once the truck stopped outside the prison grounds, Ray leaped out. Now he was a fugitive from the law.

BUNGLED SEARCHES THE SEARCH ATTEMPT FOR JAMES EARL RAY WAS BUNGLED BY DELAYS. THE FIRST REWARD FLYER POSTED AFTER THE MISSOURI ESCAPE INCLUDED AN OLD PHOTOGRAPH, OLD ADDRESSES, AND THE WRONG SET OF FINGERPRINTS. IT WAS PRACTICALLY USELESS.

Walking for six days, he ended up in Chicago with swollen and blistered feet. He took a dishwashing job under a false name. But he had a big plan, and soon he contacted his brothers to share it. He was going to kill Martin Luther King Jr. His brothers tried to talk him out of it.

Throughout 1967, Ray kept on the move—Chicago, then across the Canadian border to Toronto and Montreal. Along the way, he robbed cabdrivers and stole money orders. Back in the United States, he bought a car, using the proceeds of an Illinois bank robbery for which he was never caught. He drove to Mexico and spent a month there before returning north to Los Angeles. He'd heard that former Alabama governor George Wallace was running for president on a platform of segregation. Ray volunteered for his campaign.

Early in 1968, James Earl Ray had plastic surgery that changed his profile and reduced the size of his nose. He wrote, "I got the surgery to change my facial features so it would be harder to identify me." Although he was offered a bartending job, he turned it down and drove across the country, first to Atlanta, Georgia, and then to Birmingham, Alabama. He bought a rifle and a telescopic sight to mount on it. Spotting a story in the *Atlanta Constitution* about King's planned visit to Memphis, Tennessee, Ray packed a bag and headed to Memphis.

In Memphis, a pair of two-story buildings connected by a covered walkway stood across the street from the Lorraine Motel. Stores occupied the ground floor. Upstairs were rooms for rent. On April 4, the motel manager opened her door to a white man in his thirties, with dark hair, blue eyes, and a thin nose, who wanted a room for rent by the week. He gave his name as John Willard and paid in cash. His bland smile unnerved her.

Still calling himself Willard, the man bought an expensive pair of binoculars from the York Arms Company on Main Street. He seemed unsure how to use them. Neighbors saw a white Mustang pull in and park near the rooming house. A tenant was annoyed by the man in 5B who spent all his time in the common bathroom and flushed only once.

Then came the shot. Witnesses later said that before the shooting, they'd seen a man clutching a long, skinny object hurry along the hallway in the rooming house. A package nearby was found to contain a rifle and binoculars with Ray's fingerprints on them.

Two hundred thousand FBI posters were plastered across the country and in Canada. Spanish versions were posted in Mexico. A sharp-eyed officer of the Royal Canadian Mounted Police, examining thousands of Canadian passport applications, spotted one that matched the picture of James Earl Ray, despite his plastic surgery. The application was from a man named Ramon George Sneyd. The real Ramon Sneyd was a police officer in Toronto. Handwriting experts matched the signature on the application with a passport Ray had obtained under yet another false name.

The trail led all the way to Heathrow Airport in London, England, where Ray was arrested for carrying a firearm without a license. He claimed he was traveling to Africa. Instead, he found himself strapped into a seat on board a U.S. Air Force jet, bound for a naval air base in Millington, Tennessee, eighteen miles from Memphis. Upon arrival, he was taken right to the city's criminal courts building, where cellblock A had been specially secured for his arrival.

The day before he turned forty-one, James Earl Ray agreed to plead to the crime of killing Martin Luther King Jr. He confessed but then began to ramble. He disagreed with the prosecution, with the U.S. attorney general, Ramsey Clark, and with the FBI director, J. Edgar Hoover, all of whom accused him of acting alone. Was Ray hinting at a conspiracy, or was he trying to get out of his guilty plea? Judge Preston Battle reiterated his original question: "Are you pleading guilty of murder in the first degree in this case . . . ?" Ray nodded and mumbled a reply. He was sentenced to ninety-nine years without parole.

Later, Ray tried to recant his confession, saying his lawyer had made him plead guilty to avoid the death penalty. His story shifted. He contradicted himself. In an odd twist, members of the King family became convinced of James Earl Ray's innocence. Rumors abounded that the FBI or the Central Intelligence Agency or both were behind the assassination and that James had simply been a pawn in a larger conspiracy. Dr. King's son Dexter visited Ray in prison. Dexter King and Coretta Scott King called for a new, full-scale inquiry into the case. It never came to pass. Ray stayed incarcerated.

A brief escape from Brushy Mountain State Prison, Tennessee, and recapture within fifty-four hours added a year to his sentence. A final escape attempt was unsuccessful. In 1998, at the Lois M. DeBerry Special Needs Facility in Nashville, Tennessee, James Earl Ray died of kidney disease complications and liver failure. He was seventy years old.

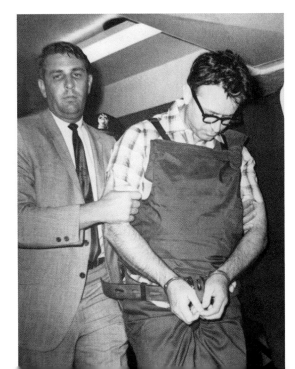

James Earl Ray's arrest photo

289

25

Spinning
New Threads of Peace

To spin thread on a spinning wheel like the one Gandhi designed when he was in jail, you begin with a roll of fluffy, carded cotton. In the Hindi language, this is called a *pooni*. You attach the pooni to a length of thread looped around a small metal spindle. You hold the fluffy cotton loosely in one hand and draw it slowly, outward and upward, to arm's length. With your other hand, you turn a flat wheel. A few turns clockwise, then a quarter turn counterclockwise, over and over, until the rhythm takes hold of you and you no longer have to think about it.

It takes patience. It takes time. Each hand has to learn to do its work without getting distracted.

At first, the cotton drifts apart. The yarn is not twisted enough. Then it's twisted too tightly. It breaks. The spindle falls off its course. The cord that drives the spinning wheel slips from its groove. But slowly, slowly, if you keep at it, the thousands of fibers contained within

Growing a Movement, Breaking the Law

Vasant Vasudev Gurjar (1916–2019) said, "When I was fourteen, I left school and began breaking the law. They sent me to jail." Gurjar, among the thousands of Indians who joined the nonviolent struggle for India's independence, went to jail four times. The first time he came home after serving a month's sentence, his father, a school principal, was furious and refused to let him back in the house. "You left school," his father said. "Now go to Gandhi's school." Young Vasant did.

On his 100th birthday, Vasant Gurjar was honored in a special ceremony held at the home of the president of India. "It was the best year of my life," he said.

a single handful of cotton begin to twist around one another, becoming one, united and strong enough to endure. The cotton springs to life, and a thread begins to form! Only inches of it, but it is real cotton thread.

The threads of peace movements are like that. They continue to spin outward over and over, long after they have been created.

In April 1968, after Dr. King's assassination, the *Chicago Sun-Times* published this cartoon:

Look at Gandhi, seated on the floor, his hand outstretched, making his point to an attentive Dr. King. You'd think they were old friends. There they are in this alternate reality, perhaps even in the

Cartoon by Bill Mauldin, Chicago Sun-Times, 1968

"THE ODD THING ABOUT ASSASSINS, DR. KING, IS THAT THEY THINK THEY'VE KILLED YOU."

artist's imagined heaven, reminding us that the voices of peacemakers can resonate long after they are gone.

Although they never met, Gandhi and King were kindred spirits. Gandhi was aware of racial injustice in the United States and hoped that Black Americans would create their own nonviolent movement.

Martin Luther King Jr. read books by and about Gandhi. He knew people who had met Gandhi. Gandhi's teaching supported King's own beliefs that grew out of the love of family, of community, of Jesus. King integrated Gandhian methods and principles into the work of his life, much as he did with the Christian gospel.

Gandhi's word, "nonviolence," is familiar to us all. With all the violence, bloodshed, and warfare running through human history, his usage of it, as a principle or practice of abstaining from violence, is only one hundred years old. Is that because nonviolence does not come easily to people? In the face of conflict, human beings, like other animals, instinctively tend to either fight or flee. Facing conflict calmly and with resolution calls for a special kind of courage.

When individuals show that kind of courage, we are tempted to idealize them, to treat them as if they were more than human. For many years following Gandhi's assassination, Indians regarded him as a kind of saint. In 2012, the United Methodist Church declared Martin Luther King Jr. a *martyr*, someone who had sacrificed his life for Jesus Christ. In truth, neither Gandhi nor King was perfect. Each struggled to find his path. Each made mistakes.

Nor should we credit the success of great movements entirely to single heroic figures. King was not the only one following Gandhi's example. Black-owned newspapers from the 1920s on had made a point of studying the Indian movement against British rule, even appointing special correspondents to India. Scholars like W. E. B. Du Bois, Howard Thurman, and Benjamin Mays had long believed that Gandhian methods could help the cause of racial justice in America. Poet Langston Hughes, sometimes critical of Gandhi, nonetheless took note of his life and actions. In his poem "Gandhi Is Fasting," Hughes compared the oppression of Indians to that of Black Americans. Both, in his words, were "jim crowed."

Vast numbers of leaders in the American civil rights movement, as well as Dr. King, deliberately and thoughtfully followed Gandhi's ideals and employed his methods. In this way, those ideals and methods not only stayed alive, but were energized and reshaped in the United States, through bus boycotts and lunch counter sit-ins, freedom rides and marches for human rights.

Protest works only when large numbers of people embrace it and brave its perils. At the very start of the bus boycott, the Black population of Montgomery showed a remarkable capacity for weaving resistance and nonviolence together in their actions. Famous as well as ordinary people worked as sisters and brothers in a common cause. Against all odds, they refused to give up. As the civil rights movement gathered momentum and more and more people joined it, the old, unjust laws were eventually dismantled and new ones framed in their place. In the process, the country was changed forever. No matter what political tides might rise and fall in the future, racial segregation and inequality were no longer encoded in American law.

Yet in 1968, King's murder left many people feeling angry and disillusioned. Riots broke out in American cities, hitting especially hard

Firefighters spraying water on shops burned during the riots that followed the assassination of Martin Luther King Jr.

in Baltimore, Washington, and Chicago. The fragile threads of peace threatened to snap.

On the night King was killed, on April 4, 1968, in Indianapolis, Robert F. Kennedy spoke passionately about two assassinations—King's and his brother's. He said, "What we need in the United States is not division; what we need in the United States is not hatred; what we need in the United States is not violence or lawlessness, but love and wisdom, and compassion toward one another, and a feeling of

ROBERT F. KENNEDY IN YET ANOTHER TRAGIC TURN OF EVENTS, ON JUNE 6, 1968, BARELY TWO MONTHS AFTER HE GAVE THAT STIRRING SPEECH, ROBERT KENNEDY HIMSELF WAS SHOT AND KILLED BY AN ASSASSIN. AT THE TIME, HE WAS RUNNING FOR THE DEMOCRATIC NOMINATION FOR PRESIDENT OF THE UNITED STATES.

justice towards those who still suffer within our country, whether they be white or whether they be black." Many listeners felt that Robert Kennedy's speech helped avert riots in Indianapolis.

In America today, racial inequality persists. In 2018, more than 90 percent of younger African Americans (ages twenty-five to twenty-nine) were high school graduates, compared with just over 50 percent in 1968. College graduation rates have also improved, yet the unemployment rate for Black workers remains twice as high as for whites.

Black Americans vote in growing numbers, but a 2013 Supreme Court ruling weakened the Voting Rights Act by striking out two key provisions that allowed the federal government to oversee how states run their elections. As a result, in the years since, many states have once again begun to impose restrictions on voting. Today's restrictions aren't poll taxes or literacy tests. They take other forms—they might require certain kinds of photo IDs, for example, or limit early or absentee voting, alter the boundaries of electoral districts in favor of a single political party, or block community groups from conducting voter registration drives.

Today in the United States, school segregation is illegal. But because many communities nationwide remain segregated, Black kids are still more likely to find themselves in neighborhoods with mostly Black schools and white kids in neighborhoods with mostly white

Sections 4 and 5 of the Voting Rights Act
Section 5 was a key provision of the Voting Rights Act of 1965. It required that if states with a history of discrimination wanted to change their electoral rules, they needed to first get "preclearance" from the federal government. Section 4 laid out the states and localities covered by Section 5.

In 2013, the Supreme Court eliminated Section 4, freeing up states to change their electoral rules as they wish, without federal oversight.

ones. Today, Black people are still more likely than whites to be shot and killed by police and to be incarcerated. The Ku Klux Klan still exists.

Police violence against Black people has given rise to Black Lives Matter—a hashtag, an organization, and a movement using the Internet to mobilize vast numbers of people in overwhelmingly peaceful demonstrations. Decades after the death of Martin Luther King Jr., it seems past time for America to come to terms with the brutal history and the unjust legacy of slavery.

Even the COVID-19 pandemic wrought deadlier damage upon Black and other racial and ethnic minority communities than white ones—more illness and more deaths. Perhaps people in those communities were poorer and more likely to have underlying health problems, such as diabetes or heart disease. After all, the conditions in which we live, learn, work, and play affect our health.

What of King's vision of the beloved community in which all people are equal and free, where justice prevails and human beings love and respect one another? Today, it is needed more than ever.

In India, Mahatma Gandhi's statues are everywhere, yet his vision of peace and love remains a dream. Hindus and Muslims in India remain divided. Kashmir is still a fiercely disputed land. For many years after independence, the Congress Party won national elections and governed the country. Its administrations were dogged by corruption and scandals, leading to the rise of strong opposition parties. The chief of these, the Bharatiya Janata Party, or BJP, is now in power. The current BJP leader, Narendra Modi, has been twice elected as prime minister. Many people accuse Modi of being against Muslims. Others say that he merely speaks for the Hindu majority. On his watch, dissenters have been harassed by police. Hate speech against journalists and minorities, especially Muslims, has been tolerated. Violence continues as well today against Muslims, Dalits, and women. The truth is, politicians in India, like politicians everywhere, want votes. If they can exploit religious hatred to get votes, many do.

Will we human beings ever rise beyond our violent instincts? Every continent has seen the rise of governments claiming strong central power and limiting the rights of their citizens. Violent groups use the mask of religion to stage and encourage terrorist attacks around the world. White supremacist groups exist across the United States and in many other countries as well. Around the world, political parties have risen to power on platforms of suspicion and distrust aimed at minorities and foreigners. And far from working toward King's dream of global peace, many nations of the world spend billions, even trillions of dollars each year on the development and maintenance of nuclear weapons.

Will the cycles of violence never end?

Perhaps the answer to that question lies in understanding that peace is a journey we can choose to undertake, as millions did in Gandhi's time and King's. Peacemakers live and work around the world in our time as well, embracing causes such as racial and ethnic discrimination, the rights of women and girls, education, humane treatment for refugees, press freedom, school safety, free and fair elections, and climate change.

Human beings are fallible. We can be kind or cruel, truthful or deceitful, moral or immoral. At some moments in history, whole societies can express values of justice, compassion, and open-mindedness. At other times, those very societies can turn toward injustice, indifference, and bigotry. Gandhi is quoted as saying, "I have nothing new to teach the world. Truth and nonviolence are as old as the hills." But so are falsehood and violence, which is why the waging of peace is a task without end.

Mahatma Gandhi and Reverend King envisioned peaceful societies with no room for hatred and disharmony. In their vision, peace is far greater than the mere absence of war or conflict. In their vision, peace walks hand in hand with justice and truth.

In response to each man's words and actions, millions of people answered the call, even at risk to their own lives. Millions took

extraordinary actions and suffered great hardships to keep threads of peace, truth, and justice spinning out into the world. Their collective work remains unfinished, waiting for each new generation to reinvent it, reshape it to new needs, and carry it on.

(Left) The memorial crypts of Dr. Martin Luther King Jr. and Coretta Scott King, in the reflecting pool of the King Center's Freedom Hall Complex, Atlanta, Georgia. The biblical verse inscribed on Mrs. King's crypt is the same one that Gandhi quoted to the Thurmans.

(Below) Rose garden at the Martin Luther King Jr. National Historic Site, near the King Center. The plaques feature children's poems about peace, freedom, and justice.

Author's Note

Some years ago, my mother gave me her old autograph book, with Mahatma Gandhi's signature on the first page. In her youth, she'd met him and had attended his prayer meetings in New Delhi, India. I took care of the precious gift, of course, but I never intended to write a book about Gandhi. Then, in 2008, I read *The End of Empires: African Americans and India* by historian and African American studies professor Gerald Horne. It was an eye-opener. I was born in India and I'd lived in the United States for nearly thirty years, but in neither country had I ever learned this history! Over the next several years, I read everything I could find about the connections in Dr. Horne's book. Among the books that shaped my thinking were *Visions of a Better World* by Quinton Dixie and Peter Eisenstadt, and *Transnational Roots of the Civil Rights Movement* by Sean Chabot.

By the time I got to Martin Luther King's *Autobiography*, a narrative began to form in my mind around the lives of two men. Two lives, unfolding on different continents, divided by both time and place, yet speaking to the world with a kind of singular urgency. I began to pore over King's writings, seeking to find both the flowering and the transformation of Gandhi's ideas and methods. In Gandhi's footsteps, I visited Sabarmati and the Aga Khan Palace; in King's, Montgomery,

Atlanta, and Boston. I bought a spinning wheel and cotton so I could feel the flawed, straggly threads emerging between my own inept fingers. I began to write drafts, many of them, drawing courage from my mother's autograph book that contained the spidery lines of Gandhi's signature. Then the COVID-19 pandemic exploded around us. George Floyd's death evoked raw memories of all those Black people who had died before him at the hands of police. People of all races thronged the streets, demanding justice. The protests spread worldwide, remaining largely peaceful. I began to see King's legacy and Gandhi's taking on new meaning, endlessly capable of being rewoven into new narratives against discrimination and injustice.

Japanese poet Yone Noguchi said, when he met Gandhi in 1935, "Without love and sympathy, you cannot give a correct picture of a people." Love and sympathy. Writing this book has made me reflect upon what it means to dedicate one's life to the pursuit of freedom and justice while holding stubbornly fast to impossible ideals of peace and love. It's a complex mix, like life itself. In this writing, I hope I've served it well.

Uma Krishnaswami learning to spin at Sabarmati Ashram.

Acknowledgments

I'm grateful to Virat Kothari and Kinnari Bhatt of the Sabarmati Ashram Preservation and Memorial Trust, Arun Gandhi for his kind encouragement, Joel Silverman for sharing his memories of growing up in Nashville, Pahlad Ramsurrun, Neelam Mahajan, and the late Vasant V. Gurjar. To Ninad and Gowri Mate, Anand Dani, and the late Saroj Dani. To Dr. Sean Chabot, Dr. Quinton Dixie, and Dr. Ramachandra Guha—deepest appreciation for expert opinions and insights regarding this work.

For help in obtaining photographs as well as permission to publish them, I must thank Peter Barr; Catherine Champion of Birmingham Public Library; Roger de la Harpe; Sujata Godbole; Anna Jedrzejowski at the Ryerson Image Centre; Angela Kepler of the Pritzker Military Museum and Library; Jonathan Gordon of the Bill Mauldin Estate; Spider Martin's daughter, Tracy Martin; Celia Pilkington, archivist at the Inner Temple; photographer Rowland Scherman; Scott Sanders of Antioch College; and Gary Truman of the Flip Schulke Archives. I especially want to thank Linda Stanley for her kindness and enthusiasm about my project, as well as for permission to reprint the work of her late husband, Vernon Merritt III. Special thanks to Andrea Morrison, Wendolyne Sabrozo, and Eric Tidwell.

As always, I'm grateful to my Autodidacts: Stephanie Farrow, Katherine Hauth, Mark Karlins, Vaunda Micheaux Nelson, and Caroline Starr Rose. To Betsy Partridge and Shelley Tanaka, who taught me so much about the art and craft of nonfiction. To Saadia Faruqi. To my students and colleagues at Vermont College of Fine Arts and my agent, Ginger Knowlton.

Blessed be the copyeditors who scour a writer's work for errors, omissions, misplaced punctuation marks, and unintended bloopers— Cindy Nixon, Clare McGlade, and Mandy Veloso, this means you. Thanks as well to Alexandria Borbolla, Michael McCartney, and Irene Metaxatos. Caitlyn Dlouhy, your editorial letters were my beacons in this work. You taught me to trust my instincts while rendering this complicated history of peaceful resistance accessible to young people. I'm forever in your debt.

To my mother, Vasantha Krishnaswami, for the stories and photographs that planted the seeds for this work. To my son, Nikhil Krishnaswamy, for help with etymological questions. Finally, Satish Shrikhande, thanks always, for everything.

I knew I'd need pictures. What I didn't expect was that each picture I found would have a story of its own. Each would be carefully curated, titled, and preserved by someone who cared about the history I was trying to understand. I began to recognize the work of certain photographers: the way they saw scenes, employed light, or rushed to snap a fleeting moment. Sometimes a photograph and its story filled a gap or brightened my text; sometimes it gave me material for a sidebar. Mostly the images made me aware of the delicate and complicated interweaving of the stories that make up history.

Threads Through Time: A TIMELINE OF EVENTS MENTIONED IN THIS BOOK

GANDHI'S LIFE AND RELATED EVENTS

1857: Rebellion against British rule in India brutally crushed

1860s: First Indian indentured laborers brought to South Africa

1869: Mohandas Karamchand Gandhi born in Porbandar, present-day Gujarat

1876: Young Mohandas begins school

1880: Takes high school entrance test

1883: Marries Kastur Kapadia

1887: Bombay University exam

1888: First son, Harilal, born; Gandhi leaves for London

1891: Qualifies as lawyer in London; returns to India

1892: Second son, Manilal, born

1893: Gandhi thrown off train in South Africa

1894: Founds Natal Indian Congress

1896: Returns to India; meets leaders of Indian National Congress

1897: Third son, Ramdas, born

1899: Forms Indian Ambulance Corps during Boer War

1900: Fourth son, Devadas, born

1904: Joins plague relief in Indian settlement in South Africa; establishes Phoenix Settlement

1906: Organizes first large-scale nonviolent resistance to Indian registration laws in South Africa: satyagraha

1908-9: Multiple arrests for disobeying registration laws

1910: Gandhi assassin, Nathuram Godse, born

1913: Marches in support of Indian coal miners—arrested three times

1914: Returns to India; start of WWI

KING'S LIFE AND RELATED EVENTS

1865: 13th amendment to the U.S. Constitution abolishes slavery

1928: King's assassin, James Earl Ray, born

1929: Michael King born in Atlanta, GA

1934: Name changed to Martin Luther King Jr.

1944: At 15, Martin makes winning speech in Dublin, GA; enters Morehouse College

1948: Ordained assistant pastor in his father's church; receives BA degree at Morehouse; enters Crozer Theological Seminary

1950: Attends Mordecai Johnson's lecture on Gandhi in Philadelphia

1951: Graduates from Crozer; begins studies at Boston University

1953: Marries Coretta Scott

1954: Pastor at Dexter Avenue Baptist Church, Montgomery, AL; in *Brown v. Board of Education*, U.S. Supreme Court rules racial segregation in public schools unconstitutional

1955: Doctorate from Boston University; first child, Yolanda Denise, born; King invited to lead Montgomery bus boycott

1956: Threatening phone call; Kings' house bombed; U.S. Supreme Court rules bus segregation laws unconstitutional; King rides first desegregated bus

1957: Appears on cover of *Time* magazine; co-founds SCLC; attends independence celebrations in Ghana; second child, Martin Luther III, born; meets James Lawson, who read about King in a newspaper in India

1958: Publishes *Stride Toward Freedom*; survives attack at book signing

1959: Month-long visit to India, following in Gandhi's footsteps

1915: Awarded Kaiser-i-Hind medal for work with the Indian Ambulance Corps

1917: Establishes Sabarmati Ashram in Ahmedabad

1918: End of WWI

1919: Rowlatt Act gives sweeping powers to British government in India; massacre in Jallianwala Bagh

1920: Launches Non-cooperation Movement; coins a new usage for the word "nonviolence"

1922: Halts movement; fasts when violence breaks out

1924: First fast for Hindu-Muslim unity

1930: Leads Salt March

1931: Sails to England to attend Round Table Conference

1932-33: Arrests; fasts against untouchability

1934: Bombing, failed attack on Gandhi

1935: Howard Thurman and delegation travel to India and meet with Gandhi

1939: Britain declares war on Germany, start of WWII

1942: Britain proposes giving India partial independence, rejected by Gandhi and Congress; Gandhi arrested

1943: Fasts, protesting detention without charges by the British

1944: Death of Kasturba Gandhi; two failed attempts on Gandhi's life

1945: United States drops nuclear bomb on Japanese cities; end of WWII

1946: Failed attempt to derail Gandhi's train

1947: Second Hindu-Muslim unity fast; partition of India; independence of India and formation of Pakistan

1948: Third and last fast for Hindu-Muslim unity; bombing attempt at prayer meeting; assassination

1968: 20th anniversary of Gandhi's assassination

1960: Moves to Atlanta, becomes assistant pastor to his father; donates farewell gift from congregation; nonviolence speech to inaugural SNCC conference; cross burned on Kings' front lawn; meets with presidential candidate John F. Kennedy; arrested during sit-in demonstration

1961: Third child, Dexter Scott, born; King addresses mass rally after assault on Freedom Riders; meets with President Kennedy; arrested in Albany, GA

1962: Arrested, spends two weeks in jail; assaulted by member of American Nazi Party

1963: Fourth child, Bernice Albertine, born; King arrested, writes "Letter from Birmingham Jail"; brutal police attack on Children's March; speech at March on Washington for Jobs and Freedom; eulogy for children killed at the Sixteenth Street Baptist Church bombing; President Kennedy assassinated; FBI wiretaps King's phone

1964: Named Man of the Year by Time magazine; meets Malcolm X; arrested in St. Augustine, FL; President Lyndon B. Johnson signs Civil Rights Act; King denounced by head of FBI; receives Nobel Peace Prize

1965: Bloody Sunday; death of Jimmie Lee Jackson; Selma to Montgomery March; President Johnson signs the Voting Rights Act

1966: King and family move to Chicago; King co-leads support for James Meredith's March Against Fear

1967: Speaks against Vietnam War

1968: Goes to Memphis, TN, to support sanitation workers' strike; final speech; assassination

THREADS OF LANGUAGE: A GLOSSARY

This list contains a selection of words significant to the lives of Mahatma Gandhi and Dr. Martin Luther King Jr. and to the movements of which they were a part.

Afrikaans: a modified form of Dutch, spoken in South Africa.

agape: an ancient Greek and early Christian concept; a higher kind of love, different from romantic love or love for a brother or sister; love for God and for all humankind.

ahimsa: Sanskrit, from Hindu philosophy; doing no harm or injury to a living being.

ashram: Sanskrit word for a place of religious or spiritual retreat or sanctuary.

Bania: term used in northern and western India for someone who is part of the trading or merchant caste.

Bhagavad Gita: Hindu sacred text; ancient Indian work of literature and philosophy.

Boer War: war in South Africa (1899–1902) between the Republic of Transvaal and the Orange Free State on one side and Great Britain and its colonies on the other.

boycott: refuse to cooperate with a person, group, or organization; refuse to participate in a policy, event, or process. Boycotting someone or something is aimed at changing the behavior of the targeted person or group.

caste: hereditary class of Hindu society; from the Portuguese word *casta*, meaning "lineage" or "race."

charkha: a hand-operated domestic spinning wheel, used mainly for cotton (Hindi/Urdu).

civil disobedience: a peaceful form of political protest; refusing to comply with laws considered unjust by the protesters.

Civil War: war in the U.S. between the northern states (known as the Union) and the southern Confederate States of America, 1861–65.

colonialism: policy or practice of acquiring political control over another country, occupying it with settlers, and exploiting it economically.

coolie: name originally given by Europeans in India and China to a native hired laborer; in South Africa, a derogatory term for all people from India.

Dalit: member of the lowest social group in the traditional Hindu caste system (also known as "untouchable").

dhoti: a seamless garment for men, wrapped around the body from the waist down (Hindi).

diwan: before Indian independence, title given to the prime minister or chief executive serving the ruler of a princely state in India.

emancipation: in U.S. history, refers to the Emancipation Proclamation, signed by President Abraham Lincoln, ordering the freeing of slaves in the Confederate States as of January 1, 1863.

Gandhian: of or pertaining to Gandhi; a follower of Gandhi.

Gujarati: a native or inhabitant of the western Indian state of Gujarat; the language of Gujarat.

Hindi: the dominant language of northern India, with numerous dialects; the fourth most widely spoken language in the world.

indentured labor: the system of binding workers by contract to work for a set period for a landowner in a British colony, often in exchange for passage to the colony.

Jim Crow laws: state and local laws that enforced racial segregation in the Southern United States.

Ku Klux Klan: American white supremacist hate group. Although African Americans have primarily been the Klan's target, it has also attacked Jews, immigrants, members of the LGBTQ community, and, until recently, Catholics.

namaste: traditional Hindu greeting, conveying respect

nonviolence: the use of peaceful means to bring about social or political change.

partition: refers to the partition of India in 1947, when an act of the Parliament of the United Kingdom divided British India into two independent dominion states, India and Pakistan.

poll tax: a fixed tax levied on every eligible individual as a precondition to voting in an election.

Quran: Muslim religious text; the sacred book of Islam.

Raj: Hindi word for British rule in India.

sari: women's garment worn in India and other South Asian countries, consisting of a length of cotton or silk elaborately pleated and draped.

satyagraha: Gandhi's policy of nonviolent resistance; from Sanskrit satya (truth) and agraha (a strong or eager inclination).

segregation: the enforced separation of different groups in a country or community (e.g., caste segregation in India, racial segregation in the United States).

sepoy: an Indian soldier serving under British orders.

sit-in: a form of protest in which demonstrators occupy a place, refusing to leave until their demands are met.

typhoid: an infectious bacterial disease resulting in fever, spots on the body, and severe intestinal irritation.

untouchable: see *Dalit*.

Urdu: a language closely related to Hindi, written in the Persian script, with loanwords from Persian and Arabic; the official language of Pakistan.

viceroy: an official who runs a country or colony in the name of and as the representative of the ruling monarch (adj. viceregal).

vigilante: a member of a self-appointed group of citizens who undertake law enforcement without legal authority.

BIBLIOGRAPHY

Arnold, Sir Edwin. *The Song Celestial: A Poetic Version of the Bhagavad Gita.* New York: Truslove, Hanson & Comba, Ltd., 1900.

Branch, Taylor. *At Canaan's Edge: America in the King Years, 1965–68.* New York: Simon & Schuster, 2006.

———. *Parting the Waters: America in the King Years, 1954–63.* New York: Simon & Schuster, 1988.

———. *Pillar of Fire: America in the King Years, 1963–65.* New York: Simon & Schuster, 1998.

Caro, Robert A. *Master of the Senate: The Years of Lyndon Johnson III.* New York: Knopf, 2002.

Carson, Clayborne, ed. *The Autobiography of Martin Luther King, Jr.* New York: IPM/Grand Central Publishing, 1998.

Carter, Lawrence E. Sr., ed. *Walking Integrity: Benjamin Elijah Mays, Mentor to Martin Luther King Jr.* Macon, GA: Mercer University Press, 1998.

Chabot, Sean. *Transnational Roots of the Civil Rights Movement: African American Explorations of the Gandhian Repertoire.* Lanham, MD: Lexington Books, 2012.

Dixie, Quinton, and Peter Eisenstadt. *Visions of a Better World: Howard Thurman's Pilgrimage to India and the Origins of African American Nonviolence.* Boston: Beacon Press, 2011.

Du Bois, W.E.B. "Strivings of the Negro People." *The Atlantic,* August 1897. https://www.theatlantic.com/magazine/archive/1897/08/strivings-of-the-negro-people/305446.

Gandhi, Arun, and Sunanda Gandhi. *The Forgotten Woman: The Untold Story of Kastur, Wife of Mahatma Gandhi.* Huntsville, AR: Ozark Mountain Publishers, 1998.

Gandhi, Mohandas K. *An Autobiography or The Story of My Experiments with Truth.* Harmondsworth, Middlesex : Penguin, 1983 (orig. 1927).

———. *The Collected Works of Mahatma Gandhi.* 100 vols. 1884–94. Publications Division, Ministry of Information and Broadcasting, Government of India. https://www.gandhiheritageportal.org/the-collected-works-of-mahatma-gandhi.

———. *Satyagraha in South Africa.* Stanford: Academic Reprints, 1954.

Gandhi, Rajmohan. *Gandhi: The Man, His People, and the Empire.* London: Haus Publishing, 2007.

Gandhi, Tushar A. *"Let's Kill Gandhi!" A Chronicle of His Last Days, the Conspiracy, Murder, Investigation and Trial.* New Delhi: Rupa, 2007.

Golden, Harry. *Mr. Kennedy and the Negroes.* Cleveland: World Publishing Company, 1964.

Guha, Ramachandra. *Gandhi Before India.* New York: Knopf, 2014.

———. *Gandhi: The Years That Changed the World.* Toronto: Random House Canada, 2018.

Hancock, W. K., and Jean van der Poel, eds. *Selections from the Smuts Papers.* Volume 3, *June 1910–November 1918.* New York: Cambridge University Press, 1966.

Hartford, Bruce. *The Selma Voting Rights Struggle and the March to Montgomery.* San Francisco: Westwind Writers, 2014. Kindle.

Herman, Arthur. *Gandhi and Churchill: The Epic Rivalry That Destroyed an Empire and Forged Our Age.* New York: Bantam, 2008.

King, Coretta Scott. *My Life with Martin Luther King, Jr.* London: Puffin Books, 1993 (orig. 1969).

King, Martin Luther, Jr. "My Trip to the Land of Gandhi." *Ebony,* vol. 14, July 1959.

———. *The Papers of Martin Luther King, Jr.* Martin Luther King, Jr. Papers Project. Stanford, CA: Martin Luther King, Jr. Research and Education Institute, Stanford University. https://kinginstitute.stanford.edu/king-papers/about-papers-project.

———. *Why We Can't Wait.* New York: Signet Classic, 2000 (orig. 1963).

King, Mary. *Mahatma Gandhi and Martin Luther King Jr.: The Power of Nonviolent Action.* Paris: UNESCO Publishing, 1999.

Lewis, David L. *King: A Biography.* Urbana: University of Illinois Press, 1978.

Lewis, John, and Michael d'Orso. *Walking with the Wind: A Memoir of the Movement.* New York: Simon & Schuster, 1998.

Oates, Stephen B. *Let the Trumpet Sound: A Life of Martin Luther King Jr.* New York: HarperPerennial, 1994.

Posner, Gerald. *Killing the Dream: James Earl Ray and the Assassination of Martin Luther King, Jr.* New York: Open Road/Integrated Media, 1998.

Pyarelal. *Mahatma Gandhi: The Early Phase*, vol. 1. Ahmedabad, India: Navajivan Press, 1965.

Ramsurrun, Pahlad. *Mahatma Gandhi and His Impact on Mauritius.* New Delhi: Sterling Publishers, 1995.

Sitkoff, Harvard. *King: Pilgrimage to the Mountaintop.* New York: Hill and Wang, 2008.

Thurman, Howard: *With Head and Heart.* San Diego: Harvest Books, 1981.

Tolstoy, Leo. "The Meaning of the Russian Revolution." In *Complete Works of Leo Tolstoy*, Oakshot Press, 2016. iBook.

Upadhyaya, J. M. *Mahatma Gandhi as a Student.* Publications Division, Ministry of Information and Broadcasting, Government of India, 1969.

Watson, Bruce. *Freedom Summer.* New York: Penguin, 2010.

Watson, Francis, and Maurice Brown. *Talking of Gandhiji: Four Programmes for Radio First Broadcast by the British Broadcasting Corporation.* Bombay: Orient Longmans, 1957.

Webb, Sheyann, and Rachel West Nelson. *Selma, Lord, Selma: Girlhood Memories of the Civil-Rights Days,* as told to Frank Sikora. Tuscaloosa: University of Alabama Press, 1980. iBook.

Wolpert, Stanley. *Gandhi's Passion: The Life and Legacy of Mahatma Gandhi.* New York: Oxford University Press, 2001.

Younge, Gary. *The Speech: The Story Behind Dr. Martin Luther King Jr.'s Dream.* Chicago: Haymarket Books, 2013.

PHOTO CREDITS

SOURCES

ABBREVIATIONS USED IN THIS LIST

CSK   Coretta Scott King, *My Life with Martin Luther King, Jr.*

CWMG   M. K. Gandhi, *The Collected Works of Mahatma Gandhi*

MKGA   M. K. Gandhi, *An Autobiography or The Story of My Experiments with Truth*

MLKA   Clarborne Carson, *The Autobiography of Martin Luther King, Jr.*

MLKE   Martin Luther King Jr., "My Trip to the Land of Gandhi," *Ebony*

MLKPP   Martin Luther King, Jr. Papers Project, Martin Luther King, Jr. Research and Education Institute, Stanford University

NYT   *New York Times*

All quotations from the words of Martin Luther King Jr. are reprinted by arrangement with the Heirs to the Estate of Martin Luther King Jr., c/o Writers House as agent for the proprietor, New York, NY.

Epigraph: "Victory attained by violence is tantamount to a defeat, for it is momentary." CWMG, vol. 15, p. 268.

Epigraph: "Christ showed us the way and Gandhi in India showed it could work." Quoted in Stanley Rowland, "2,500 Here Hail Boycott Leader," NYT, March 26, 1956, p. 27. © 1956 Dr. Martin Luther King Jr., © renewed 1984 Coretta Scott King.

p. 3: "Black America still wears chains"; pp. 3–4: "served in many of the public restaurants . . . its best citizen"; p. 4: "So, with their right hand . . . keep us in 'our places'"; "fair play"; "free opportunity." From "The Negro and the Constitution" speech, April 13, 1944. © 1944 Dr. Martin Luther King Jr., © renewed 1972 Coretta Scott King. MLKPP.

p. 7: "the guiding light of our technique of nonviolent social change." MLKE. © 1959 Dr. Martin Luther King Jr., © renewed 1987 Coretta Scott King.

p. 8: "No. I have one with me"; "Come along . . . You must go to the van compartment"; p. 9: "It was winter . . . so I sat and shivered"; p. 10: "hardship was superficial"; "only a symptom of the deep disease." MKGA, pp. 113–14.

p. 16: "restless as mercury"; "sit still . . . roaming about." Pyarelal, *Mahatma Gandhi*, p. 194.

p. 18: "The outstanding impression . . . nothing to her"; p. 19: "My intellect must have been sluggish and my memory raw"; p. 21: "Behold the mighty Englishman . . . He is five cubits tall"; p. 23: "But how were we to do it . . . an effective poison"; p. 24: "pearl-drops of love"; p. 27: "two innocent children . . . the ocean of life"; p. 28: "*make* my wife an ideal wife." MKGA, pp. 20, 21, 35, 39, 41, 26, 27.

p. 30: "Are you suggesting . . . not your mother?" Gandhi and Gandhi, *The Forgotten Woman*, p. 22.

p. 30: "completely at sea"; p. 31: "pure and simple . . . reasoning powers." MKGA, p. 31.

p. 32: "on the advantage of a cheerful disposition"; "pleonasm"; "metaphor"; p. 33: "enabling India to take her place in the new industrial world." Upadhyaya, *Mahatma Gandhi as a Student*, pp. 54, 60.

p. 34: "[T]he medical degree . . . something better"; p. 35: "I . . . was a coward . . . completely possessed me"; p. 36: "[E]ven when I understood . . . bring it out." MKGA, pp. 49, 50, 54.

p. 37: "the currency was English . . . useless here"; "The doors were opened . . . to sit for some time"; "to my great surprise . . . second floor." CWMG, vol. 1, pp. 12, 16.

pp. 37–38: "[N]ever address people . . . their masters that way"; p. 39: "eating one's terms"; p. 40: "[W]e began to get fruits and . . . vegetables." MKGA, pp. 56, 86.

p. 42: "Let right deeds be thy motive"; "the truth of truths"; "live in action"; "noble purpose." Arnold, *The Song Celestial*, pp. 18, 41, 20.

p. 42: "especially the Sermon on the Mount which went straight to my heart." MKGA, p. 77.

p. 43: "all Indians are born vegetarians"; "some are so

voluntarily . . . a heavily taxed article"; "into small equal parts . . . bake one cake." CWMG, vol. 1, pp. 19, 22.

p. 47: "tempting opportunity . . . new experience"; p. 49: "You sit on this, I want to sit near the driver"; p. 50: "I strained every nerve . . . compromise"; "I realized that the true . . . riven asunder." MKGA, pp. 105, 115, 133.

p. 52: "propagandists of agitation"; "British subjects . . . in the Colony." CWMG, vol. 1, pp. 128–31.

p. 52: "was propaganda . . . the real state of things in Natal"; p. 54: "[A] Tamil man . . . trembling and weeping"; "and I came to be regarded as their friend." MKGA, pp. 149, 150–51.

p. 55: "The only means . . . not taking part in it." Tolstoy, *The Meaning of the Russian Revolution*, Chapter X.

p. 56: "What a heavy price . . . regarded as civilized." Gandhi and Gandhi, *The Forgotten Woman*, p. 71.

p. 57: "We'll hang old Gandhi on the sour apple tree"; p. 60: "have the best medical aid at the time of her delivery"; "and some time was lost in fetching the midwife"; p. 62: "What about my daughters-in-law . . . what will happen tomorrow?"; "I am definitely of the opinion . . . accept no costly gifts." MKGA, pp. 184, 193, 209, 210.

p. 63: "a place in the sun under the pavilion of liberty." Ramsurrun, *Mahatma Gandhi and His Impact on Mauritius*, pp. 161–62.

p. 64: "I had no fear now"; p. 65: "It was a terrible night . . . vigil and nursing"; "the British Empire . . . of the world"; "rifles exploding . . . innocent hamlets." MKGA, pp. 233, 268, 287, 289.

p. 69: "for in that case . . . all the more keen." From "Proceedings of the Central Criminal Court, 19th July 1909," p. 64, https://www.oldbaileyonline.org/images.jsp?doc=190907190064.

p. 71: "Our sympathies go out to our oppressed fellow subjects." From "Editorial," *Basutoland Star*, reprinted in *Indian Opinion*, vol. 8, February 1, 1908. An extensive quote from the original can be found

in Ramachandra Guha's *Gandhi Before India*.

p. 71: "[T]he saint has left our shores—I sincerely hope for ever." Jan Christiaan Smuts to Sir Benjamin Robertson, August 21, 1914, in Hancock and van der Poel, eds., *Selections from the Smuts Papers*, p. 589.

p. 76: "the higher law . . . voice of conscience"; "[T]he people had for the moment . . . power of love." MKGA, pp. 374, 372.

p. 77: "and we should part good friends." CWMG, vol. 13, pp. 127–28.

p. 80: "an extraordinary event, a monstrous event." Quoted in Herman, *Gandhi and Churchill*, p. 255.

p. 81: "the severest penalty." CWMG, vol. 23, p. 115.

p. 86: "You must be prepared to die." Gandhi and Gandhi, *The Forgotten Woman*, p. 251.

p. 86: "With this salt I am shaking the foundations of the Empire." Quoted in Herman, *Gandhi and Churchill*, p. 338.

p. 87: "[T]he vow of silence helps in the search for truth." CWMG, vol. 31, p. 528.

p. 87: "a woolly lamb, a little doll's cradle and some other things." Muriel Lester quoted in Watson and Brown, *Talking of Gandhiji*, p. 92.

p. 90: "alarming and nauseating . . . representative of the king-emperor." Quoted in Herman, *Gandhi and Churchill*, p. 359.

p. 90: "It can be no pride . . . chaining himself." Quoted in Rajmohan Gandhi, *Gandhi: The Man, His People, and the Empire*, p. 337.

p. 91: "good and sufficient reasons." From "Gandhi Arrested," *The Guardian*, January 4, 1932, https://www.theguardian.com/century/1930-1939/Story/0,,126824,00.html.

p. 91: "sting the Hindu conscience." CWMG, vol. 51, p. 62.

p. 93: "an insane act"; "deep pity." CWMG, vol. 58, p. 109.

p. 93: "[W]e have much to talk about . . . back to Bombay." Thurman, *With Head and Heart*, p. 132.

p. 94: "more positive than electricity"; "We want you to come to America . . . we have many a problem that cries for solution and we need you badly." Quoted in Dixie and Eisenstadt, *Visions of a Better World*, pp. 104, 111.

p. 94: "You may not waste . . . trustees for the use of it." CWMG, vol. 26, p. 272.

p. 95: "a living sermon." CWMG, vol. 62, p. 201.

p. 95: "I would like a piece of cloth . . . from the flax"; "that the unadulterated message . . . be delivered." Thurman, *With Head and Heart*, pp. 134, 132.

p. 97: "I do not believe in any war." CWMG, vol. 68, p. 138.

p. 98: "perpetual vivisection of India." Quoted in "India's Reception of the New Suggestions," *The Guardian* (London), July 15, 1944, p. 7.

p. 99: "his left hand and his right hand." Quoted in Rajmohan Gandhi, *Gandhi: The Man, His People, and the Empire*, p. 473.

p. 103: "[S]he became truly my *better* half . . . non-violent non-cooperation." CWMG, vol. 77, p. 244.

p. 103: "His Majesty's hotels." *Satyagraha in South Africa*, p. 149.

p. 108: "I feel as if I was thrown into a fire pit and my heart is burning"; p. 110: "people of Kashmir should be asked . . . The people are everything." CWMG, vol. 88, pp. 84, 461.

p. 110: "the two dominions . . . find a settlement"; p. 112: "Today the poison . . . added more poison"; "I yearn for heart friendship . . . a reunion of hearts of all communities"; p. 114: "I must now tear myself away"; "Bapu, your watch must be feeling very neglected . . . my time-keepers?" CWMG, vol. 90, pp. 357, 347, 408–9, 535.

p. 121: "The community in which I was born . . . any great wealth"; p. 123 (MLK quoting his mother): "You are as good as anyone." From "An Autobiography of Religious Development" essay, fall 1950. © 1950 Dr. Martin Luther King Jr., © renewed 1978 Coretta Scott King.

p. 124: "Even as a child . . . other storybook characters." From King, "My Trip to the Land of Gandhi," MLKE.

p. 125: "Here for the first time . . . conscious of it before." From "An Autobiography of Religious Development" essay, fall 1950.

p. 125: "Someday I'm going to . . . big words like that." Quoted in David L. Lewis, *King: A Biography*, p. 12.

p. 126: "I wouldn't dare retaliate when a white person was involved." MLKA, p. 9.

p. 127: "If you persist . . . a word you are saying;" "We'll either buy . . . shoes at all"; "I don't care how long . . . never accept it." MLKA, p. 8.

p. 127: "We cannot have an enlightened democracy . . . obey no Jim Crow laws"; "they will be vigilant . . . by her enemies"; p. 128: "I with my brother . . . and yet a man!" From "The Negro and the Constitution" speech, April 13, 1944. © 1944 Dr. Martin Luther King Jr., © renewed 1972 Coretta Scott King. MLKPP.

p. 128: "I would end up . . . on the front seat"; "One of these days . . . where my mind is." MLKA, p. 9.

p. 129: "After we passed Washington . . . we want to." Letter to MLK Sr., June 15, 1944. © 1944 Dr. Martin Luther King Jr., © renewed 1972 Coretta Scott King. MLKPP.

p. 130: "I felt as if the curtain had been dropped on my selfhood." From "Pilgrimage to Nonviolence" article, April 13, 1960. © 1960 Dr. Martin Luther King Jr., © renewed 1988 Coretta Scott King. MLKPP.

p. 132: "I wouldn't go . . . to see Jesus Christ himself." Quoted in Carter, *Walking Integrity: Benjamin Elijah Mays, Mentor to Martin Luther King Jr.*, p. 12.

p. 133: "not a miraculous or supernatural something"; "inner urge . . . humanity." From "An Autobiography of Religious Development" essay, fall 1950.

p. 133: I was well aware . . . was grimly serious." MLKA, p. 17.

p. 134: "You stated . . . really hard." Letter to Alberta Williams King, October 1948. © 1948 Dr. Martin Luther King Jr., © renewed 1976 Coretta Scott King. MLKPP.

p. 134: "a serious intellectual quest for a method to eliminate social evil." From "Pilgrimage to

Nonviolence" article, April 13, 1960.

p. 134: "the gulf between superfluous wealth and abject poverty." From "Paul's Letter to American Christians" sermon, Dexter Avenue Baptist Church, November 4, 1956. © 1956 Dr. Martin Luther King Jr., © renewed 1984 Coretta Scott King. MLKPP.

p. 135: "Therefore, I must be concerned . . . economic insecurity." Preaching Ministry, fall 1948. © 1948 Dr. Martin Luther King Jr., © renewed 1976 Coretta Scott King. MLKPP.

p. 135: "During this period I had almost despaired . . . approach is necessary." From "Pilgrimage to Nonviolence" article, April 13, 1960.

p. 135: "commune with nature"; p. 136: "Sometimes I go out at night . . . There is God." From "O That I Knew Where I Might Find Him!" sermon, January 1, 1951–December 31, 1954. © 1958 Dr. Martin Luther King Jr., © renewed 1984 Coretta Scott King. MLKPP.

p. 137: "Gandhi Is Killed by a Hindu; India Shaken, World Mourns." NYT, January 31, 1948, pp. 1–2.

p. 138: "nice, attractive young ladies"; "I'd like very much to meet you and talk to you"; pp. 138–39: "You know every Napoleon . . . talk some more"; p. 139: "You have everything . . . married someday"; "Coretta is going to be my wife." MLKA, pp. 34–35.

p. 140: "Do you know . . . funeral parlor." Quoted in CSK, p. 72.

p. 142: "big little girl . . . walking the floor." Letter to John Thomas Porter, November 18, 1955. © 1955 Dr. Martin Luther King Jr., © renewed 1983 Coretta Scott King. MLKPP.

p. 144: "Young people think . . . wasn't the case at all." Quoted in Brooks Barnes, "From Footnote to Fame in Civil Rights History," NYT, November 25, 2009.

p. 146. "Martin, Martin, come quickly!" CSK, p. 105.

pp. 146–47: "They knew why . . . they carried themselves." MLKA, p. 55.

p. 147: "day of days." Letter from Hermine I. Popper, March 21, 1958. © 1958 Dr. Martin Luther King Jr., © renewed 1986 Coretta Scott King. MLKPP.

p. 149: "This could turn into something big." Quoted in Taylor Branch, *Parting the Waters: America in the King Years, 1954–63*, p. 138.

p. 149: "You know, my friends . . . iron feet of oppression"; pp. 149–50: "And we are not wrong . . . If we are wrong . . . like a mighty stream." MIA Mass Meeting at Holt Street Baptist Church, December 4, 1955. © 1955 Dr. Martin Luther King Jr., © renewed 1983 Coretta Scott King. MLKPP.

p. 152: "Christ furnished the spirit . . . Gandhi furnished the method." From "Pilgrimage to Nonviolence" article, April 13, 1960.

p. 153: "Gandhi's shadow watches over Alabama." *The Hindustan Times*, February 27, 1956, p. 1.

p. 154: "There's that damn King fellow"; p. 155: "Get out, King . . . twenty-five-mile zone"; "trembling within and without"; p. 156: "vagrants and drunks and serious lawbreakers." MLKA, pp. 73–74

p. 156: (quoting anonymous phone call) "[W]e are tired of you and your mess . . . blow up your house"; p. 157: "Lord, I must confess . . . losing my courage"; "Martin Luther, stand up for righteousness . . . the end of the world." From "Why Jesus Called a Man a Fool" sermon, Mount Pisgah Missionary Baptist Church, August 27, 1967. © 1967 Dr. Martin Luther King Jr., © renewed 1995 Coretta Scott King. MLKPP.

p. 157: "Come here, son . . . talk strong tonight." Quoted in Branch, *Parting the Waters*, p. 164.

p. 158: "Now you got your .38 . . . battle it out"; p. 159: "We believe in . . . not advocating violence." MLKA, pp. 79, 80.

p. 164: "Lord, I hope no one . . . in Montgomery." Quoted in Branch, *Parting the Waters*, p. 20; "But if anyone should be killed, let it be me!" Nelson Cole, "King Collapses in Prayer During Negro Mass Meeting," *Montgomery Advertiser*, January 15, 1957, p. 6-A. © 1957 Dr. Martin Luther King Jr., © renewed 1985 Coretta Scott King.

p. 164: "This conference is called . . . Christian understanding." From "Montgomery Improvement

Association Press Release," January 7, 1957. © 1957 Dr. Martin Luther King Jr., © renewed 1985 Coretta Scott King. MLKPP.

p. 165: "And so . . . to kill my father"; "But back then . . . and who wasn't." Interview with Joel Silverman, June 2016.

p. 166: "No man has ever . . . than you have." Clare Boothe Luce, letter to Martin Luther King Jr. (copy) MLKPP.

p. 167: "You can't legislate morality." Quoted in Harry Golden, *Mr. Kennedy and the Negroes*, p. 100.

p. 167: "It may be true that the law . . . pretty important also." From "An Address by the Reverend Dr. Martin Luther King, Jr.," Cornell College, Mount Vernon, IA, October 15, 1962, http://news .cornellcollege.edu/dr-martin-luther-kings-visit-to -cornell-college. © 1962 Dr. Martin Luther King Jr., © renewed 1990 Coretta Scott King.

p. 169: "Isn't this the time . . . civil disobedience?" Letter from Harris Wofford, April 25, 1956. MLKPP.

p. 170: "dancing with the lord on an equal plane." From "The Birth of a New Nation" sermon, Dexter Avenue Baptist Church, April 7, 1957. © 1957 Dr. Martin Luther King Jr., © renewed 1985 Coretta Scott King. MLKPP.

p. 170: "I'm very glad to meet you here . . . same kind of freedom"; p. 171: "I think this event . . . peoples all over the world." Alex Rivera, "M. L. King Meets Nixon in Ghana," *Pittsburgh Courier*, March 16, 1957, p. 2. © 1957 Dr. Martin Luther King Jr., © renewed 1985 Coretta Scott King.

p. 171: "Are you Martin Luther King?"; "I've been after him for six years." Quoted in Margalit Fox, "Izola Ware Curry, Who Stabbed King in 1958, Dies at 98," NYT, March 21, 2015.

p. 171: (speaking of Izola Ware Curry): "I bear no bitterness . . . menace to any man." From "Statement Upon Return to Montgomery" speech, October 24, 1958. © 1958 Dr. Martin Luther King Jr., © renewed 1986 Coretta Scott King. MLKPP.

p. 173: "sneezed or coughed . . . a sneeze away from death." Dr. Emil A. Naclerio, quoted in "N.Y. Police Probe Facts Behind Stabbing of Rev. M.L. King Jr." *Jet*, October 2, 1958.

p. 173: "made up a sort of three-headed team . . . looking and listening"; "down out of the clouds at Bombay"; p. 174: "The people showered upon us the most generous hospitality imaginable." From King, "My Trip to the Land of Gandhi," MLKE.

p. 174: "To other countries . . . as a pilgrim." Account by Lawrence Dunbar Reddick of press conference in New Delhi, February 10, 1959. © 1959 Dr. Martin Luther King Jr., © renewed 1987 Coretta Scott King. MLKPP.

p. 176: "strip the world bare like locusts." Gandhi, *Young India*, December 12, 1928, p. 422.

p. 176: "a better continuity . . . most of the papers in the United States." From King, "My Trip to the Land of Gandhi," MLKE.

p. 181: "Just outside the village . . . You go." From "'India's Soul'—Krishnammal Jagannathan Awarded Right Livelihood for Realizing 'Gandhian Vision of Social Justice and Sustainable Human Development,'" interview with Amy Goodman, December 8, 2008, https://www.democracynow .org/2008/12/8/indias_soul_krishnammal_ jagannathan_awarded_right.

p. 182: "one of the most concentrated and eye-opening experiences of our lives." From King, "My Trip to the Land of Gandhi," MLKE.

p. 182: "I beg of you to indulge me . . . more completely in his life"; "If you are hit . . . just keep moving." From "Palm Sunday Sermon on Mohandas K. Gandhi," Dexter Avenue Baptist Church, March 22, 1959. © 1959 Dr. Martin Luther King Jr., © renewed 1987 Coretta Scott King. MLKPP.

p. 185: "Do not strike back . . . nonviolence is the way." From John Lewis, *Walking with the Wind*, pp. 105–6.

p. 185: "shake up the world." Quoted in Branch, *Parting the Waters*, p. 273.

p. 186: "initiated, led, and sustained . . . struggle for

freedom"; "If the officials threaten to arrest us . . . fill up the jails of the South." From "A Creative Protest" speech, Durham, NC, February 16, 1960. © 1960 Dr. Martin Luther King Jr., © renewed 1988 Coretta Scott King. MLKPP.

p. 187: "a triumph of justice . . . in human good." CSK, p. 171.

p. 190: "It must be made palpably clear . . . the beloved community." From "Statement to the Press at the Beginning of the Youth Leadership Conference" speech, Raleigh, NC. April 15, 1960. © 1960 Dr. Martin Luther King Jr., © renewed 1988 Coretta Scott King. MLKPP.

p. 191: "You don't pay . . . serving the time." Interview with Loudon Wainwright Jr., *Life*, November 7, 1960.

p. 192: "King! Get up!" Quoted in Branch, *Parting the Waters*, p. 361.

p. 193: "Yes, he goes to jail to help people." CSK, p. 175.

p. 194: "How could they do that . . . on a misdemeanor." p. 200: "Martin King . . . freedom!" p. 202: "[S]ee them nonviolent rocks?" Quoted in Branch, *Parting the Waters*, pp. 365, 545, 618.

p. 204: "Every time I saw FBI men . . . local police." From "Dr. King Says FBI in Albany, Ga., Favors Segregationists," NYT, November 19, 1962, p. 21. © 1962 Dr. Martin Luther King Jr., © renewed 1990 Coretta Scott King.

p. 205: "The people of Albany . . . unless it is bent." MLKA, p. 168.

p. 205: "segregation now . . . segregation forever!" George Wallace, Inaugural address, January 14, 1963, https://digital.archives.alabama.gov/digital/collection/voices/id/2952.

p. 207: "second Emancipation Proclamation . . . second-class citizenship." Telegram signed by Dr. Martin Luther King Jr., Dr. W. G. Anderson, and Ralph Abernathy. December 13, 1961, https://www.jfklibrary.org/asset-viewer/december-13-1961-telegram. © 1961 Dr. Martin Luther King Jr., ©

renewed 1989 Coretta Scott King.

p. 210: "faith act." King, *Why We Can't Wait*, p. 81.

p. 212: "I am in Birmingham because injustice is here"; "never voluntarily given . . . demanded by the oppressed"; "The nations of Asia and Africa . . . to say, 'Wait'"; "clouds of inferiority beginning to form in her little mental sky"; "an unjust law is no law at all." From "Letter from Birmingham Jail." © 1963 Dr. Martin Luther King Jr., © renewed 1991 Coretta Scott King. MLKPP.

pp. 216–17: "Shyly but doggedly . . . blow for freedom." MLKA, p. 207.

p. 217: "for all its hopes and all its boasts . . . its citizens are free"; "Now the time has come . . . fulfill its promise." JFK, Radio and Television Report to the American People on Civil Rights, June 11, 1963, https://www.jfklibrary.org/archives/other-resources/john-f-kennedy-speeches.

p. 217: "one of the most eloquent, profound, and unequivocal pleas . . . by any president." Telegram, MLK to JFK, June 11, 1963, https://www.jfklibrary.org/asset-viewer/june-11-1963-telegram. © 1963 Dr. Martin Luther King Jr., © renewed 1991 Coretta Scott King.

p. 218: "a great shout for freedom reverberated across the land." MLKA, p. 218.

p. 219: "the moral leader of our nation"; p. 222: "to counsel with My Lord." From Clarence B. Jones, "On Martin Luther King Day, Remembering the First Draft of 'I Have a Dream.'" *Washington Post*, January 16, 2011.

p. 222: "Five score years ago . . . Emancipation Proclamation"; "languished in the corners of American society"; "promissory note"; "unalienable rights of 'Life, Liberty and the pursuit of Happiness'"; "a check which has come back marked 'insufficient funds'"; "Now is the time"; p. 223: "forever conduct . . . degenerate into physical violence"; "Go back to Mississippi . . . wallow in the valley of despair"; "I have a dream"; From "I Have a Dream" speech, March on Washington for Jobs

and Freedom, Washington, DC, August 28, 1963. ©
1963 Dr. Martin Luther King Jr., © renewed 1991
Coretta Scott King. MLKPP.

p. 223: "Yes! Tell 'em about the dream"; "These people
out there . . . ready to go to church." From Clarence
B. Jones, "On Martin Luther King Day."

p. 224: "to speed up that day . . . 'we are free at
last.'" From "I Have a Dream" speech, March on
Washington for Jobs and Freedom, Washington,
DC, August 28, 1963. MLKPP.

p. 227: "horror-filled September morning." MLKA,
p. 229.

p. 227: "I'm not for that . . . gun in her hand?"; p. 228:
"This is what is going to happen to me also . . . a sick
society." CSK, pp. 243, 227.

p. 228: "the whine of the bullet from ambush, the roar
of the bomb." MLKA, p. 235.

p. 228: "a negation of civilization." From "Letter from
Gandhi," *Baltimore Afro-American*, February 7, 1948.

pp. 228–29: "The assassination of President
Kennedy . . . spreads as a disease"; p. 233: "a bright
interlude in the long and sometimes turbulent
struggle for civil rights"; "careful practicality."
MLKA, pp. 238, 242, 243.

p. 233: "a bright interlude . . . for civil rights"; "careful
practicality." MLKA, pp. 242, 243.

p. 234: "smothered by poverty in the midst of an
affluent society." From "Martin Luther King:
A Candid Conversation with the Nobel Prize–
Winning Leader of the Civil Rights Movement,"
Playboy, vol. 12, no. 1, January 1965. © 1965 Dr.
Martin Luther King Jr., © renewed 1993 Coretta
Scott King.

p. 236: "was built by exploitation of . . . oppressed
peoples"; pp. 236–37: "quite a time getting him
ready." CSK, pp. 8, 10.

p. 237: "the tortuous road . . . to Oslo"; p. 238: "abiding
faith in . . . the future of mankind." Acceptance
speech, Nobel Peace Prize, Oslo, December 10,
1964, https://www.nobelprize.org/nobel_prizes/
peace/laureates/1964/king-acceptance_en.html.

© 1964 Dr. Martin Luther King Jr., © renewed
1992 Coretta Scott King.

p. 242: "Then they can call . . . beat you to death;"
p. 243: "his youngest freedom fighter"; "Sheyann . . .
Freedom!" Quoted in Stephen Oates, *Let the
Trumpet Sound*, pp. 337, 339–40.

p. 244: "How long are we . . . for a loooooong time!"
Bruce Hartford, *The Selma Voting Rights Struggle*,
"Bound in Jail."

p. 245: "This is Selma, Alabama . . . voting rolls." From
"A Letter from Martin Luther King from a Selma,
Alabama Jail," SCLC advertisement, NYT, February
5, 1965, p. 15.

p. 245: "to participate in the struggle"; p. 246: "If the
white people realize . . . to hear Dr. King." CSK,
p. 238.

p. 248: "Be prepared to walk . . . sleep on the highway!"
Quoted in Taylor Branch, *At Canaan's Edge: America
in the King Years, 1965–68*, p. 9.

p. 248: "the brutality of every sheriff . . . the stale bread
of hatred"; p. 249: "They had beaten us like we were
slaves." Webb and West Nelson, *Selma, Lord, Selma*.

p. 250: "Pack your bags!" p. 251: "This cause is now
submitted . . . enjoined and restrained . . ."; "I am
aware of the order." Quoted in Branch, *At Canaan's
Edge*, pp. 62, 75, 76.

p. 252: "You can have your prayer . . . to your church";
"We come . . . as a living sacrifice." Quoted in
Stephen Oates, *Let the Trumpet Sound*, p. 352.

p. 253: "We will go back to the church now!" Quoted
in Branch, *At Canaan's Edge*, p. 77.

p. 254: "Concerned, perturbed, and frustrated," *Time*
magazine, "The Central Points," March 19, 1965.

p. 254: "It is wrong—deadly wrong . . . the right to
vote"; "We *shall* overcome." The American Promise:
President Johnson's Special Message to Congress,
March 15, 1965. LBJ Library.

p. 260: "the language of the unheard." From "The
Other America" speech, Grosse Pointe High School,
March 14, 1968, http://www.gphistorical.org/mlk/
mlkspeech/index.htm. © 1968 Dr. Martin Luther

King Jr., © renewed 1996 Coretta Scott King.

p. 261: "an emotional pressure cooker." MLKA, p. 301.

p. 262: "island of poverty in the midst of a vast ocean of material prosperity." From "I Have a Dream" speech, March on Washington for Jobs and Freedom, Washington, DC, August 28, 1963.

pp. 263–64: "Why aren't you all out there tonight? . . . And I'm not going to turn my back on it now"; p. 264: "parrot racial epithets." MLKA, pp. 304, 310.

p. 266: "the first step in a 1,000-mile journey." David Halvorson, "Cancel Rights Marches: Pact Provides Equal Access to Housing, Loans." *Chicago Tribune*, August 27, 1966, p. 1. © 1966 Dr. Martin Luther King Jr., © renewed 1994 Coretta Scott King.

p. 268: "My conscience leaves me no other choice"; "a symptom of a far deeper malady within the American spirit." From "Beyond Vietnam" speech, Riverside Church, New York City, April 4, 1967. © 1967 Dr. Martin Luther King Jr., © renewed 1995 Coretta Scott King. MLKPP.

p. 270: "Something is happening in Memphis, something is happening in our world"; "I've been to the mountaintop." From "I've Been to the Mountaintop" speech, Bishop Charles Mason Temple, Memphis, TN, April 3, 1968. © 1968 Dr. Martin Luther King Jr., © renewed 1996 Coretta Scott King. MLKPP.

p. 272: "I tell you tonight I want that song . . . I mean it." Interview with Ben Branch, Rhodes College Digital Archives. http://hdl.handle .net/10267/33850.

p. 277: "My life is my message." CWMG, vol. 89, p. 529.

p. 277: "I want you to say . . . serve humanity." From "The Drum Major Instinct" speech, February 4, 1968. © 1968 Dr. Martin Luther King Jr., © renewed 1996 Coretta Scott King. MLKPP.

p. 281: "They are children . . . what the old man said was right." Report of Jeevan Lal Kapur Commission of Inquiry into Conspiracy to Murder Mahatma Gandhi, Vol. 2, p. 187.

p. 283: "attitude . . . violates all of them"; "Repulsive"; "a somewhat disturbed child"; p. 287: "I got the surgery . . . harder to identify me"; p. 288: "Are you pleading . . . in this case . . . ?" From Gerald Posner, *Killing the Dream.*

p. 291: "When I was fourteen . . . sent me to jail"; "You left school . . . to Gandhi's school"; "It was the best year of my life." Interview with Vasant Gurjar, March 2016.

pp. 294–95: "What we need in the United States is not division . . . whether they be white or whether they be black." Audio recording, Senator Robert F. Kennedy, announcing the news of the assassination of Martin Luther King Jr. during a presidential campaign speech in Indianapolis, IN, April 4, 1968, https://www.jfklibrary.org/asset-viewer/statement-on-the-death-of-martin-luther-king-jr-april4-1968.

p. 298: "I have nothing new to teach . . . old as the hills." Quoted in Mary King, *Mahatma Gandhi and Martin Luther King Jr.*, p. 231.

INDEX

Page numbers in **bold** indicate glossary terms.

A

Abdulla, Dada, 7, 47–50, 52

Abernathy, Ralph
> Birmingham protests, 207
> bus boycotts, 144–45, 156–57, 162
> Freedom Riders protests, 200, 202–03
> integrated schools, 233
> Memphis march, 269–72
> Selma protests, 244–46, 252
> white-only businesses, 240–41

Afrikaans language, 51, 61, **308**

agape, 152, **308**

ahimsa, 80, 94, **308**

Ambedkar, Bhimrao Ramji, 84, 90–92

Apte, Narayan, 279–80

ashram, 77–79, 179–80, **308**

Asiatic Registration Act, 66

B

Bania, 20, 35, **308**

bar examination, 42

Bevel, James, 187, 213, 243, 248, 271

Bhagavad Gita, 41–42, 68, 111, **308**

Bible, 42, 94, 111, 124, 150

Birmingham protests, 205–17

Black Lives Matter, 296

Black Power, 267

Boer War, 61–62, **308**

boycotts, **308.** *See also* civil disobedience

Brown v. Board of Education, 142

C

capitalism, 134

Carmichael, Stokely, 266–67

caste system, 20, 80–81, 91–94, 111–13, **308**

Central Intelligence Agency, 289

charkha (spinning wheel), 83, 93–95, 290–91, **308**

Children's Crusade, 214–17

Churchill, Winston, 67, 79, 90, 98, 100, 196

civil disobedience
> defined, **308**
> Gandhi, caste system and, 82, 91–94, 111–13
> Gandhi, India's independence and, 72–91, 97–104, 174
> Gandhi, India's partitioning and, 104–13
> Gandhi, *satyagraha* movement, 67–71, 94–97, **309**
> King, Birmingham protests, 205–17
> King, Freedom Riders protests, 197–204
> King, housing discrimination, 261–66
> King, March on Washington and aftermath, 218–32
> King, Memphis march, 269–72
> King, Montgomery protests and aftermath, 5–7, 143–69, 176–77
> King, Selma right to vote campaign, 239–58
> King, sit-in protests, 185–92

Civil Rights Act (1964), 232–33

Civil Rights Act (1968), 272

civil rights movement
> bus boycotts, 147, 150–51, 160
> Kennedy and, 191, 217
> March on Washington and aftermath, 218–32
> Nixon and, 170
> Rabbi Silverman and, 165
> voting rights, 239–58

Civil War, 126, 245, **308**

colonialism, **308**

Colvin, Claudette, 144, 160

Congress of Racial Equality (CORE), 198, 234

Congress Party, 96–100, 296

Connor, Eugene "Bull," 198–99, 208, 214–15, 236

coolie, 8, 84, **308**

Crusader Without Violence (Reddick), 173

D

Daley, Richard J., 262–63, 266

Dalit. *See* untouchables

Desai, Mahadev, 77, 95, 99

dhoti, 72–73, **308**

diwan, 16, **309**

Du Bois, W. E. B., 94, 130

E

East India Company, 14, 44

Ebenezer Baptist Church, 121–22, 133

Eisenhower, Dwight D., 166–67

emancipation, 126, 207, 222, **309**

Evers, Medgar, 219

F

Fair Housing Act (1968), 272

fasting, Gandhi and, 82, 91–92, 111–13

Federal Bureau of Investigation (FBI), 204, 231, 234–35, 251, 268, 289

Fifteenth Amendment, 242

Freedom Riders protests, 197–204

Freedom Summer campaign, 234

G

Gandhi, Abha, 114

Gandhi, Devadas, 60, 91–92, 102–03

Gandhi, Harilal, 34, 62, 64, 74, 91, 102

Gandhi, Indira, 174

Gandhi, Karamchand, 15–16, 19, 24, 26–27, 31–32

Gandhi, Karsandas, 16, 21–23, 26

Gandhi, Kasturba (Kapadia), 25–30, 34, 46, 54–57, 60–62, 66, 69, 74, 77, 86, 96, 102–03

Gandhi, Laxmidas, 16, 45, 94

Gandhi, Manilal, 47, 62, 64, 91–92, 102, 282

Gandhi, Manu, 102, 114

Gandhi, Mohandas K.

    arrests/imprisonment, 67–71, 76, 81, 87, 91, 96, 98–103

    assassination attempts, 93, 113–15, 228, 280–81

    awards and recognition, 72, 80–81

    civil disobedience and. *See under* civil disobedience

    death of, 115, 137, 281

    early life in Porbandar, 13–18

    early life in Rajkot, 19–27

    education in India, 19–21, 30–35

    education in London, 36–45

    India's partitioning and, 104–13

    influential books/stories, 24–25, 41–42, 54, 65, 68

    King and, 136, 166, 169–82, 205, 291–93

    law practice, 46–60, 64–66

    married life and children, 25–30, 34, 58–61

    publications written by, 55–56, 64–65

    in South Africa, 7–10, 47–62, 64–71

    vegetarian lifestyle, 16, 21–23, 35, 38, 40, 43–44

Gandhi, Putliba, 15–18, 35, 45

Gandhi, Raliat, 16

Gandhi, Ramdas, 60, 64, 69, 102, 282

Ghana, 170–71

Godse, Nathuram Vinayak, 114–15, 277–82

Gokhale, Gopal Krishna, 63, 73–74

Gujarati, 16, 29, 33, **309**

H

Harijan. *See* untouchables

Hindi language, 113, **309**

Hindu caste system. *See* caste system

Hoover, J. Edgar, 204, 234–36, 288

Hughes, Langston, 261, 293

I

"I have a dream," 223–24

indentured labor, 51, 54, **309**

Indian Independence Act, 106

Indian National Congress, 52–53, 63, 73–74, 87

India's independence, 72–91, 97–104, 174

Interstate Commerce Commission, 200

J

Jackson, Jesse, 250, 262, 271

Jackson, Mahalia, 223–24, 264

Jallianwala Bagh massacre, 78–80

Jim Crow laws, 119–20, 122, 230, **309**

jimsonweed *(dhatura),* 23–24

Jinnah, Muhammad Ali, 74, 90, 96, 104, 279

Johnson, Lyndon B., 230, 232–33, 235, 254, 258, 260, 272

Jones, Clarence, 211–12, 222

K

Kashmir, 109–12

Kennedy, John F., 190–97, 203, 207, 212–17, 228–30

Kennedy, Robert, 193–94, 204, 212, 236, 294–95

Khan, Khan Abdul Ghaffar, 90–91

King, A. D., 241

King, Alberta, 122–23, 126

King, Bernice Albertine, 208

King, Coretta (Scott), 138–42, 158–59, 173–78, 192–93, 208, 245–46

King, Dexter, 197, 289

King, Martin Luther, III, 167

King, Martin Luther, Jr.

    arrests/imprisonment, 155–56, 159–60, 187, 191–94, 201–03, 210–11

    awards and recognition, 230–31, 235–38

    civil disobedience and. *See under* civil disobedience

    death of, 272

    early childhood, 121–25

    education, 125, 128–29, 131–38

    Freedom Summer campaign, 234

    Gandhi and, 136, 166, 169–82, 205, 291–93

    incremental change, 218–32

    influential books/works, 124, 134–35

    interviews with, 153, 166, 171

    marriage and children, 138–42, 167, 197, 208

    ministry studies and profession, 133–37, 140–42

    post-India visit, 183–96

    publications written by, 169, 171, 182, 211–12, 228, 244–45

    segregation experiences, 3–7, 125–30, 143

    speeches by, 3–4, 127–28, 148–50, 165, 178, 182, 186, 200–01, 222–26, 234, 237–38

    threats and violence against, 156, 158, 163, 171–73, 187, 206, 219, 228, 231, 241, 264, 270–72

    timeline of events, 306–07

    travels abroad, 169–82

King, Martin Luther, Sr., 121–23

King, Yolanda, 142, 158, 212, 218

Ku Klux Klan, 156, 187, 192–93, 198–99, 231–32, 252, 283, **309**

Kyles, Samuel, 270–71

L

Lawson, James, 153, 165, 183, 185, 189, 268–69

Lenin, Vladimir, 134

"Letter from a Birmingham Jail," 211–12

"Letter from a Selma Jail," 244–45

Levison, Stanley, 187

Lewis, John, 183, 187, 198

literacy tests, 119–20, 245

Luther, Martin, 123–24

M

Malcolm X, 166, 213, 245–47

March on Washington and aftermath, 218–32

Marx, Karl, 134

Mays, Benjamin, 94, 132, 136

Meredith, James, 206, 219, 266–67

Mississippi Burning, 234

Mississippi Freedom March, 267

Modi, Narenda, 296–97

Montgomery Improvement Association (MIA), 148, 150–51, 154, 156–57, 159–60, 184

Montgomery protests and aftermath, 143–69, 176–77

N

namaste, 114, 281, **309**

Narmad (poet), 21, 33

Nash, Diane, 187, 189, 206

Natal Indian Congress, 52, 61, 64

National Association for the Advancement of Colored People (NAACP), 122, 133, 143, 212, 217, 234

Nehru, Jawaharlal, 74, 90, 92, 98, 111, 114, 174, 176, 282

Nixon, Edgar D., 144, 159, 162

Nixon, Richard, 170

Nkrumah, Kwame, 170, 179

Nobel Peace Prize, 235–38

Non-cooperation Movement, 80–81

nonviolence, 80, 94–95, 135–36, 292, **309**. *See also* civil disobedience

P

Pakistan, 105, 108–10, 113

Parks, Rosa, 143–44, 149, 154, 164

partition of India, 104–13, **309**

Patel, Vallabhbhai, 77, 111, 114, 281–82

peaceful resistance. *See* civil disobedience

perjury, 187

poll tax, 119, **309**

pooni, 290

Poor People's Campaign, 268

Prasad, Rajendra, 76, 177

Pritchett, Laurie, 201–03, 208

Project C (SCLC), 207–08

Q

Quit India Movement, 98–99

Quran, 18, 111, **309**

R

Radhakrishnan, Sarvepalli, 177

Raj, 14, 21–22, **309**

Ray, James Earl, 282–89

Reddick, Lawrence, 173, 180, 222

roti, 43

Rowlatt Act, 78–79

Rustin, Bayard, 169–70, 187, 198, 222

S

salt tax, 41, 85–87, 106

sari, 102, **309**

satyagraha, 67–71, 94–97, **309**

Savarkar, Vinayek Damodar, 69, 84, 279, 282

Scott, Coretta. *See* King, Coretta (Scott)

segregation

defined, 119, **309**

protesting. *See* civil disobedience

Selma right to vote campaign, 239–58

sepoy, **309**

sharecroppers, 122

Shuttlesworth, Fred, 164, 185, 198, 206, 241

sit-ins, 185–92, **309**

Smuts, Jan Christiaan, 67, 71

Southern Christian Leadership Conference (SCLC), 164, 184, 204, 206–10, 213, 216–17, 231–32, 248–49

Stride Toward Freedom (King), 169

Student Nonviolent Coordinating Committee (SNCC), 189, 198, 234

Supreme Court, 160–61, 197, 295

T

Thoreau, Henry David, 68, 132, 145

Thurman, Howard and Sue Bailey, 93–95, 136, 226

Till, Emmett, 143, 219

Tolstoy, Leo, 54–55, 65

topi (white hats), 226

typhoid, 64, 91, **309**

U

untouchables (Dalit), 20, 77, 84, 90–92, 181, **308**, **309**. *See also* caste system

Urdu language, 113, **309**

V

vegetarian lifestyle, Gandhi and, 16, 21–23, 35, 38, 40, 43–44

viceroy, 87, 98–100, 105, **309**

Vietnam War, 267–68

vigilante, 156, **309**

voting rights

in America, 94, 119–22, 127, 190, 207, 217, 220, 234, 239–58, 266–67, 295

in India, 92

in South Africa, 50–52, 64

Voting Rights Act, 258–59, 266, 295

W

Wallace, George, 205, 240, 255

Watts riots, 259–61

"We Shall Overcome" song, 186, 201, 219, 238, 254, 266

Williams, Adam Daniel, 121–23

women, India and, 28–29

Women's Political Counsel, 144–45

World War II, 96–98, 131

Y

Young, Andrew, 204, 213, 216, 246, 253, 272

Z

Zulu Rebellion, 66